The Eye of the Cinematograph

To Nasser, Mehrvash and Kamyar

The Eye of the Cinematograph

Levinas and Realisms of the Body

Keyvan Manafi

Edinburgh University Press is one of the leading university presses in the UK. We publish academic books and journals in our selected subject areas across the humanities and social sciences, combining cutting-edge scholarship with high editorial and production values to produce academic works of lasting importance. For more information visit our website: edinburghuniversitypress.com

© Keyvan Manafi, 2023, 2024

Edinburgh University Press Ltd
13 Infirmary Street
Edinburgh EH1 1LT

First published in hardback by Edinburgh University Press 2023

Typeset in 12 on 14pt Arno Pro and Myriad Pro
by Cheshire Typesetting Ltd, Cuddington, Cheshire

A CIP record for this book is available from the British Library

ISBN 978 1 3995 0724 0 (hardback)
ISBN 978 1 3995 0725 7 (paperback)
ISBN 978 1 3995 0726 4 (webready PDF)
ISBN 978 1 3995 0727 1 (epub)

The right of Keyvan Manafi to be identified as author of this work has been asserted in accordance with the Copyright, Designs and Patents Act 1988 and the Copyright and Related Rights Regulations 2003 (SI No. 2498).

Contents

List of Figures vi
Acknowledgements viii

1. The Ethical and the Image 1
2. The Image and the Body 35
3. The Body and the Camera 67
4. Literal Durations and Cinematic Parallelism 99
5. The Inhuman Eye and the Formless Body 123
6. Re-enactment, Proxies and the Facing Image 154
7. The Withdrawal of the Body 177
8. The Offscreen and the Promise of the Image 205

Coda 224

Bibliography 227
Index 240

Figures

1.1	Persistence of the offscreen stare in the opening shot of *Ossos*	2
1.2	Extended shot that presents the profilmic act in its entirety in *Jeanne Dielman, 23 quai du Commerce, 1080 Bruxelles*	3
2.1	Unable to tell his own story to contest the existing narratives, Sabzian in jail asks Kiarostami to narrate the story on his behalf in *Close-Up*	47
2.2	Extended use of frontal, static shots that emphasise the staging of bodies in *Still Life*	50
2.3	The woman trying to thread a needle in an extended scene in *Still Life*	51
3.1	Edie Sedgwick in Andy Warhol's *Screen Tests*	80
3.2	Restoring the variable of duration by the staging of tableaux in *Thérèse*	90
4.1	Camera as static witness truncating the body in *Jeanne Dielman, 23 quai du Commerce, 1080 Bruxelles*	107
4.2	The final scene of *Jeanne Dielman, 23 quai du Commerce, 1080 Bruxelles*	116
5.1	Inscription of bodily gesture in *Umberto D*	126
5.2	Capturing the habits as ingrained in the body in *Mouchette*	127
5.3	Staging of the sex act in open nature in *Flandres*	134
5.4	The human figure dwarfed by the landscape in an extreme long shot in *L'humanité*	134
5.5	Lingering on body parts in *L'humanité*	136
5.6	Tight framing of the body in *Hors Satan*	136
5.7	The body reclaimed by the material world in the finale of *La vie de Jésus*	142
5.8	Following her spiritual journey, Céline is saved by David in the finale of *Hadewijch*	143

5.9	Returning the body to formless precarity released from mediation and sustained by the image in *Jeannette, l'enfance de Jeanne d'Arc*	146
6.1	Introducing multiple characters through title cards and extended screen time in *Elephant*	160
6.2	The breaking of the fourth wall does not necessitate second takes in *Elephant*	171
7.1	Marcos and Anna, the unlikely couple in *Battle in Heaven*	188
7.2	Distinctive bodily presence of Pharaon that defies the conventional figure of detectives in *L'humanité*	190
7.3	Capturing the lethargic rhythms of the non-actor's body in *Crimson Gold*	192
7.4	Ecstatic bodily expressions of Amiru that defies the activity of the viewing subject in *The Runner*	196
8.1	Frame-within-a-frame compositions in *Ossos*	207
8.2	Pauses that emphasise the weightiness of onscreen bodies in *Ossos*	212
8.3	The prevalence of stares into the offscreen space in *Ossos*	216

Acknowledgements

This project began life as a doctoral dissertation that I completed at the University of New South Wales, Sydney, and revised into this book with the addition of several new chapters and case studies. My dissertation was supervised by Lisa Trahair to whom I particularly feel indebted because of her invaluable advice and support throughout my doctorate adventure. I am grateful to James Phillips, who agreed to come aboard as my co-supervisor and assisted me to critically revisit my ideas. I also want to thank George Kouvaros, who was a great reader of my work, and Chris Danta and Meg Mumford, who as research coordinators assisted my candidature at the School of the Arts & Media. I am grateful to Sarah Cooper (King's College London) and Sam B. Girgus (Vanderbilt University) for their advice and comments as the examiners of my dissertation.

I would like to thank Gillian Leslie, Sam Johnson and the Edinburgh University Press team for their encouraging support and remarkable work during all stages of the book's production. I also thank the anonymous readers of the book proposal and the draft manuscript for their illuminating suggestions.

1

The Ethical and the Image

A woman is sitting on the edge of a bed in a relatively dark room, against a blue wall that emphasises and helps to set off not only the poor conditions of the room she is in but also her sad face, greasy hair and gloomy red eyes. The static, extended shot of the woman lasts for one minute before the next shot presents the title. The initial shot can be said to represent destitution, poverty and pain. There is something else to it, however, that provides the grounds for representation but also works to disrupt it. The woman is looking offscreen, and even though she is mute, expressionless and immobile, the persistence of her stare subtracts something from the representational thrust of the image. The shot is reduced to a persistence within the image, not only of the body of the woman, but of her looking offscreen – a look that can be said to be sad or in pain, but is devoid of content, does not resonate with anything on- or offscreen and disrupts the meaningfulness of the shot by its mere persistence.

This first shot seems to reaffirm something of the image, something of its structure beyond what the image is or signifies. The frame of the image separates it from the surroundings and gives it an irreducible position within my frontal visual field. At the same time, the image appears to be irreducible to an image about the world it shows; it is not merely a derivative of the world it represents. Prior to being a representation of the world or an object within my vision, the image appears to be presenting itself to my eye, referring to itself as what is self-presenting. The shot contains the body of the woman, and her looking offscreen is there within the image. But it is precisely because of its being within the image, being a constituent of what the image contains, that the looking offscreen emphasises the address of the image, its opening towards me, beyond whatever is revealed to me or exposed within the image as visual content. The looking seems to resonate with the image itself: it asks me something but what it asks or demands remains untold. Or perhaps it is not something to be told. Sitting in the dark theatre and being visited by the image, I become a viewer predominantly in

2 The Eye of the Cinematograph

Figure 1.1 Persistence of the offscreen stare in the opening shot of *Ossos* (Pedro Costa, 1997).

debt to the image being opened to me while the woman's looking offscreen leaves me clueless and unarmed in dealing with the image before me. It is not to say that the image is hiding something from me. Even if it was, its impact seems to lie elsewhere. In a position of having to respond, I encounter a human presence that is already affirmed by the image and, in a certain sense, is already turned to me and imposed on me. Whatever I might read into the body's image would be a failure of that reading, would be an exposure of my failure, as it fails to exhaust the looking, one that addresses but refuses to be filled with content. The significance of the looking, in a certain way, is indissociable from the event of the body's image opening up within my visual field and its duration. Persisting onscreen, the woman's image is in front of me, yet I cannot merely point at it, for its persistence is before me but also towards me.

Or consider a woman being watched by a static camera as she is washing the dishes in the kitchen of her apartment in 23 Commerce Quay, 1080 Brussels. She is turned away from the camera and I have no access to a view of her face. The shot lasts for several minutes. The woman exits the frame while the shot continues, showing a frame devoid of human presence. I may connect this shot to other shots in which her body appears and persists onscreen, cooking, dusting, making the bed or taking a shower. After all, the woman seems to be following a daily pattern and her daily tasks are presented to me not only in a detailed manner but also in their complete duration. The information that the shot is to convey is so rarefied that it is absorbed by me in a couple of seconds. However, the shot lasts for minutes as the action onscreen is presented in its entirety. I am exposed to watching the woman doing the dishes in real time rather than being simply informed about this act in an elided manner.

After the potentially dramatic aspect of the shot is absorbed, I am left with nothing but the sheer fact that the woman is washing the dishes. I might decide to focus on the details of how she is doing what she is doing, which is itself dramatically insignificant. After a short while, however, I am once again left with the bare fact of what persists onscreen. I begin to ask myself if the camera functions here as that which is supposed to construct the images that effectively progress the drama through exposition, suggestion and allusion or, perhaps, it is only assigned the task of merely filming what is before it. It is as though the camera is, curiously, obsessed with its own power to record automatically yet indifferently what is made available to its gaze. Turning away from the camera, the woman seems to be indifferent to the camera's presence too. But having made her body available to the camera, the actor renders tenuous the character's apparent indifference to the presence of the camera and its recording. Her body is unable to escape the fact of its being staged for the look of the camera. Acting as a woman doing the dishes, the body becomes a filmed body placed within the image to be rewatched.

Figure 1.2 Extended shot that presents the profilmic act in its entirety in *Jeanne Dielman, 23 quai du Commerce, 1080 Bruxelles* (Chantal Akerman, 1975).

After a short while the sheer fact of washing the dishes is also redundant as I start to find myself exposed to the physical qualities of the image, of the woman's figure, the movements of her body, her inexpressive gestures and postures, the sound of water dripping, and to the setting. I am confronted with details while they do not yield discernible meanings or contribute to the dramatisation. These do not seem to be *a priori* details that are now presented to me – ones that are pre-scripted and now actualised within the image I have before me. The details are themselves an effect of the persistence of the image, of its extended duration that frustrates my scanning for meaningfulness. This persistence instead appears to claim the significance of the physical qualities, which are utterly uninterested in a story that I have presumed to be on its way to being told. The visual and aural details of the woman's figure and movements while doing the dishes are, in a certain sense, contingent insofar as their sheer presence onscreen and the particular qualities they present to me are not necessitated by the progression of the drama or any meaning-making framework. The shot makes room for the contingent as the profilmic, staged to be recorded, is given the privilege of being justified in its own right beyond whatever I can make of it. It is included in the composition of the shot because of the sheer fact of its being recorded and then carried within an image that is now opened up to me. What the shot does is not simply present a surplus of details that would deliver something beyond their mere physical thereness. The details flood in just because the extended duration of the shot welcomes the indifferently copied details, allowing them to occupy the screen. The materiality of the profilmic calls attention to itself as the protracted shot releases the contingent from being forced to be motivated and justified. The contingent is not domesticated – it breaks through the image, but is allowed the room to stubbornly resist rationalisation and *withdraw*.

How are these modes of presentation of the body of the other significant? If an image extends duration by presenting actions in their entirety, protracts the shot length and disrupts the viewer's expectation to find meaning and significance, what are the alternative possibilities in the viewer–viewed relation that are brought forth? More accurately, if an image is set up in a way that something is substantively subtracted from whatever is rendered visible within the frame of the image, what is the relation between the viewer and the filmed body that this mode of setting up shots and durations has established?

Furthermore, what is the promise that resides in the structure of the image? What is it that happens when the other makes its body available to the gaze of the camera for it to be automatically recorded, and this giving of the body is preserved within the image, juxtaposed with other images to allude to a story that might otherwise remain untold? What if the other in the image is impoverished, underprivileged, insignificant or marginalised, socially unremarked, invisible or forgotten, mute, inarticulate or not necessarily making sense? What if the body in the image does not conform to the sacrosanct codes of presentation of bodies, or does not exactly belong to a screen onto which their image is projected? What if the body is captured without any aestheticising filter, in its mundane moments, and the appearance and persistence of its image defies cultural and aesthetic validation but also adamantly resists meaning and significance? Having been exposed to the above shots, I might wonder if it would be possible for me as the viewer to imagine cinematic images as equipped to tell the precarity of the human other, not through a confirmation of what I already know, but through what cannot be properly known, a story that is untold, but is not exactly told through proper telling: that the unremarked suffering of the other embodies a certain materiality whose ethical address cannot be adequately told but is indissociable from the body's image opening up within the visual field and the duration of my exposure to it.

It is my contention in this book that Emmanuel Levinas's ethical philosophy offers responses to these questions and raises further enquiries to film studies predominantly with respect to the body of the other and its relation to the cinematic image. More significantly, Levinas's ethical thought provides the premises for a new appreciation of the complexities of the cinematic image. Of course, Levinas famously sees ethics as 'a vision without image'. Calling artistic activity a fixity and immobilisation, seeing it as a degradation, 'a fall into the world of forms', Levinas is most unapologetic when it comes to the visual image in particular. He notoriously derides the image by understanding it as necessarily acquisitive and reductive. What is banished by the image is a genuine otherness that resides in the immediacy of the encounter with 'the face' of the other and the call to responsibility that this encounter involves. The image, for Levinas, is closely bound to visibility and form. It is an exhibition, while underneath it conceals the originary expression of the face.[1] It therefore seems from the outset contradictory to ask what Levinas's ethical philosophy has to say about cinema. After all, what does it mean to ask an iconoclast for assistance to ethically engage with film while his thought explicitly manifests a biblical prohibition of images and a strong condemnation of the image as an inherent violence against the human other? What would an iconoclast with grave concern for absolute alterity have to say about the submission of the body of the other to the gaze of the cinematographic machine, about the automatic formation of the body's image that is to be stored and then endlessly projected to be looked at?

In the introduction to the special issue of *Film-Philosophy* journal dedicated to investigating the intersection of film and Levinas, Sarah Cooper stresses this difficulty by reminding us that there is something provocative in 'wanting to ask what Levinas's philosophy has to say about cinema, if we understand this realm as the location *par excellence* of the moving image'. Insisting on the possible usefulness of Levinas's thought in philosophical reflections on cinema seems a matter of risk. As Cooper notes, Levinas's philosophy 'bears a challenging relation to questions of vision and the phenomenological world of appearance, tending towards the anti-ocular and revealing an iconoclastic approach to images'.[2] This challenging relation is fundamentally rooted in Levinas's understanding of ethics, his suspicion of the image, and ultimately the altericidal violence exerted on the other through representation and form.[3]

To stage any encounter between film and Levinasian ethics, it is therefore essential to account for the foundational underpinnings and broader implications of Levinasian iconoclasm. A genuinely fruitful engagement between film and Levinas has as its substantial requirement not only an investigation of Levinas's philosophy with regard to the visual but also a certain critique of the shortcomings of his iconoclasm. As Libby Saxton points out, '[v]iewing films with Levinas always involves a degree of viewing against the iconoclastic thrust of his writings'.[4] Moreover, as Melissa Raphael reminds us, while it might seem to be an easy task to disparage or dismiss Levinasian 'image polemics as antiquated and excessive', at the same time we should be mindful that Levinas is 'often right about so much that is wrong with images'.[5] The problems that Levinas brings forward must be taken seriously not as dilemmas to resolve or put aside but as what make evident the tensions that are already present within the visual.

To take the current Levinasian film scholarship forward and draw out a new dialogue between his ethics and film theory, I demonstrate that what Levinas's ethical thought presents to film studies is beyond an iconoclastic critique of the visuality of the image. Nor can the insights Levinas potentially offers to our thinking about film be limited to a mere appreciation of filmic practices that self-critically expose the violence of the image from within. An unorthodox reading of Levinas's ethical philosophy demonstrates that his ethics does not banish vision altogether but bears directly on the viewer's relation to the image. It is particularly through the concept of the face in this book that Levinasian ethics can be taken to propose new affirmative ways to think and experience the cinematic image and its relation to the other.

Critical space for an investigation of Levinas's ethical thought in connection to film is opened up only if the foundations of his thought are exposed to encounters with concrete filmic practices that aesthetically engage with the materiality of the film medium. This is an encounter according to which film must be considered as a realm whose aesthetic potential cannot be either subordinated to the alleged mastery of theoretical reflections or be reduced to mere illustrations of philosophical themes or arguments.[6] It does not seem viable to speak of the possibility of 'cinematic thinking' without considering films that, according to Robert Sinnerbrink, resist 'theory' insofar as they evoke 'an experience that is aesthetic and reflective, yet where the former cannot be reduced to, or even overwhelms, the latter'.[7] Cinematic thinking resides in an endeavour in which the aesthetic experience cannot be exhaustively translated or paraphrased by another 'language' that is deemed to be adequate.[8] With respect to film–ethics encounters, Kristin Lené Hole interestingly sees this approach as a giving 'flesh' to ethics: 'Putting philosophy in contact with cinema gives flesh – both metaphorically and also literally, in the sense of centring the material body – to the concept of ethics.'[9]

To locate the ethical at this intersection of the body and the aesthetic, I intervene in the field of film and ethics by staging an encounter between Levinas's ethical thought and the automatic formation of the body's image by the cinematographic camera. It is my argument throughout this book that exploring the possibilities of film to question and subvert our established ways of forming and viewing the body's image and affirm new modes of encountering the other is rooted in an investigation of the specificity of the cinematic image, its technological formation and aesthetic use and the relation of the machine to the body. This new engagement with film through Levinasian thought requires an exploration of the theories of cinematic realism, not least a revisiting of André Bazin's film theory. It is my contention that there exists at the core of these theories a fundamental ethical concern with alterity. The cinematic image involves responsibility, for the filmed body is always already the real body of an other that is given a renewed life within the image. In dialogue with Bazinian film theory and several film philosophers and scholars, I make a case for the hospitality of the cinematic image and explore the ethics of the cinematograph. I argue that the cinematic image is distinctively able to affirm the body of the other prior to its identification and, more outstandingly, to sustain the body within filmic durations without the body having to be necessarily recognised as familiar or appearing as intelligible. There is an originary welcoming at the core of the filmic rendition of the body, an originary 'yes' that is pronounced (by the machine) before there is a self to decide to embrace or reject the other. Certain engagements with realisms of the body in this book will demonstrate how the viewing subject's authority over the body of the other is already tenuous, as the freedom (to say 'no!' to the visitation of the other) relies on the originary passivity of ethical exposure, which the cinematic image is uniquely equipped to restage.

In this chapter, I map out the core setup and structure of Levinasian iconoclasm and review the existing enquiries into the consequences of Levinas's philosophy of ethics for cinematic aesthetics. I then conclude the chapter by proposing aesthetic realisms of the body as affirmative responses to Levinasian iconoclasm. While acknowledging the deliberate non-systematicity of Levinas's thought, I investigate his redefinition of ethics on the basis of the self–other paradigm and his not always easy use of the term the face to refer to a revelation of the other precedent to consciousness and irreducible to representation. I mainly focus on Levinas's *Totality and Infinity: An Essay on Exteriority*, his first of two major philosophical books first published in 1961. Pointing out the presuppositions underlying the iconoclastic thrust of his philosophy, I stress the paradoxical nature of the concept of the face. I show how this difficulty problematises a common understanding of the visual as a domain of appearance reducible to the rule of frontal vision. It is this uneasy conceptualisation that led to the marginalisation of the term in Levinas's second major book, *Otherwise Than Being, or, Beyond Essence*, first published in 1974, which is the focus of the next chapter. It will be my contention that Levinas's attempt to establish a not always tenable but significantly revealing distinction between 'the saying' (*le dire*) and 'the said' (*le dit*) in the second book does not necessarily undermine his earlier insistence on the centrality of the concept of the face for his ethical thought. Rather, this distinction establishes the parameters of the self's bodily exposure to the other. It helps to revive radical potentials of the notion of the face by understanding it as the agonised vocalisation of the other that can be traced on the body, one that defies meaning but needs the image to find a channel into being. This approach requires an understanding of the face as a noun that essentially embodies a verb within itself. To have a face, to be a face, is also to face – it is a *facing*. This notion of the face as facing underscores and appreciates the images that are aesthetically set up to make present the tensions between the ethical and the visual and thus subvert the violence of vision.

Levinas: ethics as critique

Levinas's philosophy primarily gains its distinction through its endeavour to bring the importance of ethics to the fore of philosophical discussions by giving it a new life and a decisive twist and redefinition. Ethics as a critical idiom, as Simon Critchley reminds us, had either been absent from intellectual spheres or only present precisely as 'a term of abuse' in what he calls 'radical anti-humanism'.[10] This idiom once again became acceptable and this acceptance was, to a considerable extent, indebted to Levinas's reworking of the concept. Levinas reformulates ethics as that which precedes ontology, and deems it as 'first philosophy'. He revives ethics by thinking it away from sets of pre-established and predefined moral codes aimed at preserving a certain form of community or sense of the self. Levinas 'does not posit, *a priori*, a conception of ethics that then instantiates itself (or does not) in certain concrete experiences'. The ethical is, rather, 'an adjective that describes, *a posteriori* as it were, a certain event of being in a relation to the other irreducible to comprehension'.[11]

Ethics is the putting into question of 'the same' – the latter as that which includes both the consciousness and the *for*-consciousness. The spontaneity of the same is put into question by the other precisely because the other cannot be reduced to the self as it escapes and overflows its power. Ethics is, as Levinas remarks, this calling into question that 'cannot occur within the egoist spontaneity of the same brought about by the other'. He continues, the 'strangeness of the other, his irreducibility to the I, to my thoughts and my passions, is precisely accomplished as a calling into question of my spontaneity, as ethics'.[12] The other's originary foreignness to the cognitive capacities of the self and its indifference to cognition bring forth the question. Ethics is not an *a priori* set of norms or a thought that is digestive insofar as it centres around a subject that is 'the melting pot of Being'. It is, rather, the very condition in which the sovereignty of the self is exposed to doubt and incompleteness by the presence of the other.[13] Ethics is a *critique* that does not 'reduce the other to the same as does ontology, but calls into question the exercise of the same'.[14] Originated by the other, ethics puts into question the self that 'seeks to reduce all otherness to itself'.[15] The egoist spontaneity of the self forecloses the possibility of critique. By contrast, ethics as critique is a rupture within the flow of the ego. It is a disturbance. A disruption from the outside, ethics is not what takes place within the egoist flow of the subject. It is what happens to the self from a foreign position, from an 'exteriority'.[16]

Levinas's approach initially recalls the Husserlian terminology as he brings to fore the paradigm of the same (*le Même*) and the other (*l'autre*). Despite his great debt to Edmund Husserl, however, Levinas formulates his philosophy by breaking with Husserlian phenomenology. According to Husserl, the domain of the same includes not only *noeses* (intentional acts of consciousness) but also *noemata* (intentional objects that give meaning to those acts). This distinction acknowledges that the domain of the same maintains a relation with what is other. Yet, most significantly, it is a relation in which, according to Levinas, 'the ego or consciousness reduces the distance between the same and the other',[17] thus overrunning what is exterior about the other. On the other hand, however, Levinas's involvement with otherness as absolute alterity resides in his conviction that the other is not a phenomenon but an 'enigma', something 'ultimately refractory to intentionality' and 'opaque to the understanding'.[18] His conception of otherness not only moves beyond the phenomenological relation of intentionality but also problematises any notion of relation between the same and the other. It argues instead for a non-relationality based on the radical alterity of the other.[19]

The fundamental axiom of phenomenology is the intentionality thesis: all thought, regardless of its potential content, is fundamentally characterised by its being directed towards its various matters. Levinas's contribution to the discussion is rooted in his attempt to rethink the (non)relation to the other away from a relation perceived as phenomenological. The other is not a given. Givenness reduces otherness to being a matter for thought, to an object of intention or reflection.[20] In his reading of Levinas's ethics, Philippe Crignon argues:

> Phenomenology, which describes the constitutive activity of consciousness in each of its acts, shows its limits when faced with the unconstitutable. In other words, it fails when, in the heart of my world, there arrives what I could not draw from myself, an existent [*etant*] whose meaning cannot be attributed to the power of a transcendental subject.[21]

What concerns Levinas is the necessity of differentiating this phenomenological intentionality from the face of the other. While the former involves the intentional object as a phenomenon and the presence of the object to consciousness, the latter implies trace. The face presents the other as absent or withdrawn, as that which is beyond the grasp and possessiveness of consciousness.[22] Otherness, according to Levinas, is what overflows any thought. His philosophical endeavour is concerned with that which is the 'unthinkable par excellence', and is thus irreducible to an object of contemplation. It is through this conception that Levinas's thought situates itself against the ontological tradition dominant in Western philosophy – a tradition that, in Levinas's view, is fundamentally aimed at thinking the other, and thus inevitably results in compromising the latter's alterity. Levinas's critique is rooted in his understanding of this tradition as the dominion and kingdom of the same, of the thought that is objectifying and totalising. It is a tradition in which self-identification as a process tends to subsume alterity by making it 'merely a necessary part in the self-conscious play of the subject'.[23] Thought comprehends what is foreign to it by rendering it familiar and grasping it by a return to what is familiar. The price of this process is, inevitably, otherness.

Every ontological relation to that which is other than the same is necessarily a relation of comprehension and, as a result, is disposed to form totalities and amounts to violence. Rendering the other as an object of knowledge and comprehension, Western thought, as Levinas tells us, concerns itself with eradicating the constitutive alterity of the other.[24] This is a thought that has most often been an ontology – by which Levinas means any attempt aimed at comprehending and grasping the being of that which *is*. The other is thus reduced to an object that is for consciousness, as that which can and must be formed and fall under a concept. The ontological act not only reduces but also suppresses otherness by a return to the same. Ontology is 'the movement of the hand, the organ for grasping and seizing' by which 'the other is assimilated to the same'.[25]

Ontology designates a whole. But a whole that is also a totality – that is, in Levinas's words, 'a multiplicity of objects' that form a unity, coming 'without remainder under a sole act of thought'.[26] This disposition towards totality, towards a whole that is predominantly constituted by its own intolerance for and thus the exclusion of what remains, overruns otherness through its own abstract purity. Levinas is therefore wary of a thought that is all-encompassing.[27] The true function of totalising thought does not consist in an innocent looking at and encountering being, but in 'determining it by organizing it'.[28] Totalising thought is a determination that also forms and brings into being what it reduces.[29] Totality is what gives thought the necessary confidence to render the unintelligible intelligible and ultimately to return home. What underlines Levinas's conception of ethics is his contention that this totality, while being resilient, can be disrupted. It might be said, of course, that this totality is always already being disrupted but only by that which 'lies outside of it'.[30] Yet, what is it that lies outside of totality?

The non-relation between the same and the other precedes the emergence of self-consciousness. This is where a Levinasian intervention begins to take hold through the concept of the face. It is early on in the introduction of *Totality and Infinity* that the question of the face emerges:

> We can proceed from the experience of totality back to a situation where totality breaks up, a situation that conditions the totality itself.

> Such a situation is the gleam of exteriority or of transcendence in the face of the other.[31]

The same/self is not to be taken as that which absorbs and digests what lies outside of it and Levinas's philosophical mission is to attempt to think of the other as other. The conception of ethics that Levinas tries to bring forth acknowledges the way the face of the other puts the same/self into question while warning against the violent absorption and dissolution of the other into the same. The aim of Levinas's philosophy, according to Krzysztof Ziarek, is 'to treat the other in such a way that he would remain "unthinkable", absolutely exterior and non-thematizable'.[32]

Levinasian thought therefore differentiates between two levels of otherness. Opposed to the radicality of the constitutive alterity of the other as other (revealed in the face) is the merely 'apparent' otherness as what is present in the play of the same where the same/self identifies 'itself with itself through the necessary "detour" of the alterity of objects'.[33] Having a self has as its condition for possibility a certain levelling of otherness. Privileging the same over what is other is fundamental to this condition. As a threat to the cohesiveness of the self, otherness is inevitably reduced and compromised to the extent that it is stripped of its exteriority.[34] This otherness, an apparent one, is foregrounded and ultimately produced to provide the other pole which is vital and necessary for the realisation of the same. The same/self depends on the other 'precisely to seize it, to take possession of it, to represent and think it'.[35] The other is not the other *per se*, but an other that is reduced, tamed and digested so that it can provide the condition for the process of self-identification. The second level of otherness, by contrast, is a matter of non-relation that is manifested in an encounter with the face of the other. This non-relation, as Jill Robbins remarks, is a 'relation without relation'.[36] It does not enable the same to identify itself and return to itself. The absolutely other is 'indifferent to representation', overflowing and exceeding any plot of identification.[37]

Iconoclasm: a vision without image

If vision is to be understood as 'the master sense of the modern era', as Martin Jay suggests, then a critique of modernity would inevitably involve an investigation of 'the hegemony of the eye'.[38] At the core of this investigation is the question of the image, and the Levinasian concern with the other is predominantly rooted in a critique of the visibility and domination with which he associates the image.

Ethics, as articulated in *Totality and Infinity*, is primarily conceived of as 'a "vision" without image, bereft of the synoptic and totalizing objectifying virtues of vision, a relation or intentionality of a wholly different type'.[39] In essence, the revelation of the face of the other is, from the outset, alien to the domain of the visual[40] – hence the founding stone for Levinas's hostility towards the image, his strong prohibition against representation, and his iconoclasm:

> the way in which the other presents himself, exceeding the idea of the other in me, we here name face. This mode does not consist in figuring as a theme under my gaze, in spreading itself forth as a set of qualities forming an image . . . The face of the other at each moment destroys and overflows the plastic image it leaves me.[41]

Levinas's concern with otherness and exteriority complicates the relation between the visual and the other. For him, the visual is a matter of egology, evoking the same and the totality that elsewhere he associates with the conceptual: 'vision is not transcendence. It ascribes a signification by the relation it makes possible. It opens nothing that, beyond the same, would be absolutely other, that is, in itself.'[42]

Levinasian ethics is abidingly suspicious of figurality, of the realm of the visual and the aesthetic. It embodies a rigid iconoclasm and a deep suspicion according to which images are inherently violent.[43] As Hagi Kenaan points out, one of the pivotal presuppositions that structures Levinasian iconoclasm is that there is an 'essential connection between the intentional, object-directed structure of consciousness, visual content, objectification and the imposition of power'.[44] This connection stands out as a mediation – it is what, following Maurice Blanchot's approach to the violence of seeing, will be referred to later in this book as the third that mediates the immediacy of the encounter with the face and puts it under a form.[45] This conception of ethics associates the aesthetic and the visual with forms of domination and violence. It issues a taboo on visual representation, questioning the legitimacy of representation and, in particular, of the visual image. This iconophobic approach, as Saxton reminds us, sees representation as 'liable to "thematize" and thereby reduce the "visage" [face] to a projection of the Same',[46] thus considering images as a certain reductive, acquisitive mode of thought. Representation is reconfigured as 'thought thinking the thing', bringing forth what is fundamental to its own structure: *adequation*. Representation is 'the adequation of thought with its other'. It involves intentionality and is a thematisation and identification of 'what lets itself be designated', what can be referred to through a 'demonstrative', or 'with the index finger'.[47] This adequation gives the self, through representation, its power. As Diane Perpich notes, adequacy implies a thought that 'never fails to give itself the object as an ideal unity of meaning' imposed on the other.[48] The other's status as an object is an effect of representation, while representation, by delivering the object over to thought, reveals itself as a 'creative mastering of the world in the production of intelligibility'.[49] In Levinas's words, intelligibility is a 'giving of meaning' – it is a 'total adequation of the thinker with what is thought', where the thinker's mastery is exercised on its object such that the latter's 'resistance as an exterior being vanishes'.[50] The self, therefore, determines the other in representation. In representation, as well as in cognition, the other, which is first exterior, is given and delivered over to the self as though the other owed its existence to the constitutive activity of consciousness.[51]

As a Levinasian corrective to representational thinking, the critical endeavour is to strive to imagine a thought that is freed of all the dominating aspects of representation, one able to infer 'a meaningfulness prior to representation'.[52] What is at stake here is that which cannot give itself in representation: 'the uniqueness of the unique that is expressed in the face'.[53] The face of the other is thus fundamental in this correction. It is where the other presents itself and, at the same time, exceeds the idea that the self might have of the other. The face is that which cannot be comprehended through representation.[54] The face can be said to be present but only in 'its refusal to be contained'.[55] Thereby, the encounter with the other cannot be reduced to a question of comprehension. The other already moves beyond any cognitive act and cannot be grasped as a theme or concept. The face is substantially a resistance against consciousness.[56]

Levinas's understanding of the face as the site in which this non-relation to the other takes place is rooted in a complicated terminology – one that reflects the uneasy relation between the ethical and the visual in his philosophy. Using the face as the term implying the revelation of the other evokes a certain visuality. But the face is not a visual phenomenon. Quite the contrary is the case: the face gains its importance through its problematic relation to the visual domain and phenomenality. Oddly, as Critchley reminds us, Levinas understands the face in terms more of speech than of vision[57] – a proposition to which I return in the next chapter to establish the face as a wordless vocalisation that can be traced not only on the face but also on the body of the other. The face is not, strictly speaking, a visual phenomenon. It is not something that can be said to be visible. According to Crignon, Levinas's hostility towards the image is most evident in his efforts to found ethics by 'wresting the Face of man from visibility, by freeing it from the image that it is forever tempted to lapse into'.[58] The face must be distinguished from the form and surface of any imagehood and visuality for it to maintain its ethical charge and claim.[59] The alterity of the other is not to be equated with what can be perceived since, according to Levinas, 'to see is already to have' and therefore 'to possess and to grasp, to dominate and keep'.[60]

The paradox revolves around the fact that the other, as that which cannot appear and resist any sort of appearance, 'must nevertheless break in, and thus break in somewhere' – that is, in the face.[61] In Levinas's words, the other 'who manifests himself in the face as it were breaks through his own plastic essence'. The presence of the other 'consists in divesting himself of the form which, however, manifests him'.[62] The face affects and concerns the self, yet at the very same time escapes reduction to form, or whatever related to the domain of the visible. The way the face gives itself is excessive. Through its excessiveness, as Gabriel Riera remarks, the face introduces the collapse of 'subject/object polarity' since the face is that which cannot be 'fixed' in a form, while, at the same time, 'the face looks at me and concerns me'.[63] Speaking of the face necessitates a certain understanding of this excess precisely because, through the face, the other exceeds form and representation, overflowing any attempt to contain it. The other escapes from the grasp of the self, yet, at the very same time, it affects the self. How is the face to affect the self by giving itself to the gaze while not appearing to it in any form?

It is by employing the notion of 'expression' that Levinas tries to respond to this paradox. As Crignon argues, Levinas understands the face to be 'pure expression'. Expression, unlike signification, 'does not succeed the form it animates'.[64] Yet, what is crucial is the fact that what precedes still emerges as that which affects. Most importantly, its mode of affecting is predominantly indebted to its being alien to the domain of signification. The face leaves an impression on me precisely due to its being 'inconceivable and unforeseeable', because 'none of my horizons makes it possible'.[65] The other affects the self, but precisely because the other escapes the grasp of it. Exceeding the boundaries of the self and its power of comprehension does not result in a haven for the self that is built upon its self-sufficiency. The opposite is the case: the self is afflicted by the other because the other and the pure expressivity of its face resist being reduced to a necessary stage in the process of self-identification.

The face of the other cannot be contained or framed. It is neither conceptual nor phenomenal. It is not visible as any other visual phenomenon can be said to be. Its signifyingness is unique. The face 'enters our world', but not as an object appearing in the frontal visual field.[66] Levinas explains this peculiar mode of signifyingness as a 'signification without context'. While all signification is relative to a context where an object gains its meaning through its embeddedness within a matrix of relations, the face is, by contrast, 'meaning all by itself'.[67] It is in this respect that the other is

> what cannot become *content*, which your thought would not embrace; it is uncontainable, it leads you beyond. It is in this that the signification of the face makes it escape from being, as a correlate of knowing. Vision, to the contrary, is a search for adequation; it is what par excellence absorbs being.[68]

A binary opposition in Levinas's thought between objects and the face emerges here – one that Levinas relies on to further specify the irreducibility of the face to the visible. The signifyingness of the face is unique precisely because it is heterogeneous to the domain of signification, the latter governing the meaningfulness of objects. The object can be identified and located as something with recourse to its relation to other objects. It is in this regard that the object can never be considered as the origin of meaning. Its meaning is dependent upon its position within a broader network of objects. It is always seen and perceived as against a background. The face, however, is from a different order. Its meaning does not rely on its relation with other faces. It is irreducible to what we perceive as face precisely because it can be regarded as an object specified on the basis of its characteristics and relational bonds with other faces as objects. The face is, in a certain sense, the singular. It is neither similar nor different – adjectives that depend on the possibility of ascribing objective attributes to an entity from a totalising perspective. The singularity of the face resides in its uncontainability, the latter itself, as we see in the next chapter, stemming from the facingness of the face.[69] However, and more importantly, the face as meaning *per se* is also 'the origin of meaning'. The face, even though invisible, is itself 'the origin of visibility'. Devoid of form, it 'makes forms possible'.[70] Expression of the face is pure meaning in the sense that not only is it without context[71] but it also initiates meaning, standing out as its origin. In Levinas's words, the face 'signifies by itself'[72] – it is a meaningfulness prior to representation.

There is a certain interconnection between signification and phenomenality that belongs to the world of objects and breaks down in the face of the other. The face of the other can be seen as an object, as that which gains its meaning through its embeddedness within a matrix of relations. It can be said to appear in a manner that dominates the appearance of objects in front of us. Yet the face of the other resists the location we ascribe to the other in the world. It is not to be regarded as a signifying phenomenon. The face, strictly speaking, is not seen. Precisely because of its uncontainability, the face is not visible – it cannot be rendered visible. The face has 'its way of incessantly upsurging outside of its plastic image'.[73]

The enigma of the face therefore rests upon its problematic relation to the visual. The face, as what does not enter into a relation and is not relative to anything including me, 'comes to me nevertheless'.[74] It is not of this world, it is beyond the world; yet it 'springs up in a place within my world'.[75] Indeed, the face can be said to have a form. But the face, understood as expression, 'undoes this very form'.[76] In Levinas's words, the face 'breaks through the form that nevertheless delimits it'.[77] The face is not a phenomenon and is, strictly speaking, invisible. It is unfigurable, unless, as Crignon reminds us, it is forced to be 'reduced to its plastic mask'.[78] Therefore, representation of the face, one might say, *all* figuration, 'participates in a certain violence'. Representation is 'an impulsive wounding', insofar as each representation is understood as an activity that aims at reducing alterity to a plastic form.[79] Representation tames that which precedes form precisely through formalising it, thus exerting violence on that which does not belong to, thus uncompromisingly resisting, the world of forms. Levinas associates form with objects, since form belongs to the things that we can, essentially, see and possess. The face, however, resists form. The fact of being without form is what ensures that the face remains irreducible to the world of phenomena.[80]

Film–ethics encounters

Even if the face of the other is more a matter of speech than vision, it still would not be sufficient to oversimplify Levinas's use of the term, and its obvious visuality by emptying the face of any visual connotation that it certainly brings forth. Of course, the path to casting further light on Levinas's ethics necessitates an investigation of his understanding of speech and language to which I return in the next chapter. It will be my contention that the implications of the distinction that Levinas establishes between the saying and the said are fruitful in bringing to attention the way he conceives of the face as facing and reformulates the encounter with the other in bodily terms.

This is an encounter that, of course, takes place before the face of the other, yet stands in a problematic relation with the visual. As Kenaan argues,

> [t]he troublesome presence of internal tension is fundamental to Levinas' own project. The tension between the visual and the non-visual dimensions of the Other's face is not only a problem but also an expression of the Other's form of appearance, its mode of givenness. The Other is what is present and revealed, according to Levinas, through the tension between the visible and the invisible, the phenomenal and the transcendent, the conceptual and what cannot be conceptualized.[81]

The tension between the visible and the invisible is at the heart of the Levinasian understanding of ethics. Most significantly, this tension is a fundamental aspect of any critical engagement with the image through Levinas's thought. The iconoclastic thrust of Levinas's thought should not amount to a suspension of seeing according to which seeing must be somewhat put on hold to turn to the face of the other, but to thinking a tension. Thereby, the primary question is whether it is possible to counter the gaze's inclination to objectification. Similarly, it is important to investigate whether it is possible to speak of the cinematic image without shutting down the possibility of a revelation of alterity.

Reading Levinasian iconoclasm without succumbing to a rigid prohibition of images is a position that, as briefly mentioned earlier, has been adopted in recent film scholarship. This approach has taken the iconoclastic presuppositions of Levinas's thought seriously yet also has endeavoured to open up room for the possibility of thinking non-violent images. What enables us to speak of the latter rests upon providing the grounds for envisaging a connection between the ethical and the visual that does not treat the two realms in merely antagonistic terms. The equation of the image and the visual with visibility, and ultimately with comprehension and violence, is a Levinasian assumption that this book attempts to further unsettle.

The face of the other eludes representation and cannot be encountered in images, whereas film is essentially intertwined with the image. The most pressing question that arises at the intersection of film and ethics is therefore whether the cinematic image can reveal alterity in a way that it might expose us to the face of the other without reducing the face to a mere object. The pivotal question, as Saxton accurately formulates it, is

> how could a visual medium reveal alterity or call us to responsibility in the manner described by Levinas? Is it possible to conceive of ways

> in which cinema might expose us to this face without 'defacing' or 'effacing' it – without reducing it to an object of perception? Is the prohibition against representation signified by the face not always already violated as images of the other are captured on celluloid or translated into digital data?[82]

One response to this question would claim that film is incapable of emulating the 'immediacy and spontaneity of the "face-à-face"', as it is conceived by Levinas, insofar as 'the camera mediates otherness and manipulates our look'.[83] The camera and its approach to the world are always already charged and informed by subject/object relations, generating objects for consciousness.

An ethically inspired theory of viewing, however, would necessarily 'posit a space beyond subject/object relations'. This space is crucial for 'an opening to otherness', for the proximity and separation proper to what might be called 'the revelation of the Other' as a relation irreducible to the subject/object structure.[84] Perhaps, as Lisa Downing observes, 'precisely by being suspicious of the image', Levinas can help us to think film 'in the awareness of the ethical dangers of unproblematic viewing'.[85] Levinas's often iconophobic rhetoric then should not foreclose the possibilities inherent in staging encounters between his thought and film. By contrast, the fruitfulness of introducing Levinas's thought to film studies particularly resides in his hostility towards the image. It is his suspicion of the image that opens up new critical spaces insofar as it allows us to not only foster an awareness of the risks associated with image-making/viewing but also make present and appreciate the cinematic achievements that have put into practice these ethical concerns. In his discussion of the intersection of Levinas's thought and the image, Crignon points to a similar potentiality of Levinas's iconoclasm as he refers to him as 'the only philosopher of modernity who did not share in the general enthusiasm for the arts'.[86] Yet, Crignon argues, the fact that Levinas 'was a fierce and unwavering iconoclast leads us to suspect that he perceived, perhaps better than others, something considerable at stake in the image'.[87] Not sharing the enthusiasm for the arts turns Levinas into an asset for critical engagements with art. This approach strives to explore the underpinnings of Levinasian iconoclasm yet refuses to reiterate his proposed prohibition. Aiming at revealing the limits of his iconoclastic assumptions, this response examines how the Levinasian assumption that 'looking equates always with possessing', that 'to have before one's eyes is to have', can and must be exposed to critical investigation. According to Downing, this possessive and acquisitive characteristic of the look should not be considered as 'a transcultural and ontological absolute', but rather as an inclination that has deep historical roots, as 'culturally constructed and specific', most clearly emerging 'when the look manifests as the gaze'.[88] It may be better after all to understand the Levinasian deep suspicion of the image and representation as a critique of specific cultures, of specific tendencies in framing and encountering images, according to which 'looking equates with possessing'.[89]

According to Sinnerbrink, cinema might be able to suggest this immediacy of the face-to-face, but only indirectly. From a Levinasian perspective, he argues, the 'challenge for cinema' would be to find alternative ways 'to evoke indirectly this face-to-face encounter'; to materialise 'a moment of ethical transcendence in which what is conveyed on screen overflows the narrative framework or the explicit representational content of the image'. This is a moment that might offer 'a transcendent experience of ethical responsibility towards the Other'.[90] This response to iconoclasm is also underlined in Saxton's effort in staging an encounter between Levinas's theoretical endeavours and Claude Lanzmann's cinematic practice in *Shoah* (1985). Lanzmann's take on the Holocaust and the challenges it poses to representation inevitably leads to a more rigorous engagement with iconoclasm in which visual representation is embraced 'to reflect on its perceived limitations from within'.[91] Saxton interrogates whether and how images reduce their subject matters to objects of perception and knowledge, and whether and how they would be able to elevate themselves to the point of resisting this reduction. She maps the ways in which the face resists 'reduction to visible phenomena, sources of knowledge or objects of aesthetic contemplation and the possibility that this preserves an opening onto alterity'.[92] *Shoah* exemplifies how film can transpose the ethical concerns regarding 'the potential for treachery and violence inherent in images' into the visual register itself, while presenting us with strategies by which film 'might expose us to alterity without domesticating or simply effacing it'.[93] Film is thus considered as capable of implicating our gaze and charging it with responsibility. This can be undertaken precisely by 'impeding our vision and frustrating our desire to see', and by 'rehabilitating vision without instrumentalizing the image, by visualizing others without reducing them to projections of the self, and by envisaging an ethical "optics" which illuminates the visible as much as the invisible'.[94] Sinnerbrink similarly argues that 'visual art might be regarded as ethical in this distinctively "Levinasian" sense' only if there is a possibility of an 'indirect evocation' of the invisible, of what remains 'unacknowledged' or 'unknowable' – as 'the materiality of things but above all the alterity of individual human beings'.⁹⁵ What merits most attention is therefore the importance of a reconceptualisation of optics with regard to the question of the invisible. It is vital to ask what it means to speak of an image that 'illuminates the visible as much as the invisible'. What does the invisible mean in this investigation? Is there something in the unrepresentability of the exposure to alterity that constitutes the invisible of the image? Or further, is the invisible not the uncontainability of the address of the image and the responsibility that it calls forth? These questions are further elaborated in the next chapter.

Sam B. Girgus considers film as an artform that, from its outset more than a century ago, has 'set forth a new scene for ethical and moral engagement', providing the premise for 'enacting ethical and moral conflicts and dramas'.⁹⁶ While reminding us that Levinas, unlike most of his contemporaries, never really wrote on cinema or exclusively spoke about it, Girgus turns to his philosophy and interestingly picks up on Levinas's use of the term *mise en scène* in several works, spotting what can be considered as 'an inherent compatibility between film as thought process and philosophy'.⁹⁷ According to Girgus,

> Levinasian metaphysics has the potential for presenting an alternative to André Bazin's classic theory of cinema ontology in the form of an ethically-based appreciation of film. Such an effort to conceive of a non-ontological approach to film compares to Levinas's overall attempt to counter ontological language.⁹⁸

Girgus specifically focuses on what he terms 'the cinema of redemption' and the concept of time to demonstrate how time relates to absolute alterity and revisits the Levinasian stance on the feminine in particular. Time, for Girgus, is essential in his Levinasian engagement with film as it connects the material and the transcendental by suggesting 'a relationship of "holiness" that connects people to each other and infinity'.⁹⁹

Cooper identifies in the cinema of the Dardenne brothers an approach that introduced Levinas's ethical thought into their film practices prior to the emergence of Levinasian film-philosophy, taking the fundamental ethical question 'Thou shall not kill' and turning it into a 'mortal ethics'. Remarkably, as Cooper observes, what the Dardennes achieve in terms of cinematic ethics is a profound attempt to relocate the ethical from the face to the body 'without a loss of connection to the transcendent ethical dimension'.¹⁰⁰ Referring to the close shots where fragments of bodies are foregrounded, Cooper notes a framing where cinematic identification with fictional characters is reworked through images that literally fail to contain the bodies as the latter 'overflow the edges of the frame, rather than being contained within the shots'.[101] Cooper continues:

> By choosing to focus frequently on the backs of the characters, the Dardenne brothers steer us down, rather than up, the topography of the body, from the face to the back . . . The commandment of the Levinasian face speaks through the movements of the bodies in the diegetic space, as well as through the movements of the film (furnished by the camera, then enhanced by the editing), and the back is the point of origin of this mode of address.[102]

The Dardennes' cinema has also been the subject of Joseph Mai's discussion of pre-ontological ethics in film. Mai finds a Levinasian approach to the film particularly useful to avoid a reduction of the film's protagonist to a series of political positions of race or gender on the one hand, and, on the other, a more traditional ethical approach to film that is solely interested in reading the characters' trajectories as representing 'a moral conundrum' that is offered for analysis.[103] Levinas, as Mai demonstrates, can offer us the chance to think of ethics not as a 'cold moral deliberation by an autonomous individual', but as 'the restless perception that one's "own" self is living for another growing within it, taking it over'. According to this alternative conception of cinematic ethics that shows how a film can contribute to the ethical consciousness of its implied viewer, a film 'should not reinforce our political or intellectual habits' but rather 'persecute us and goad us into a confrontation with the other who constitutes us'.[104] In the dark theatre, the Dardennes 'are not striving to force their viewers into an intellectual . . . or entertainment experience'. They, rather, 'hope to force the viewer into giving up her "self", and confront an "other" as constitutive of the self'.[105]

Mai moves further to suggest that cinema is able to provide the premise for an encounter with the other onscreen where a coexistence with the time of the other is possible in what he terms a 'borderless region' without penetrating it. Citing Bazin's investment in deep-focus photography that encourages an active viewer who vigorously engages with reality onscreen, Mai admits that a Bazinian view 'flirts with a reliance on the type of conscious self that Levinas has rejected'. What is assumed in this standpoint are 'an intentional subject that is free to impose a meaning on reality' and film as what 'gives objects over to our understanding'.[106] Drawing on Dudley Andrew's reading of Bazinian theory, however, Mai observes that metaphors like trace, fissure, deferral and apparition in Bazin's works offer a more subtle understanding according to which realism is not so much a demonstration of 'a viewer's mastery of the world' as 'a disturbing and uncanny encounter with other faces, places and times'. Cinematic realism, therefore, resides in a certain 'dislocation in time and space' – it is, by essence, a mode of 'being torn from our daily selves and brought to times and spaces manifestly beyond our control'.[107]

To propose a feminist cinematic ethics, Hole notes a 'non-normative ethics' in the works of Claire Denis that works to disallow 'propositional morality or knowledge' and instead entails an exposure to the world that cultivates 'an attentiveness towards others'.[108] Hole draws on Diane Perpich's reading of Levinas to suggest a notion of 'alterity aesthetics' to locate the ethical in relation to the cinematic image:

> Both identity politics and a politics of recognition rely on a notion of the subject that posits her in relation to an unmarked subject or, in the Levinasian lexicon, 'the Same'. Identity politics typically defines significant categories of identity relative to the dominant subject group... Similarly a politics of recognition demands recognition as like the other, again, typically a dominant subject group conferring recognition on marginalised or under-represented peoples... these strategies fall into the logic of relativising difference, ultimately diminishing the singularity of the other, be it through defining oneself as different in comparison to the other or by demanding recognition as *like* the other.[109]

As a correction to this dominant conception of otherness that is based on notions of 'shared universal subjecthood', Hole suggests thinking of a deconstructed subject whose otherness is 'uncategorisable'.[110] She argues that we can envisage 'representational practice of alterity' that does not reside in 'identity or recognition', one that 'respects the very impossibility of capturing the other'.[111] Hole conceptualises alterity aesthetics based on the idea that singularity is what overflows categories by citing Perpich's reading of Levinasian ethics:

> Singularity – *who* one is – is always excessive with respect to *any* characterization of what one is or of the groups with which one identifies or is identified... But nor can my singularity be understood without recourse to socially, politically, and culturally salient facets of my experience. Singularity is not meant to convey some abstract otherness or merely formal alterity, it is the concreteness of my life, my lived bodily experience.[112]

I take this position further, and this is where the concept of facing will be central to my arguments in this book, by contending that a representation that fails to capture the other and shows its failure is ultimately not a representation, as the latter still presupposes that otherness pre-exists the exposure to the other. In this view, the image (of the body) is still, albeit implicitly, read as a lack, yet, not as a lack that calls for the meaningfulness of intentionality, but one that shows its inadequacy in capturing the singularity of the other. The precedence of the other, however, does not precede the encounter with the face of the other. Understanding the face as facing and the saying not as the absolute alterity of the other but as the originary structure of exposure in the next chapter demonstrates that singularity resides in the encounter with the other. The other precedes the self; yet the other is not dissociated from its movement of facing. The failure of representation is therefore not a representation of the singularity of the other. Rather, the ethical failure is a testimony to the singularity of the exposure. This line of enquiry problematises prohibition of images by speaking of the inevitability of the image but also of its ethical necessity – the image is what has the potential to stage the breakthrough but also the withdrawal of the other.

Realisms of the body

It is imperative to ask whether certain images can bring forth the ethical epiphany. Reading Levinas against the grain demonstrates how he himself treats the critique of the visual in less prejudiced and more nuanced ways than the condemnations that often surface in his works. It is problematic to reduce the image to visibility, to uncritically state that the image is always already trapped in an economy of violence that fosters visibility. The image is irreducible to an act of bringing its subject matter to light and stripping it of its alterity, and it is problematic to assume the image to be essentially representational and thus closely connected to the violence of comprehension and grasping. In particular, a reduction of the densely audiovisual register of the cinematic image to visibility is symptomatic of a theoretical self-assuredness that denies the specificity of the cinematic image and the innovative ways it has been put into practice. Visibility is not the definitive materiality of the film medium, but rather is what has historically been both staged and critically interrogated by certain cinematic practices. The cinematic image does something to the visual – it is not only capable of self-reflectively questioning its own violence but also has the potential to exert a certain affirmative violence on our habituated vision; the latter dominated by, as is established in the next chapter, the rule of 'the frontal'.

Levinas can help us affirmatively reconceive the cinematic image as a gift – not a representation of the other that renders the latter as a given for consciousness, but a giving of the body revealed to be rewatched and borne witness to in its precarity. Following Kenaan's notion of facing images, I dissociate the cinematic image from being merely *of/about* the world (a copy) or *in* the world (an object) and approach it as that which bears a certain analogy with the face. The structure of the image has an inherent tie with the condition of being viewed. Capable of establishing a relation with its viewer irreducible to subject/object dynamic, the image addresses the eye without the address being necessarily containable in terms of what is posited within the image. In other words, the image is what can stage the breakthrough, but also the withdrawal, of the other.

This attention to the image-as-face will allow me to treat the ethical of the cinematic image as irreducible to the self/other dynamic present in the diegetic world, and instead theorise film as the location in which the ethical exposure to the other takes place. I enquire what happens when the body of the other is submitted to the gaze of the camera, the image of the body is formed and projected onscreen, and is offered to be rewatched during the rituals of film viewing in the dark theatre whose duration is fixed and the attentiveness it implies involves a certain passivity. Exploring the self/other paradigm in film is therefore inseparable in my study from an investigation of what happens to the affirmation (welcoming) of the body of the other that takes place in the moment of the formation of the image when the body is recorded.

Bazin's regard for film's inherent realism and the works of scholars who have contributed to the revival of the aesthetic theories of realism in recent film theory are chiefly instrumental in my task at hand in demonstrating the ethical implications of this trust in the inhuman machine (against what often seems to be a Bazinian anthropocentric adherence to 'natural' perception). I will take as my point of departure Bazin's renowned investment in the photographic basis of the film medium to demonstrate that there is an otherness intrinsic in the way the camera encounters the fragments of the real in the world. I will draw on Bazin's analogy of 'bricks' and 'stones' in his seminal book *What is Cinema?* to demonstrate the precedence and persistence of the fragments recorded by the camera. According to Bazin, the brick is a basic unit whose being is thoroughly absorbed and exhausted from the outset by the totality it enters into, whereas the metaphor of rock brings our attention to a fragment of reality that is found in the world and therefore precedes and persists beyond the articulations it takes part in. I rely on this line of enquiry to state that at the core of the film medium there is a non-interrogatory attentiveness to the fragment as a found thing and that the cinematographic machine embodies a preoccupation with the filmed thing prior to the emergence of representational drives. The inhuman eye of the camera transfers the thing as a fragment of the real offered to its gaze, without questioning what the thing is or signifies. At its degree zero, what is made present within the image is not primarily framed for the human eye but, if opened onto the eye, will constitute a certain imposition of a cinematic presence anchored in materiality and duration. There is a coming into being of things in their thingness, imposing a presence that defies objecthood by its onscreen weightiness. Revisiting Bazin's interest in film's ability to faithfully record the real, I argue that this automatism works against representation – it is not a reproduction of verisimilitude, but a mechanical making-unfamiliar. Similarly, I will rely on an alternative notion of indexicality that thinks it away from semiosis – that is, approaching the indexicality of the cinematic image as index-as-testimony that is tied to the actuality of the profilmic thing and therefore frustrates the abstraction that is key to representation.

I draw on Bazin's attentiveness to the actuality of filmmaking, Stephen Heath's understanding of film's materiality as fundamentally heterogenous, Jean-Louis Comolli's emphasis on the precedence of the profilmic body, and Ivone Margulies's notion of body-too-much to demonstrate that there is an affirmative maladjustment at the heart of filmic renditions of bodies. Not produced by or for the film, the profilmic body does not inherently bear the traces of the film as a whole. While representation is based on a conversion of the real profilmic body and its reduction to what can be recognised by recourse to what is for consciousness, the precedence of the profilmic body disrupts representation as a work that is always incomplete. The camera provides the premise for a giving of bodies that, by essence, is inexhaustible by what is rendered as given and thus bears the seeds of an interruption of givenness. The body of the other is therefore an insurmountable problem for an ontology of film that reduces the cinematic image – the parameters of its being and what it does to vision – to the telos of meaning and visibility. While obsessive concerns with readability and continuity work to deny the problem, alternative approaches, as illustrated by the examples in the opening of this chapter, do not shy away from the problematic but intensify it. They put into practice this irreducibility of the camera's giving and rely on the automatic 'making present' prior to representation to enact a parallelism between the profilmic body and the body of the character. In so doing, cinematic parallelism testifies to the fact that film bears the marks of two heterogeneous realities – that film is an oscillation between a documentation of filmed bodies and a fictionality of characters. Parallelism exercises pressure over film's constitutive duality and theatricalises the stubborn persistence of the filmed body of the other. The cinematic image, if set up by the artist to make the bodily surplus perceivable, can potentially stage the withdrawal of the filmed body from the visual field.

I am intrigued by Bazin's understanding of cinematic images as peculiar amalgams of literalism and referentiality, and by his investment in images that bear the heterogenous realities of the filmic and profilmic, with the quotidian and the non-professional actors as those whose life experiences weigh on their bodies. Enthralling for me as well is the status of the body in Bazinian thought as that which fills the cinematic image, as what, in its contingency, manifests a certain weightiness that does not readily necessitate a call for meaningfulness. Opposing revelation to meaning, Bazin is conscious of a certain weightiness that releases the body-thing[113] from the necessity to signify a lack. I draw on Karl Schoonover's work on the neorealist body to argue that the body, filling the image without necessitating a call for meaningfulness, registers parallelism with greatest force as it blurs the boundary between the intended and the unintended, the fictional and the documentary. This understanding of the body will be instrumental in demonstrating how the body of the other is not merely a vehicle for the filmic event but, in a certain sense, is the event itself. This involves a preoccupation with the body that is, in a certain sense, non-anthropocentric, and its realism is other than a recognition of familiarity. Affirmed by the automatic recording, the body of the other is what provides the documentation of the fragments of the real with certain evidence. As a found thing not enacted through signifying processes, the body becomes the site in which indexing physiognomic peculiarities take precedence over meaningful articulation of bodies, resulting in the breakdown of top-down semantics, the latter crucial to the viewer's mastery over the body viewed. Rooted in the inhuman eye, this viewing dynamic becomes fundamentally dissociated from a reproduction of frameworks of familiarity. It is in this regard that Bazinian humanism, as a belief in the inhuman machine, will be essential for me in demonstrating that there is something ethically profound in the submission of the body of the other to the camera and, through parallelism, in a retention of something that the cinematic image has earned prior to an interrogation of the body.

Equally important for me is the Bazinian obligation to respect the integrity of profilmic time and space and to preserve the wholeness of a profilmic act. Beyond a mere illustration of a set of specific cinematic conventions, presenting an act in its entirety demonstrates the ontological indeterminacy of the cinematic time – the latter as what has to be tamed for the meaning to emerge, and as what alternatively bears the seeds of an interruption of intelligibility if it resurfaces. To respect the wholeness of a profilmic event, as Bazin reminds us, a film must remain faithful to the profilmic that it automatically records by regarding it as what is given and pre-existing rather than exploiting its own ability to facilitate meaning-making. That is, the film should subordinate itself to the profilmic events rather than merely create them. This is an obligation whose seeds the cinematographic machine bears in its degree zero: an automatic recording of the profilmic that preserves the wholeness of the filmed event. Bazinian attentiveness to the profilmic finds its most evident manifestations when an event or action is shown in its entirety in an unbroken shot. A demonstration of the irreplaceability of a unique instance taking place in the profilmic space and the irreversibility of the time of its actual happening, this adherence to the integrity of the profilmic act disrupts the abstraction and repeatability that are central to any formation of meaning. This mode of presentation is not necessarily, as I contend, anti-narrative – rather, it works to introduce a tension within the narrative structure by creating de-hierarchised space and ontological equity. Irreplaceability and irreversibility are therefore less a property of the unique other but reside in the filmic encounter with a body whose actual materiality and duration is preserved and repeated. Singularity resides in the claim of an image that repeats and sustains what is unrepeatable, therefore providing the grounds for the withdrawal of the body from the domain of the visible.

    I argue that this withdrawal exists as a potential in the cinematic image. Automatism brings forth a too-muchness that must be exhausted to render readability – a work that is always incomplete. Sheer recording of the profilmic, however, does not automatically result in the withdrawal of the other from the domain of the visible. An alternative approach is required to negotiate with the realism that film as a medium achieves technologically. I further my argument by drawing on recent scholarly works that problematise the realist–modernist binarism and demonstrate that this negotiation places the question of aesthetics at the core of ethical engagement with film. There is a tension in Bazin's film theory between two different notions of realism, mechanical and aesthetic, which assists me in arguing for realism as a plural aesthetics and its openness to artistic experimentation with the image. There must be a coupling of what the machine brings to life technologically and an aesthetic use of the latter by the artist so that the ethicity of the interaction between the camera and the body will be brought forth.

    An exploration of the materiality of film as the medium that hosts experimentations with the body is therefore accompanied in my study by an emphasis on the role of the aesthetic in absorbing Levinasian concerns without falling prey to iconophobia. I will argue that realism, understood not as a set of recognisable norms but as aesthetic endeavours to question recognisability, is where the ethical and the aesthetic intersect. Experimental realisms of the body involve an openness and exposure to what is other, to what precedes and faces, therefore staging the withdrawal of the filmed body from the 'body as given'. I will therefore argue that the cinematic image's originary concern with alterity is not simply because of film's presumably faithful and objective recording of appearances (mechanical realism), but precisely due to its capacity to host and enact distinctively rich negotiations with the profilmic body (aesthetic realism). While representation locates and pins down the body as an object in the frontal visual field and in meaningful relations to the elements of a given image, realisms of the body stage the encounter with the other where the other faces (the viewer). They rescue the facing of the other from reduction to an object within a frontal visual field by emphasising the materiality of the body over conscious articulations and expressions of text-bound meaning and characterisation.

Expanding the existing enquiries into the consequences of Levinas's ethical thought for aesthetics, this book studies selected films and cinematic approaches exemplifying realisms of the body that are consistent with the ethics drawn from the notion of facing. I approach Chantal Akerman, Bruno Dumont, Pedro Costa, Gus Van Sant, Sohrab Shahid Saless, Abbas Kiarostami, Amir Naderi, Jafar Panahi and Carlos Reygadas as philosophical interlocutors engaged in thinking how film is particularly equipped to affirmatively expose the tensions between the ethical and the visual. In their differing engagements with cinematic realism and manipulations of the image, their films involve certain critical negotiations with the surplus of film's presentation of the body to stage the withdrawal of the other. Bringing about an ethical resonance between the automatism of the camera and the face of the image, the films studied in the book demonstrate the ethical significance of experimentations that aesthetically earn what the cinematographic machine technologically achieves – a sort of appreciating the body of the other that precedes and remains inexhaustible by any recognition or identification of the body. Endorsing the essential part that the aesthetic plays in this appreciation, I propose an aesthetics of incompleteness and contend that respecting the human other requires a recounting of their story but also a breakdown of intentional meaning and a retention of something of the inhumanity of the eye of the machine. Countering a looking that reduces the image to enclosed visual content and turns vision into objecthood and domination, I make a case for aesthetic experiments that turn the image into an active gift – a giving of bodies to be borne witness to in their precarity and openness, irreducible to a rendition of visible, meaningful givens.

Before exploring in depth how the cinematic image is capable of this encounter with the other, it is crucial to revisit the Levinasian face in relation to bodily exposure to the other and demonstrate why the body is central in Levinasian ethics. It will be my contention that the face is, in a certain sense, a body, whereas the body is a wordless vocalisation of suffering indissociable from the body's image. This proposition will require a redefinition of the visual being of the image and what it does to vision – it is precisely through the image that the body of the other is able to withdraw from the visual. This understanding of the image in connection to the dynamics of breakthrough and withdrawal, as we shall see, resonates with the saying–said distinction in Levinas's thought and with what the image-as-facing does to vision.

Notes

1. The work of art, in Levinas's terms, 'substitutes an image for the troubling depth of the future'. Levinas, *Totality and Infinity*, 263. In 'Reality and Its Shadow', his most notorious argument against art, Levinas sees this fixity as an idolatry of fate, as a fostering of a sense of inevitability that is in clear opposition to creation and revelation, the latter terms intimately linked with futurity. According to Levinas: 'A being is that which is, that which reveals itself in its truth, and, at the same time, it resembles itself, is its own image. The original gives itself as though it were at a distance from itself, as though it were withdrawing itself, as though something in a being delayed behind being. The consciousness of the absence of the object which characterizes an image is . . . is equivalent to an alteration of the very being of the object, where its essential forms appear as a garb that it abandons in withdrawing.' See Levinas, 'Reality and Its Shadow', 6–7. Levinas sees artistic activity as 'a plastic immobilization, a molding of what, by essence, could not and should not be fixed'. See Crignon, 'Figuration', 112.
2. Cooper, 'The Occluded Relation', i.
3. I take the notion of altericide from Colin Davis, who uses the term 'to describe the possibility for violence inherent in the fraught relations between selves and others, texts and readers'. See Davis, *Ethical Issues in Twentieth-Century French Fiction*, 1–2.
4. Saxton, 'Blinding Visions', 105. Also, see Saxton's article in *Film-Philosophy*, 'Fragile Faces'.
5. Raphael, *Judaism and the Visual Image*, 37.
6. See Bergren-Aurand, 'Film/ethics', 459. Also, see Tuck and Carel, *New Takes in Film-Philosophy*.
7. Sinnerbrink, *New Philosophies of Film*, 141.
8. As Sinnerbrink and Lisa Trahair contend in the introduction to *SubStance*'s 'Film and/as Ethics', 'many theorists are now engaged in what has come to be known as

"film-philosophy", developing philosophical insight out of their close engagement with film, and bringing philosophical concepts to bear on the aesthetic experience cinema affords'. See Sinnerbrink and Trahair, 'Introduction: Film and/as Ethics', 3.
9. Hole, *Towards a Feminist Cinematic Ethics*, 2–3.
10. Critchley, 'Introduction', *The Cambridge Companion to Levinas*, 2.
11. Ibid., 12.
12. Levinas, *Totality and Infinity*, 43.
13. Ibid. Also, see ibid., 173.
14. Ibid., 43.
15. Critchley, 'Introduction', *The Cambridge Companion to Levinas*, 15. Also, for a discussion of ethics as a process of self-questioning, see Garber, Hanssen and Walkowitz, *The Turn to Ethics*.
16. Exteriority, that which 'cannot be reduced to the same'. See Critchley, 'Introduction', *The Cambridge Companion to Levinas*, 15.
17. Levinas, *Totality and Infinity*, 126.
18. See Levinas, 'Enigma and Phenomenon'.
19. For a critique of the hyperboles of Levinas's conception of otherness, see Treanor, *Aspects of Alterity*.
20. See Critchley, 'Introduction', *The Cambridge Companion to Levinas*, 8.
21. Crignon, 'Figuration', 102.
22. See Levinas, 'Enigma and Phenomenon', 109.
23. Levinas, *Totality and Infinity*, 35–9.
24. Western philosophy, as Levinas observes it, is the 'plot of the ego'. See Levinas, 'Philosophy and the Idea of Infinity', 50.
25. Critchley, 'Introduction', *The Cambridge Companion to Levinas*, 16. Also, see Levinas, 'Transcendence and Height'.
26. Levinas, *Alterity and Transcendence*, 39. Also, see Wyschogrod, 'Language and Alterity in the Thought of Levinas', 190–1.
27. As Wyschogrod observes: 'the intellectual act that intends the whole', according to Levinas, 'loses touch with the world in its concreteness' and thereby is 'left with the pure form of the thinkable'. See Wyschogrod, 'Language and Alterity in the Thought of Levinas', 190–1.
28. Levinas, *Alterity and Transcendence*, 47.
29. As Levinas remarks, the object is 'engendered in the gratuitous spontaneity of a thought that thinks it'. See Levinas, *Totality and Infinity*, 127.
30. Wyschogrod, 'Language and Alterity in the Thought of Levinas', 191.
31. Levinas, *Totality and Infinity*, 24.
32. Ziarek, 'Semantics of Proximity', 213.
33. See Levinas, *Totality and Infinity*, 36–7.
34. Levinas's rhetoric reflects this violence: 'the foreign being, instead of maintaining itself in the inexpugnable fortress of its singularity . . . becomes a theme and an object'. See Levinas, 'Philosophy and the Idea of Infinity', 50.
35. Ziarek, 'Semantics of Proximity', 215.
36. It is a separation that can be grasped and captured neither by the colonising domain of the same nor by a third that, by falsifying definition, is assumed to be on the outside. For Levinas, non-relation is 'the nontotalizing relation to the face of the other'. See

Robbins, 'Aesthetic Totality and Ethical Infinity: Levinas on Art', 356. Also, see Levinas, *Totality and Infinity*, 36.
37 Ziarek, 'Semantics of Proximity', 215. Also, see Levinas, *Totality and Infinity*, 39 and Wyschogrod, 'Language and Alterity in the Thought of Levinas', 188.
38 Jay, *Downcast Eyes*, 543.
39 Levinas, *Totality and Infinity*, 23.
40 Ibid., 85.
41 Ibid., 24–5.
42 Ibid., 191.
43 See Downing, 'Re-viewing the Sexual Relation', 50.
44 Kennan, 'Facing Images', 153.
45 To articulate Blanchot's antipathy for the violence of vision in his *The Infinite Conversation*, Ullrich Haase and William Large argue: 'The unity of seeing is explained by the fact that in comprehension there are not two terms but three: the two terms in relation and the third term that mediates and forms the unity between them'. See Haase, Large, *Maurice Blanchot*, 75–6. Indeed, my use of the notion of the third must not be conflated with the notion of the third party (*le tiers*) in Levinas work that refers to all the others (other than the self and the other in the face-to-face non-relation) who constitute the community. See *Totality and Infinity*, 212–14 and *Otherwise Than Being* 156–62.
46 Saxton, 'Blinding Visions', 95–7.
47 Ibid., 98.
48 Perpich, 'Sensible Subjects', 298.
49 Ibid.
50 Levinas, *Totality and Infinity*, 124.
51 Ibid., 123.
52 Cited in Saxton, 'Blinding Visions', 99.
53 Ibid.
54 See Levinas, *Totality and Infinity*, 50. Representation is a reduction of the face to 'immobility' – it is a reappropriation of alterity and a silencing of the face's address. See Saxton, 'Blinding Visions', 99. On the notion of infinity, see Levinas, 'Philosophy and the Idea of Infinity', 54.
55 Levinas, *Totality and Infinity*, 194–5.
56 In the face, the absolutely other resists consciousness 'to the extent that even this resistance is not convertible into a content of consciousness'. See Levinas, 'Meaning and Sense', 97.
57 See Critchley, 'Introduction', *The Cambridge Companion to Levinas*, 12.
58 Crignon, 'Figuration', 101.
59 See Steimatsky, *The Face on Film*, 13.
60 Crignon, 'Figuration', 102.
61 Ibid.
62 Levinas, 'The Trace of the Other', 351.
63 Riera, '"The Possibility of the Poetic Said"', 22.
64 Crignon, 'Figuration', 103.
65 Ibid.
66 The face's signifyingness is, therefore, 'extraordinary, outside of every order, outside of every world'. See Levinas, 'Meaning and Sense', 96.

67 Levinas, *Ethics and Infinity*, 86.
68 Levinas continues: 'But the relation to the face is straightaway ethical. The face is what one cannot kill, or at least it is that whose meaning consists in saying: "thou shall not kill".' See Levinas, *Ethics and Infinity*, 86.
69 The face-to-face [*vis-à-vis*] as the ethical relation introduces that which is 'not integrated into the world of significations because it is the absolute expression of a presence'. See Crignon, 'Figuration', 108.
70 Ibid., 108.
71 Ibid., 103.
72 Levinas, *Totality and Infinity*, 261.
73 Ibid., 262. Also, see ibid., 200.
74 Ibid., 198.
75 Crignon, 'Figuration', 103.
76 Ibid.
77 Levinas, *Totality and Infinity*, 198.
78 Crignon, 'Figuration', 103.
79 Ibid., 104.
80 See ibid.
81 Kenaan, *The Ethics of Visuality*, 10–11.
82 Saxton, 'Blinding Visions', 100.
83 Ibid.
84 Ibid. Also, see Cooper, *Selfless Cinema?*, 19 and Levinas, *Totality and Infinity*, 73. For a study of visibility and invisibility, documentation, absence, trace and ethics, see Saxton's monograph *Haunted Images*.
85 Downing, 'Re-viewing the Sexual Relation', 50.
86 Crignon, 'Figuration', 101. Seán Hand interestingly points out that Levinas's mistrust of art can also be seen in the immediate post-war context where Levinas had witnessed what her termed 'the cowardice, evasion and even wickedness of certain artists during the Shoah'. Hand, *Emmanuel Levinas*, 65.
87 Crignon, 'Figuration', 101. As Colin Davis notes, 'Levinas reminds us that philosophy's distrust of the arts has not simply disappeared; . . . the ancient quarrel is by no means settled, and the philosophical seriousness which some thinkers now seem eager to accord to literature and film may in fact mask a continuing rivalry.' See Davis, *Critical Excess*, xiii.
88 Downing, 'Re-viewing the Sexual Relation', 51.
89 Ibid.
90 Sinnerbrink, *Cinematic Ethics*, 152.
91 Saxton, 'Blinding Visions', 101.
92 Ibid., 102.
93 Ibid., 104.
94 Ibid., 105.
95 Sinnerbrink, *Cinematic Ethics*, 153.
96 Girgus, 'Beyond Ontology', 88. Also, see Girgus, *Levinas and the Cinema of Redemption*.
97 Girgus, 'Beyond Ontology', 91.
98 Ibid., 96.

99 Ibid., 90. More recently, Girgus's work on Laura Mulvey's notion of 'delayed cinema' and the existential coming of being and cinematic presence envisions a 'new ontology of cinema' that can enable us to bring forth new ways of thinking about ethics, otherness and being. See Girgus, 'Existential Presence and the Cinematic Image'. Also, see Girgus's book *Time, Existential Presence and the Cinematic Image* that studies Mulvey's theory in relation to the idea of time and the other in dialogue with Levinas, Jean-Luc Nancy and Julia Kristeva.
100 Cooper, 'Mortal Ethics', 74.
101 Ibid., 72.
102 Ibid., 74.
103 Mai, '*Lorna's Silence* and Levinas's Ethical Alternative', 436.
104 Ibid., 438.
105 Ibid., 447. Also, see Mai, *Jean-Pierre and Luc Dardenne*.
106 Mai, '*Lorna's Silence* and Levinas's Ethical Alternative', 448.
107 Ibid., 448–9.
108 Hole, *Towards a Feminist Cinematic Ethics*, 45.
109 Ibid., 109.
110 Ibid.
111 Ibid., 110.
112 Perpich, 'Levinas, Feminism, and Identity Politics', 33. Cited in Hole, *Towards a Feminist Cinematic Ethics*, 110–11. Kelly Oliver's study of witnessing beyond recognition interestingly emphasises 'the unseen in vision and the unspoken in speech' and associates witnessing with address and response. See Oliver, *Witnessing: Beyond Recognition*.
113 I take this concept of body-thing, as opposed to body-object, from Davis's reading of Jacques Derrida's approach to alterity and the question of meaning. To refer to the absolute otherness of a poem and the inexhaustibility of its ethical address in order to contest the adequacy of interpretation, Davis argues: 'The poem-thing is absolutely other, it addresses me without speaking to me, it is mute but its silence issues an imperious command, it offers and withholds itself at the same time, it commands us to listen to what does not speak and to submit ourselves to what is never entirely present.' See Davis, *Critical Excess*, 30. In *Signéponge/Signsponge* Derrida writes: 'Thus the thing would be the other, the other-thing which gives me an order or addresses an impossible, intransigent, insatiable demand to me, without an exchange and without a transaction, without a possible contract. Without a word, without speaking to me, it addresses itself to me . . . the law of the thing is singularity and difference as well. An infinite debt ties me to it, a duty without funds or foundation. I shall never acquit myself of it. Thus the thing is not an object; it cannot become one.' See Derrida, *Signéponge/Signsponge*, 14.

2

The Image and the Body

In Levinasian iconoclasm, the image fixes and masks, and is therefore the paradigmatic illustration of what is suspicious and condemnable about vision.[1] The ethical revelation of the face, as Emmanuel Levinas conceives it, is evidently different from the always already mediated experience that an image offers. However, as Lisa Downing suggests, it may also be possible to consider 'certain cinematic images which foil our desire to interpret, name and understand' as analogous to a movement 'from the meaningfulness of intentionality to the ethical of epiphany'.[2] Downing points out the potentialities inherent in a resistance towards interpreting the image according to discourses that are established and familiar. She contends that, through such a resistance, there may emerge the possibility of being 'affected *beyond* the level of meaning and intellect'; of being 'interpellated at the level of ethics without social positions of subjectivity and objectivity being predefined for us'.[3] Identifying innovative framings of the body in the works of Claire Denis and Catherine Breillat where 'the human body is subjected to a radical making-unfamiliar', Downing demonstrates the aesthetic possibilities where bodies 'may appear in the realm of the visible *qua* face, precisely in so far as their appearance confounds the Looking–Knowing relation', therefore disrupting the violence of the gaze.[4] Opposing ethical epiphany to 'content', Downing proposes a Levinasian 'gaze-as-caress' where the camera moves away from the 'acquisitive familiarity of possession'.[5] In this proposition, Downing reworks the ethical investigation of the image by stating that this critique interrogates not so much 'looking *per se*' but rather 'processes of meaning-making that accompany it'.[6]

Similar to the responses to Levinasian iconoclasm reviewed in the previous chapter, Downing's approach demonstrates reverence for Levinasian concerns yet does not shy away from the aesthetic possibilities that can help us read Levinas against himself. The face resists the gaze; however, it 'may appear in the realm of the visible', but only insofar as its appearance undermines the gaze.[7] How is the body significant in engaging with Levinasian anti-ocular concerns and in thinking the image otherwise? Why is the body pivotal in resisting the 'Looking–Knowing' relation and in the disruption of meaning-making processes in the image? Is the Levinasian face a body? And how is it possible to think film–ethics encounters in affirmative ways through an understanding of the face as a revelation of alterity that can be traced on the body?

To investigate the paradoxical visuality of the face and cast light on the relation between the ethical and the body, this chapter reads the face through the philosophical insights Levinas puts forward in his second major book, *Otherwise Than Being, or, Beyond Essence*. Even though the face becomes an evidently marginal term in the book, it is my contention that thinking the invisible aspect of the face depends on a certain revisiting of the latter through what Levinas calls forth in his discussions of language. In *Totality and Infinity: An Essay on Exteriority*, the face is already tied to language and speech. It is in *Otherwise Than Being*, however, that this tie is further explored, and its fullest implications begin to emerge despite the marginalisation of the face as a critical idiom in the second book. As an implicit correction to the binary oppositions Levinas brought forward in *Totality and Infinity*, between the ethical on the one hand and the ontological and visual on the other, *Otherwise Than Being* presents a more nuanced treatment of these terms. It provides the grounds for opening up a space in which the ethical relevance of the visual can be highlighted not only through Levinasian ethics but ultimately against his iconoclasm. Associating the face with speech is paradoxically a reaffirmation of the visuality of the face, as the latter is the wordless vocalisation that can be traced on the body of the other. As I will demonstrate, this nuanced understanding is instrumental in revisiting the body's image and in determining its ethical relevance.

In what follows I propose to map the ethical in the originary structure of exposure to the body of the other and establish the ethical necessity of the body's image. This approach will show that the relation of the face to the body is central to an account of Levinas's thought. Attentiveness to the structure of exposure provides the premise for my contention throughout the next chapters that ethical engagement with film is indissociable from an examination of the aesthetic implications of the formation of the body's image. Film is equipped to release the ethical from the flatness of abstract language, as Kristin Lené Hole rightly observes, by illustrating the 'reality of bodies' in material terms. Film can stage an encounter with alterity, with our bodily and felt 'openness and vulnerability' – it is at the same time what has the potential to render evident ethical tensions.[8] I take this position further by arguing that a Levinasian engagement with the ethics of film requires a certain understanding of filmic otherness where the latter does not predate the filmic encounter with the body of the other. What film does through the image is reaffirm the originary exposure beyond recognition of identity and evoke a self that is hosting the other prior to assuming the capacity to actively accepting or rejecting the other. Before turning to discussions of the visual being of the image, it is therefore crucial to investigate this structure of exposure as what resonates with the viewing self's relation to the image and, most remarkably, with the film viewer's lack of control over the automatically formed image of the body and the imposing duration of its persistence onscreen.

The structure of exposure: hospitality and the body

At the core of the tension between the ethical and the visual is the invisibility of the face. The way the concept of the face evolves and stands out in Levinas's philosophical endeavours removes the term from its common implications:

> To manifest oneself as a face is to impose oneself above and beyond the manifested and purely phenomenal form, to present oneself in a mode irreducible to manifestation, the very straightforwardness of the face to face, without the intermediacy of any image.[9]

Levinas does not simply oppose the invisible to the visible. Nor does he reduce the invisible to what is not visible – the non-visible. Rather, Levinas's use of the term uncovers a paradox. As Hagi Kenaan notes, the face

> is seen in being invisible. It is seen as the invisible . . . Even if what is central in the face is not visual (as Levinas argues), this non-visuality is located at the very core of the visible. The ethical dimension has no other place to reveal itself and, in this sense, Levinas' use of the face cannot be understood without addressing the unique form of its visual presence.[10]

The face, even though it is not to be equated with face as a visual object, with countenance, and even though it is more a matter of speech (as exposure to the other) than of seeing, has a visual connotation. It is precisely its relation to visuality that problematises the relation between the ethical and the visual. In a certain way, the face needs the visual to reveal itself. However, it does not reveal itself as an object within vision, as what can be located within the frontal visual field. What Levinas tries to bring our attention to is that the face reveals itself within the visual, yet it also disrupts and ruptures the visibility of the visual through its revelation. The face is 'the vanishing point of the visual'.[11] How is the face capable of this disruption? How is the face to be taken as the invisible while it nevertheless breaks into the visible?

The invisible of the face is its address. It is what wrests the face away from being a visual object. Yet how is the encounter with the face of the other harbouring an address that is structurally absent in encounters with other objects? Furthermore, it is crucial to investigate how the face of the other, despite its irreducibility to a visual object, *concerns* the self, and how the attributes of a self that is receptive to the claim of the face must be reconceived. Responding to these questions is bound up with the question of language – with an ethical condition preceding all meaning and visibility.

Irreducible to thematisation or any sort of comprehension, the non-relation to the other involves not vision but language. Entering the face-to-face non-relation, I do not see the other – despite the ocular connotations of the face-to-face encounter. Nor do I turn the other into an object of contemplation.[12] Levinas distinguishes between two aspects of language: the saying (*le dire*) and the said (*le dit*) – respectively understood as the originary structure of exposure (to the other) and the designative, communicative aspect of language that, in simple terms, cannot exhaust but only suggests this structure.[13] The said is closely tied to the world of objects, thus making possible a certain mastery of the world.[14] Just as the object is conceived in *Totality and Infinity* as what gains meaning through its embeddedness within a matrix of objects, as what can be pinned down as a something, the said of the language in *Otherwise Than Being* involves objective and contained forms of meaning. The said can be understood as an ontological process in which the active subject intends, and thus brings into light and being, an intended object.[15] The said renders the object by identifying it as this or that, by referring to it by an index finger, ascribing to it a location within the frontal world of objects.

More significantly, however, there is another side to language – a passive one opposed to the aforementioned activity. The saying is the revelation of an ethical aspect of communication that works as the 'precondition of every communicative situation';[16] a saying that might be referred to as 'the saying without the said'.[17] Just as whatever the face has to say or signify, or whatever its visibility contains as visual content, rests upon an encounter with the face, every said is based on and is made possible by a fundamental saying that is a saying without the said – that is, what is without content yet makes the content possible. There is a receptivity at the heart of the subject that precedes yet persists beyond the activity of meaning-making, of forming and rendering objects for consciousness.[18] The saying first and foremost signifies an exposure (to the other). It is the site where the encounter with the face of the other takes place. As such, the saying implies 'a possibility of being addressed by the other'; an address that, most importantly, happens 'prior to any intention, need, or demand of the subject'.[19]

The saying is ethical and the said is ontological. This is a designation that not only sheds light on Levinas's approach to ethics but further complicates the relation between the ethical and the ontological. The said, as the ontological, appears to leave no room for exposure to the other while the saying constitutes language as proximity to and contact with the other. While an object owes its meaningfulness to a context, to an order of meaningful objects, the face, breaking with every context, is meaningful without context – it harbours a meaningfulness prior to any meaning.[20] The saying, as Levinas reminds us, is the 'very signifyingness of signification'.[21] The said is being, whereas the saying is otherwise than being.[22]

Language is therefore key to Levinas's concern for preserving the irreducible alterity and exteriority of the other as what precede thinking and thematisation. Through the face-to-face non-relation, the face of the other makes possible the originary meaning and signification. It founds language, not by conveying a linguistic meaning or a message that is simply translatable into words, but through issuing a command. This initial word exists in the encounter from the very beginning, precedent to a subject that seems and claims to have or possess language. Language is always already an address from the other.[23] It is a proximity that is not established through moral or conscious elaboration or initiative whereas, most interestingly, '[c]onsciousness in all its forms – representational, axiological, practical – has already lost this close presence'.[24] Responsibility arrives prior to the self's having a choice to assume anything. It therefore implies a proximity that consciousness, from its very moment of constitution, is bereft of. It is by this token that the first word of the other possesses a meaning in itself, that it has a meaning immediately, since it 'arrives before any constitutive act of my consciousness'.[25] The self is only the recipient of language as a gift since the latter is founded by the arrival of the other. It is in this regard that Levinas sees the essence of language 'as the welcoming of otherness, of the visitation of the other'.[26]

The saying is in close affinity with hospitality, for proximity implies that the self is always already hosting the other, is touched by it, prior to consciousness. According to Jacques Derrida, hospitality constitutes the core of

Levinas's approach to ethics. It is a giving up of a closeness to the other and keeping a space of unconditional openness towards the other before they are identified.[27] The welcome is not a derivative as 'there is no face without welcome'.[28] Hospitality, in this originary sense, implies that the subject is, as Levinas asserts, not only a host but a hostage.[29] It is always the other who can say the first 'yes' – the self has received the other prior to being able to assume its own powers. According to Derrida,

> there is no *first yes*, the *yes* is already a response. But since everything must begin with some yes, the response begins, the response commands. We must make the best of this aporia, into which we, finite and mortal, are *thrown* and without which there would be no promise of a path. It is necessary to *begin by responding*.[30]

The saying–said dynamic therefore deconstructs the host–hostage binary. The self is not simply a host inviting the other; it is taken hostage by the arrival of the other.[31] This originary hospitality assumes a self that is embodied. A body, the self is always already exposed prior to the constitution of its consciousness. The Levinasian ethical subject is a 'sensible' subject, not a conscious one. Sensibility is what Levinas calls the way of my subjection, 'a sentient vulnerability or passivity towards the other'.[32] For Levinas, sensibility implies an originary openness and receptivity to the world.[33] Subjectivity in Levinas's account is thus irreducible to the intentional structures of consciousness – it implies an 'affective knowledge'.[34] It is in this respect that ethics is 'lived in the sensibility of an embodied exposure to the other';[35] that is, ethics is dependent on an originary vulnerability and openness as its condition for possibility.[36] The sensation that sensibility involves is essentially heterogeneous to meaning and signification, even if it functions as the condition for meaning mainly due to the *response* it necessitates.

The saying exposes an alternative mode of sensibility as 'the capacity for being affected by the other'.[37] As Ewa Ziarek contends, the saying is a pre-reflective sensibility characterised by touch rather than by vision. In starting with touching, understood not as palpation but as caress, and language, regarded not as a channel of communication or a mere traffic of information but as contact, proximity is irreducible to consciousness.[38] This returns us to the paradox that seems to govern the whole Levinasian account of the relation between the ethical and the visual since, as Philippe Crignon observes, what 'takes us beyond phenomena manifests itself – exhibits itself – in the sensible world that it rends'.[39] It is in a close affinity with the caress that Levinas tries to think the approach to the other in a tangible, material way. Indeed, how could the face of the other touch me if it is 'without a body'? In other words, if the other can touch the self, if the face, in a certain sense, *is* body, and if the non-relation to the other is always a carnal matter, then we might say that the face is always already 'a tangible production', even a 'figuration'.[40] The ethical breaks through the visual as its only way of manifestation. Therefore, one might ask whether the ethical epiphany of the face is always already a figuration, contesting the absolute dissociation of the ethical from the image commanded by iconoclasm.

The non-frontal: the face of the image

This nuanced relation between the saying and the said casts light on what the face does to vision. Reconceiving the face through the pre-reflective and embodied exposure to the other demonstrates how the face cannot be dissociated from the movement of *facing*. As Kenaan argues, the face is never a given but is always

> part of a becoming, involved in its own revelation. The face is part of a movement that unravels the mesh of the visual, but is not itself entwined in the visual web. The face erupts into the visible and leaves clear traces, but is never found in the visual field as an object of vision . . . While showing itself, breaking into the frame of the visual, the face never coalesces into a visual object. The face's form of appearance is not the form of a 'something'.[41]

While the visible can be located within the viewer's frontal visual field and pointed at as an object occupying a certain space, the face has a non-frontal aspect that renders it unlocatable and invisible. Invisibility is not a matter of not being visible. It is not that the face has an aspect that is not visible – which is to say, an aspect that is yet unrevealed and non-visible, and therefore is yet to be illuminated. Nor is it that the face hides and masks something, that the face is a surface that hides a space behind itself. The non-visible still belongs to the rule of the frontal and cannot break with it. The fact that the face is concealed, or that it is what conceals, implies that the face refuses to belong to my frontal visual field. The face is non-frontal in the sense that it is a movement that cannot be located in the same way as an object can be. The movement of the face removes it from belonging to objecthood. As opposed to objects that acquire meaning in relation to the world of objects, Kenaan reminds us,

> the epiphany of the other involves a signifyingness of its own independence of this meaning received from the world. The other comes to us not only out of the context, but also without mediation; he signifies by himself... This presence consists in *coming toward us*, in *making an entry*... the phenomenon which the apparition of the other is also a face... the epiphany of a face is visitation.[42]

The face is not simply and unproblematically positioned within the frontal visual field. The face is a becoming, involved in its own revelation. The movement of the face is not the movement of an object travelling through a space of objects, traversing them. Its movement is making an entry, thus already involving a coming from elsewhere. While appearing in our frontal visual field, the face breaks through, yet its non-frontality is not dissociable from the movement itself. The meaningfulness of objects, as Kenaan observes, requires a certain frontality: objects appear in the context of 'a world of sense that unfolds *in front of us*'. The presence of the face, by contrast, is its coming towards us – the face is not, strictly speaking, 'located anywhere, at least not in the ordinary sense of things filling up a given space with their mass. Rather, the face is present as a kind of movement, the crossing of a border.'[43] And just as the saying is ontologically precedent to the said, the singularity of facing is prior to the particularity of what a face could contain in terms of meaning. The face establishes proximity and hospitality, regardless of the content of the face. The face is an expression prior to expressing any content in particular.

Levinas reminds us that no other object possesses the movement in the face that gives it a non-frontal aspect. The face can be thought to embody the non-frontal despite its obvious belonging to our frontal visual field only if the face is not simply approached as a noun. The face is a noun that at the same time is a verb. The face has in its very root and structure the verb *to face*; that to have a face, to be a face, is at the same time a facing. As Kenaan reveals to us, this understanding of the face as facing resides in *panim* (the Hebrew word for 'face'), which implies 'a specific kind of movement involved in [face's] revelation'.[44] *Panim* is revealing in making present the event quality of the face of the other. The term teaches us, as Levinas would have intended, to appreciate a turning (*peniyya*) within the face of the other. Reminiscent of the tense relation between the saying and the said in the event of language, 'the turning of the face, the *peniyya* of the *panim*, always comes with a double meaning: it consists of both a turning toward and a turning away from, an approaching and a taking leave'.[45] This event quality explains the uneasy relation of the face to the visual – the face does belong to the visual not only as an object yet also as that which problematises objecthood and disrupts the visual field. The mode in which the face of the other enters the visual field is not a matter of appearance. Appearance assumes a certain *for*-consciousness structure, while the event quality of the face of the other is better to be understood as revelation. Unlike appearance, revelation acknowledges the movement, the making an entry. Similarly, while what appears belongs to the world of objects and is reduced to visual content, the face of the other, because of its movement, takes leave and is thus uncontainable. There is a 'reverberation of alterity that cannot be framed as content'.[46] The thing that remains irreducible to a 'something' is the presence of the non-frontal. It is what any framing of the frontal visual field fails to grasp and exhaust. The relation of the face to the visual therefore simultaneously harbours the two movements of breakthrough and withdrawal.

What is the relation of the image to the non-frontal? To argue that an analogy between the image and the face is possible requires an alternative understanding of the image. The common, age-old paradigm that has persisted in conceptualising the image has reduced the term to representation. Often referred to as Platonic, this approach considers the image as that which draws its significance from its derivative, secondary relation to what it is presumed to be a representation of. The object of representation is deemed as primary, while the image is relegated to a secondary state of being. The image is a copy. By contrast, there has been a rival approach, more commonly accepted in the contemporary philosophy and cultural theory, according to which the ontological inferiority that the first paradigm ascribes to the image should be problematised so that a certain space for conceiving the autonomy of the image is opened up. While image-as-representation sees the image as simply reducible to an image of or about the world, as a copy that is constituted by what it is not, the second approach endeavours to understand the autonomy of the image by theorising its objecthood. The image is no longer a picture or reflection of reality but reconsidered as part of the real in the world.[47]

While the second paradigm achieves freeing the image from merely representational understandings, objecthood cannot do justice to the unique being of the image, for it cannot account for the image's problematic relation with other objects. It fails to acknowledge how the image is not simply part of our frontal visual field but is, most importantly, a potential disruption of it. An interrogation of what constitutes an image is indissociable from the way it opens up visually. According to Kenaan, the question of the being of the image necessitates a certain engagement with the points in which the image diverges from the world of objects: 'Being an image is being visual in a very specific way', while this being can be articulated 'in terms of the image's turn to its viewers, its manner of facing us.'[48] The manner in which the image faces the viewer stems from the image's departure from objecthood. Admittedly, images and objects are similar insofar as they both could be said to be positioned in our visual field. Yet, there is a fundamental difference between them in terms of the manner they present themselves to the eye:

> [U]nlike objects, images are in essence visual entities. Images are visual at heart. They are not only perceptible or visible but they specifically meet the eye as that which offers itself to sight. That is, the being of images is always already tied up with the fact that we have eyes that see and that can respond to the image's offering. The question of vision is internal to the image's visibility.[49]

The image has an inner, essential bond with the condition of being viewed. It is an entity that is 'never just present but always already self-presenting, addressing itself to the eye' – it is 'a turning toward the eye, a facing of the viewer'.[50] This movement is, to borrow from Michael Fried, 'a shift of emphasis from considerations of psychology or social identity', to something more 'surface-oriented',[51] something that is 'noncommunicating, without psychological interiority of any kind',[52] that goes beyond the limitations of mere representation by prioritising facingness over closure.[53] This approach assists to conceptualise an alternative possibility in the image according to which the surface is irreducible to whatever the frame might contain in terms of visual content. The image can establish a relation with its viewer that addresses the latter without the address being containable in terms of the meaning of what is conveyed within the image as content.

This distinction between the image and the object is analogous to what I have discussed with respect to the irreducibility of the face to objecthood. The way the image is taken to have a specific relation to the visual field no less shares a structural similarity with the way the face problematises visibility. Just as the face of the other precedes the self's inviting powers and happens to the self as visitation, the image is what the viewer looks at yet is always already addressing the eye. More remarkably, the way the image opens up visually is inseparable from its meaningfulness. Just as the face of the other is a testimony to a meaningfulness prior to meaning, an image, by its very structure, is a facing whose significance resides in the manner in which it faces us. The image is what has a face, or at least it is what manifests a certain facingness, and it is associated with not just the face of the other but also its body. Just as the face of the other is essentially a *peniyya* (a facing), it is possible to think the image away from representation and objecthood by seeing in the image the movement of a turning. This movement introduces the non-frontal. As Kenaan contends, the image is extrovertly visual – which is to say:

> Unlike objects, they are never just there in our field of vision but always show themselves in a manner that is, already, intricately tied to the condition of being viewed. Being an image is being turned – a turning – toward the eye.[54]

The image turns our relation to the frontal visual field into an uneasy, troubled one precisely because the image is never simply present – it is always self-presenting. The image is not, by its structure, visual content always already framed by the eye. Its being resides in its being towards a viewer. The image is therefore a *gift*, yet one that actively disrupts the frontality of the visual field, introducing another aspect that cannot be simply grasped or contained: 'what we face when we look at pictures is never a given, but, alternatively, a *giving*.'[55]

Locating the ethical in the image: *Close-Up* and *Still Life*

There lies an alternative ethical possibility precisely within the visual field that the gaze operates. This possibility 'is not of our making but is already open toward us',[56] resonating with the originary structure of exposure. It is the existence of what is never a given, just as an object is, but a giving. Reading Levinas, Kenaan fleshes out this tension at the heart of his philosophy: 'the face can remain hidden from us precisely because it is in front of us, because the eye has become fixated on its relationship with it, particularly because the gaze is locked in a frontal relationship with the face.'[57] The image is where this frontal relationship is staged but is also potentially exposed to failure.

Let me briefly look at two films here before turning to a discussion of an ethics of failure that disrupts the frontality of vision. Abbas Kiarostami's *Close-Up* (*Namaye nazdik*, 1990) and Sohrab Shahid Saless's *Still Life* (*Tabiate bijan*, 1974) explore the risks and possibilities of the image while each exemplifies a different account of the ethics of the image. Their differing aesthetic approach can be instructive at this point in envisaging responses to iconoclasm from within the image.

Kiarostami's *Close-Up* is a remarkable example of cinema's engagement with the ethics of representation. The film poses questions about what it means to bring the other into the image and project their body's image onscreen. It recounts the real-life story and trial of poor, unemployed cinephile Hossein Sabzian in Tehran. Impersonating the well-known Iranian filmmaker Mohsen Makhmalbaf, Sabzian approaches the Ahankhahs, a middle-class family, while pretending to be involving them in his next project. Kiarostami's film begins when Sabzian is arrested and a legal case is opened against him following his ultimate failure to keep up the pretence. Persuading the people involved in these events to play themselves, Kiarostami documents Sabzian's actual trial with his camera while reconstructing the scenes that led to his detention.

In a key early scene, Kiarostami meets Sabzian in jail for the first time, letting him know about his interest in the story and his willingness to assist in the case. In arguably one of the most moving and self-reflexive scenes in the history of cinema, Sabzian admits that what he did looked like fraud, but only 'from outside'. Reiterating his passion for cinema, he turns to Kiarostami and suggests, 'You could make a film about my suffering'. Rejecting the narratives around his 'real' story, from a journalist's report published in a popular magazine to the Ahankhah's account of what took place, Sabzian welcomes Kiarostami's approach. In return, Kiarostami makes his film – which, as an attempt to give voice to Sabzian's narrative, is concurrently his own commentary on cinema. Kiarostami collides documentary with fiction to pose questions to our assumptions about filmic practices of truth. He deliberately manipulates the economy of withholding and revealing information to expose the paradoxes of cinema as well as our investment in cinematic deception. Laying bare the artifice of filmmaking, Kiarostami playfully refuses to conform to conventions of fictional and documentary films and subverts the optics and power dynamic of courtroom dramas.

In her reading of *Close-Up*, Elizabeth Hope Finnegan draws on Ludwig Wittgenstein's notion of aspect-seeing and Stanley Cavell's notion of aspect-blindness to show that the question of representation is always an ethical enquiry. As Finnegan argues, *Close-Up*'s investigation of the ethics of representation is done through a deliberate disruption of chronological recounting and a multiplication as well as a restriction of perspectives. Particularly in *Close-Up*'s earlier sequences, scenes are set up to ensure that we as the audience are 'almost always seeing only one person's point of view at any given time, while the other point of view is withheld from us'.[58] Each perspective is presented through re-enactments, but each time in the absence of other perspectives, leading to an awareness of the existence of multiple perspectives (literally cut out and not yet framed), while the film

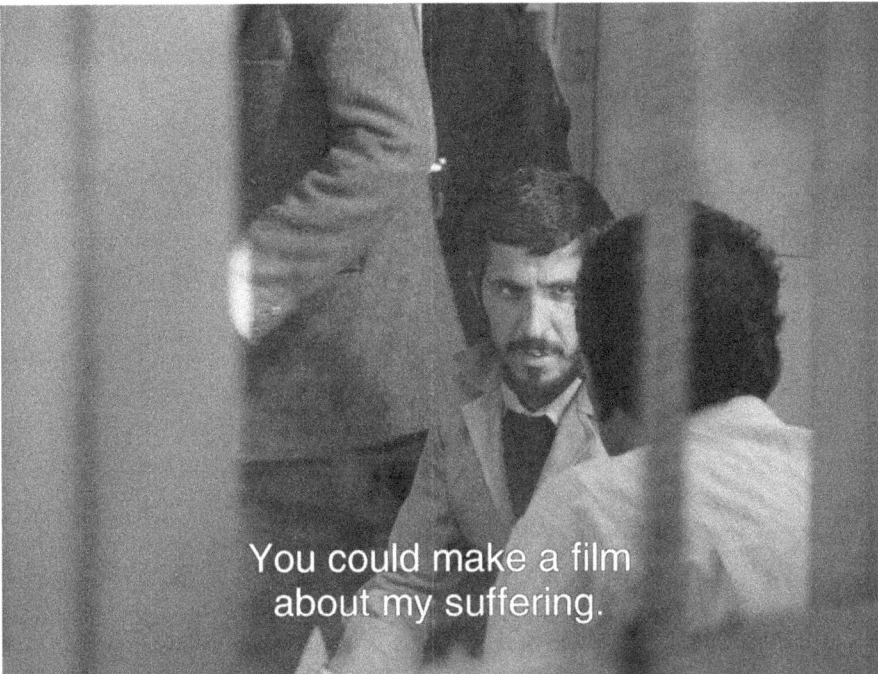

Figure 2.1 Unable to tell his own story to contest the existing narratives, Sabzian in jail asks Kiarostami to narrate the story on his behalf in *Close-Up* (Abbas Kiarostami, 1990).

deliberately denies the viewer access to them. As a correction to the existing narrative lapses, Kiarostami achieves to open up an alternative space in which Sabzian can be recognised as himself through Kiarostami's filmic experimentations:

> The story of Hossein Sabzian as depicted in *Close-Up* is the story of how he has been seen and not seen by others. Almost every character in this film suffers from aspect-blindness with regard to Sabzian; we could say that Kiarostami's attunement to Sabzian's humanity – his suffering – provides the filmic evidence of these lapses.[59]

While 'Sabzian-as-Sabzian' does not exist for other characters in the film and each sees him differently, Kiarostami ultimately shows us how to see him as himself beyond all the blindness and lapses. Assigning to Sabzian in the courtroom a separate camera with a close-up lens (the central scene in the film), which allows him to speak on his own terms and 'to tell the audience facts and feelings that are legally unacceptable but nevertheless true', Kiarostami grants voice to testimonies and gives the film a redemptive quality.[60] Moreover, deliberately rejecting 'conventional editing by not cutting Sabzian's close-ups and his speech to the facial expressions and reactions of the other attendants', Kiarostami allows Sabzian to speak while ensuring that his comments are not reappropriated through the reactions of others.[61] The scene, as Ivone Margulies remarks, 'reveals a critical sensibility attuned to Sabzian's pathos – to his love of films and his inability to make them', while Kiarostami's intervention 'transforms the trial from an accusation of fraud into an exploration into the nature of belief'.[62] By acting as a lawyer, as Finnegan observes, Kiarostami presses Sabzian 'to reveal himself'. He manages to help Sabzian 'make himself intelligible'.[63]

Close-Up exposes the masquerades of filmmaking to probe the ethical tensions inherent in representing the underprivileged other. It achieves to save the other from oblivion and to perform an ethical stepping back (by the filmmakers) for the other to attain its distinctive voice.[64] As Vered Maimon notes, Kiarostami allows Sabzian 'to become an actor who watches himself playing and to play himself rather than be himself, thereby allowing him to become-Other, not be an Other, a fixed emblem of an Iranian poor man',[65] therefore regaining his singularity in debt to Kiarostami's negotiations with narrative composition.

Despite its triumph in empowering the other, *Close-Up* ultimately remains tied to the rule of the frontal. Seeking more adequate and truthful images, the film reduces the exposure to the other to the question of representation and limits the justice of the image. Despite showing the complexities of reading the other by locating the ethical in the necessity of images that correct the existing ones and by allowing the other to take part in the formation of readability, the film in its due course does not contest the centrality of meaning. According to *Close-Up*, the other can be recognised, but this recognition must be delayed until after the other is able to speak and have his said heard so that he can make sense and reappear as intelligible. This is most evident in Kiarostami's close-up camera, which appears as a certain compassionate audiovisual device that opens up space for an alternative narrative to be heard. The close-up camera ultimately works as a device of interrogation precisely because it sets up an encounter with the other according to which the other must make sense before recognition can be conferred on him (and before he can be conditionally forgiven and ultimately return to the very community that has denied him the privilege of telling his own suffering).[66] This aesthetic outcome is compounded by the film's contrived finale where Sabzian's demonstration of regret and his redemption are delayed until after he reappears as making sense.

With a similar attention to the marginalised, Shahid Saless's *Still Life* exemplifies a different response to iconoclasm and the acquisitive impulses inhabiting vision. The film is a demonstration that otherness in film is irreducible to a recognition of sameness/difference in the face of the other, but in fact resides in the alternative temporality of ethical exposure. *Still Life* tells the uneventful story of an ageing railroad guard at a quiet train station in a remote, unidentified area in Iran and his wife who weaves carpets day and night. The couple's livelihood and their belonging to the town is endangered when the man receives the news that he must pass on his responsibility to someone else. With an aesthetics of monotony and banality, *Still Life* foregrounds the *temps mort* through its excessive focus on the everyday and the quotidian, the latter often framed within long takes. In the absence of camera movements, each shot is set up with static *mise en scène* and often symmetric composition, creating a powerful effect of stillness.[67] The characters/bodies rarely move, and if they do their movements are slow and often within confined spaces. If there is any action, they are so mundane that the viewing experience of the film turns into a sort of spending time with the characters in their raw, mute and tedious durations to the extent that one might even question if there is any point in the camera being there at all.[68]

Moreover, Shahid Saless does not invite reading into the stillness and blankness of his images. As Hamid Naficy observes, Shahid Saless's films are

> concerned with the life of ordinary people and their daily routines, rendered with an ironic and objective distance. Space is closed and pre-ordained; time is still or passes slowly. Unlike some [Iranian] New Wave filmmakers, Shahid Saless generally shunned symbolism.[69]

Still Life locates the ethical revelation not in what the image posits but in what the image does to vision. The specific form of witnessing (to the body of the other) that *Still Life* encourages makes the camera function as a sort of compulsion to testify and appreciate, as opposed to comprehend, the meaningfulness of what is normally considered too banal or too insignificant to be shown or looked at. As one of the lesser-known progenitors of what is now referred to as 'slow cinema', *Still Life* attests to this alternative sense of significance by reducing the representational content. Through its deceptively simple but deliberate stylisation, it makes room for a fullness that is dramatically rarefied since it does not pay off. The sense of fullness it brings forth is tied to a material presence that defies exhaustion by content. What is 'more' and 'too much' is not what the images contain in terms of visual content – it is, rather, the duration of the viewer's exposure to bodies. The sense of fullness that *Still Life* gives the figures and things onscreen resides in their unmotivated presence enveloped in the actuality of the film's duration: a sort of thereness that seems to be irreducible to, if not independent of, any justification, since it is as it appears.

Either through static frontal shots of the man walking, drinking tea, or simply sitting or sleeping, *Still Life* is a staging of bodies before the camera that exceeds the function of a mere representation of the everyday. Consider the scene in which the man is sitting in the middle of the cottage, smoking a cigarette after he finishes dinner. He repeatedly coughs while continuing smoking for a relatively prolonged time. Here, coughing does not necessitate a second take – its contingency is preserved and emphasised in a long, uninterrupted shot where the same symmetric, frontal and eye-level composition makes the staging of the body more emphatic. Or, reminiscent of the famous scene in Vittorio De Sica's *Umberto D.* (1952) in which the maid, a periphery character, attempts to strike a match but fails several times to light it, consider the static shots of the woman in *Still Life* slowly trying to thread a needle; with her 'weak eyesight and trembling fingers she tries many times but misses; she wets the thread and tries again and again, the camera holding the shot'.[70] A mundane, dramatically insignificant action is presented in extended shots. Monotony is not merely what the film represents (as a pre-existing part of the lives of its characters) but works as a cinematic force. Irreducible to a derivative of the real-life monotony, the

Figure 2.2 Extended use of frontal, static shots that emphasise the staging of bodies in *Still Life* (Sohrab Shahid Saless, 1974).

Figure 2.3 The woman trying to thread a needle in an extended scene in *Still Life* (Sohrab Shahid Saless, 1974).

monotonous image does something to vision through a surplus of bodily presentation, disrupting a habituated look that is contingent on motivating the appearance and persistence of bodies onscreen.

Similarly, *Still Life* does not deploy the everyday in place of the eventful and the spectacular simply to represent banality so that the images would bear more resemblance to 'reality' and look more lifelike for an eye that recognises a familiar image of reality. The everyday is not an introduction of a healthy dose of contingency within the film – an everydayness that can be digested by the film as a contingency that reinforces the representational as its constitutive outside. Nor should it be overlooked that watching empty and dead time onscreen is significantly different from experiencing such dullness and emptiness within one's own life. The everyday evoked by *Still Life* is already contaminated by its being staged for the camera and ultimately facilitates the withdrawal of the bodies. Through the reduction of character presentation to an emphasis on their banal activities or their craft of operating the tracks or sewing, the recurring long shots of bodies that further accentuate their slow movements in space, or framings that do not discriminate bodies and inanimate things, *Still Life* achieves its ethico-aesthetic effects by retaining the *thingness* of the face and the body of the other.

It is crucial to associate visibility with the viewing subject's desire to establish authority over the world viewed. Visibility turns the viewed into what stands out as a lack and therefore calls for meaningfulness – a critique of the image that *Close-Up* overlooks despite its best intents. More significantly, the problem with the violence of visibility is not challenged merely through some sort of unconcealment – by an exposition of the artifice of framing the other, or a revealing of interiorities through facilitating the other's voice. The hiddenness of a positive content, a concealment contrary to what the Levinasian face involves, takes place not when 'a positive content eludes the eye but rather the opposite – it occurs when a positive content "seizes" our eye'.[71] The habituated relation of the eye to the visual field is characterised by its desire for adequation. Insofar as adequation is what defines the viewer–viewed relationship, the invisible is just a circumstantial failure. It is just that what is simply not visible owes its non-visibility to a defect that is, by essence, rectifiable. By contrast, Levinasian ethics as an alternative optics is an opening of the eye onto what cannot be framed as content. It is a testimony to the trace that the address leaves within the frontal visual field. The invisible is therefore not simply an unlit or covered aspect of the visual, not what awaits illumination. It is that which persists despite the illumination of the frontal visual field.

A subversive image involves a problematisation of the apparently innocent but suspicious desire to see (and grasp). It exposes the limits of seeing within the site where seeing is expected to take place – within the frame that presumably brings the world into visibility. Neither being within the image nor having the image before one's eyes is to be reduced to visibility. The latter has a certain requirement – to be visible is to be mediated by the third beyond the immediacy of ethical exposure. For Maurice Blanchot, influenced particularly here by Levinas, seeing is a matter of subsumption, absorption, fusion, unity and thus violence:

> [L]ight gives pure visibility to thought as its measure. To think is henceforth to see clearly, to stand in the light of evidency, to submit to the day that makes all things appear in the unity of a form. It is to make the world arise under the sky of light as the form of forms, always illuminated and judged by this sun that does not set.[72]

The third is not a matter of a thing merely appearing within the visual. It is a mediation, craving the thing to call for form, thus to be reduced to an object that has to be located within a matrix of relations, and to be illuminated. *Still Life* disrupts the power of the third through its anti-psychological approach, rarefied narrative exposition and reluctance to dramatise already uneventful situations. As Hamid Dabashi contends, in *Still Life*

> what we see is not even the perceptible things themselves but things *before* their metaphysically mediated perceptibility – *before* they are perceived, understood, analyzed, judged. The sheer physicality of being, prior to any attribution of meaning and significance, is what begins to surface in his cinema.[73]

The body-thing not only appears within the frontal visual field before it is understood but, more significantly, it persists beyond subsequent mediations. The image is no longer an uncovering of an unlit aspect of the visual that essentially awaits illumination, and bodies no longer stand out as lacking form and in need of a revelation of their interiorities in order for them to belong to the screen. The image becomes the event of giving bodies within the frontal visual field but equally resisting the solace of givenness.

Despite its preoccupation with time, *Close-Up* does not adequately interrogate the prevailing modes of experiencing time and its relation to the other. Its cinematic time remains normative and teleological, governed by the principles of functionality – a time that in the final analysis, even if not efficient or economical, pays off; a time that delays but eventually reinstates the rationalisation of bodies' persistence onscreen. Shahid Saless, however, resists visibility through a certain weightiness of onscreen presences and the duration of their persistence, which work against the taming force of the third. Shahid Saless avoids fashioning the precarity of the lives he portrays into a 'story proper'.[74] The body in *Still Life* is returned to a material status whose precariousness is vocalised paradoxically through an erasure of the voice. The other is not merely identified through the image – Shahid Saless seems to be most interested in the actuality of the bodies staged for his camera to be rewatched. By implicating the everyday within images that equally evoke and disrupt the familiarity of everydayness, *Still Life* brings forth an ontological equality that resides in an alternative temporality. As Dabashi argues, Shahid Saless's relation to time is an 'unmasking of the real by a deliberate emphasis on the material endurance of the present'.[75] Indeed, present tense is no longer a mere unfolding of a life in its everydayness. Rather, it is the duration of the flow of time that makes the viewer attest to the fact that something exists or is taking place, that bodies appear and persist onscreen, even though they are too particular and contingent to be pinned down. Rather than producing givens, the images reassert their state of giving bodies, things and fragments in duration.

This is not to suggest that story is a burden for Shahid Saless. *Still Life* tells a story through certain narrative punctuations; yet the experience it puts forward keeps exposing the story to a certain level of indeterminacy. There is a story on the way to being told, but what the story claims to be about is not exactly a story that makes exhaustive sense. Telling a story is no longer a totality that renders what is told meaningful. It is primarily tied to what is in the profilmic, what is staged and performed for the camera. The body calls the viewer to attend to a story that is on the way to being told while the story that the body hosts is not a story proper. The story that the filmed body promises is tied to its radically minimised gestures and postures, and its exhibitions of fatigue and stasis, all of which are enveloped in extended durations. It constructs itself out of the recorded fragments of reality found in the world while harbouring a withdrawal that is simultaneous with the construction of the story. Screen duration hosts both movements of giving and withdrawal.

Shahid Saless endeavours to present the precarity of life while performing his own anxiety in exercising authority over the bodies whose suffering his images seek to bear witness to. Stillness, therefore, is not merely a theme but an approach, a way of seeing things that is ethical precisely because it demands a commitment that is not exhaustively compensated. While the viewer/self that *Close-Up* assumes is an active one (reading into images to make the other intelligible) who is eventually rewarded when the other onscreen is understood and forgiven, *Still Life* encourages a certain passivity, demonstrating the redundancy of exhaustively subjective activity, instead restaging the exposure that resides in the originary encounter with the other. Story becomes the promise of a certain making-available of bodies to be borne witness to. It is indebted to the images of bodies while the latter are in return indebted to a filmic documentation.

The ethics of failure: betrayal and the imprint

Levinas unsurprisingly tries to shield and protect the face and the body of the other from the risk of visibility. But this struggle may not be as rigid an iconoclastic position as it would seem initially. Levinas tries to think and examine a tension. This tension, as Crignon suggests, can be rethought as one between the 'impossibility of separating the image from the body' and the 'necessity of not assimilating them, of not incorporating them'. The image, however, is always 'an image of the face'.[76] This is where the tension is most remarkably announced: the image is also that 'from which the face must be saved'.[77] It is therefore important to redefine the invisibility of the face, its non-phenomenality:

> The face is no longer invisible because it would disintegrate as an image but because it is caressed or touched, because it abandons

> itself to a sensibility that does not turn into perception . . . It is precisely because the face is a body in this sense that it cannot be seen and that it escapes images.[78]

Levinas is not an iconoclast so much as a thinker whose main concern involves not necessarily a position, but an effort aimed at diverting our attention to, and warning us about the necessity of, thinking a tension. Despite its radical elusiveness, unrepresentability and irreducibility to plastic forms, the face of the other breaks through the visual nonetheless. It happens to the self, affecting and concerning the latter.

If the face of the other breaks through the visual despite not being an object within the visual, how is it possible to speak of the face, or to turn the face into an image, as *Close-Up* and *Still Life* endeavour, or think of the body as already implicated within its image, without reducing the other to the plastic form that is left behind? The saying–said distinction is once again helpful in showing how the other breaks through the visual despite its invisibility. In particular, it must be asked how it is possible to say the ethical exposure to the other, to say the sensible, corporeal exposure that is originary, and bring it under ontology, and at the same time avoid betraying the saying.[79]

Levinas's response would initially seem surprising as he posits the necessity of betrayal: 'Everything shows itself at the price of this betrayal.'[80] According to him, '[t]he correlation of the saying and the said, that is, the subordination of the saying to the said . . . is the price that manifestation demands'.[81] The saying, to manifest itself, is destined 'to fix itself in a said', thus becoming a theme, the 'object of a narrative'.[82] The other side of the necessity of betrayal, however, appears to be that something is nevertheless borne witness to through the betrayal. Levinas employs a notion of 'reduction' as the manners in which the said can be unsaid, thereby letting the saying circulate as a 'residue' or 'interruption' within the said.[83] The signifyingness of the saying cannot be exhausted and thus a thought that is concerned with *otherwise than being* should be aimed at practising a 'saying that must also be unsaid'.[84]

Levinas appears to have avoided here the binary oppositions of his earlier works and adopted a more affirmative path. Ethics is no longer conceived, as it perhaps seemed in *Totality and Infinity*, as an attempt to overcome ontology or abandon it through the immediacy of ethical exposure.[85] The translation of the saying into the said is a necessary betrayal – 'a performative disruption of the language of ontology, which attempts to maintain the interruption of the ethical saying within the ontological said'.[86] Even though the saying is always already mediated by the said, it nonetheless preserves in its withdrawal the trace of the exposure to the other.[87] The saying must, in one way or another, find a channel into the language of the said and be thematised.[88] However, if the said is thought to betray the saying in the act of translation, Levinas assures us that 'the said in absorbing the Saying does not become its master'.[89] The saying is 'not exhausted in the said' but, most significantly, 'imprints its trace in the said'.[90] This trace is a matter of epiphany, rather than content.[91]

Most significantly, this dynamic reflects Levinas's concern with the face of the other. The face withdraws from the visual. Moreover, the face withdraws, yet leaves a trace within the visual precisely because the visual is incapable of exhausting the face. While not belonging to the domain of the visible, the face must somehow break through the visual field. It certainly does break through, Levinas believes, even though the peculiar mode of its revelation removes it from a reduction to visual content, and thus disrupts the visual field. Rather than being reduced to an object within the visual, the face withdraws from the realm into which it has broken through. Just as the saying comes as an interruption of the rule of the said through its harbouring of proximity and responsibility, the face acts as the interruption of the visual.

The face in *Still Life* does not manifest itself in a visual sense despite its breaking through the image. Nor is it associated with speech as an evocation of what makes sense through what the other has to say within the constraints of linguistic articulation. If the other is to be said through the image, marked and remarked, it can be a delineation, a punctuation – a desire to render the other visible, to illuminate the other by the benevolent light of the privileged self who has access to the means of storytelling and cultural production. *Still Life* is evidently frustrating because it is not a proper bringing of the other's precarity under a totalising said. Nor is it a bringing of the other onscreen so that they can adequately express the suffering. The filmmaker is not simply a channel with narrative privilege who recounts the lives of those who do not have access to the means of self-narration. It is equally inaccurate to say that the images of *Still Life* capture the 'unspeakable' suffering of the other through emphatic stress on the faces and bodies; as if 'showing', not telling, can address the ethical risks of rendering suffering meaningful. What this view overlooks is the critical fact that showing does not simply escape the totalising power of meaning-making, the latter often presumed to be exclusive to telling. Showing, insofar as it is limited to what is rendered visible as visual content within the frontal visual field, insofar as it works to illuminate the frontal vision without leaving the trace of what cannot be mediated, is fundamentally tied to the question of meaning, to a desire to make the other accessible through representation. The bodies of *Still Life* are often sustained by only the image itself, for there is an affirmation of their existence that is inexhaustible and thus sustained originarily by their being within the image – an exclusively cinematic capacity to which I return in the next chapter in my discussion of André Bazin and aesthetic theories of realism.

Despite its radical stillness, the life onscreen is still a life being lived before the camera, the value of which is not tied to compelling the body to make sense despite its appearance within the visual field. The image enacts as well as re-enacts real life, not to represent it but, to the contrary, to further expose its inaccessibility. *Still Life* brings into being a viewer who is visited by the world due to cinematic exposure, prior to having the privilege to assume their being affected, and beyond being able to exhaustively translate this exposure and represent it. In *Still Life*, the claim of the image is irreducible to what is shown and said, to what is rendered visible within the visual field. There is a failure at work that stages the breakthrough and withdrawal of the other.

Still Life's commitment to say the other through the face is accompanied by a certain unsaying. The revelation of the other in the facing of the image is a vocalisation – one that is wordless but is indissociable from the body's image. Through this unsaying and the disruption of the third, the body is returned to a precarious state where it is predominantly sustained by nothing but the image itself. The giving of the body within the image becomes a grave concern for the other, the latter not as having to reveal interiorities to be recognised, but as a body that is, by essence, precarious and exposed to harm and destruction. According to Judith Butler, if the Levinasian face is a matter of speech rather than vision, and if what the speech communicates is, in a certain sense, wordless and beyond content, then it could be argued that the face of the other is not only irreducible to the visible face but is also indissociable from a body that is agonised. The face

> describes the human back, the craning of the neck, the raising of the shoulder blades like 'springs'. And these bodily parts, in turn, are said to cry and to sob and to scream, as if they were a face or, rather, a face with a mouth, a throat, or indeed, just a mouth and throat from which vocalizations emerge that do not settle into words. The face is to be found in the back and the neck, but it is not quite a face. The sounds that come from or through the face are agonized, suffering. So we can see already that the 'face' seems to consist in a series of displacements such that a face is figured as a back which, in turn, is figured as a scene of agonized vocalization.[92]

The face is not to be equated with the countenance or conflated with the face that can be referred to by an index finger within the visual field. Nor is it merely a face with a mouth that rescues the other from oblivion by positing a distinctive voice. The face as facing, as ethical exposure, is a wordless expression that is non-frontal but can be traced upon the body of the other. According to Butler,

> it is precisely the wordless vocalization of suffering that marks the limits of linguistic translation here. The face, if we are to put words to its meaning, will be that for which no words really work; the face seems to be a kind of sound, the sound of language evacuating its sense.[93]

Resonating with Levinas's attention to the face, Butler's notion of the body is an attempt to locate the other beyond recognition and in the originarity of the event of facing. The facing of the face is a kind of sound. It is a turning that punctuates the inadequacy of whatever the face contains as meaning. It is wordless, yet it is a vocalisation. It is a call, an address. Yet its address is irreducible to whatever could be found in the face. The visible face does not absorb the facing of the face. It does not become its master precisely because facing withdraws and disrupts the visible, while the inscription of the trace of the withdrawal is retained within the visual.

Reading the body through this lens not only indicates that the other appears within the visual but also demonstrates the ethical necessity of bringing the other within the image. The Levinasian face, in a certain sense, speaks through the body while the body is always already implicated within its image. The other not only leaves an image behind, but its being given within an image is an ethical imperative – it is through the image that the ethical exposure to the other is restaged. While acknowledging the risks inherent in the production of the other's image, Butler significantly undermines prohibition of images by bringing forth the analogy of 'the obituary':

> If there were to be an obituary, there would have had to have been a life, a life worth noting, a life worth valuing and preserving . . . I think we have to ask, again and again, how the obituary functions as the instrument by which grievability is publicly distributed. It is the means by which a life becomes, or fails to become, a publicly grievable life, . . . the means by which a life becomes noteworthy.[94]

For Butler, the other must break through since the image is, in a certain sense, the basis for a recognition of not sameness/difference, but the value of life. The image-as-obituary essentially harbours an ethical address as it testifies to a life that counts and qualifies as a life. The image of the body assumes grievability as a condition for both the emergence and sustenance of the other while presupposing 'a life has been lived' as the future anterior. In the absence of the image, the other is 'sustained by no regard, no testimony, and ungrieved when lost'.[95]

The image is therefore a gift, not only because it is a giving of the face but also because it stages the withdrawal of the giving from the frontal visual field. The face withdraws from the image but not every image is the same in terms of making present the withdrawal of the face and the trace it leaves. The facing of the image can be concealed through a *capture* of the face. The giving of the image is what, as Kenaan tells us, 'all too often remains hidden by the manner in which what is given captivates the eye'.[96] Even though facingness and self-presentingness reside at the heart of the image, these ethical conditions cannot be taken for granted. Not every image can retain its facingness, which is to say, makes present the way it disrupts the rule of the frontal within our visual field. The *peniyya* of the image is more often than not concealed and ultimately denied precisely because what the image itself is reduced to what the image contains. Something to be achieved rather than given, the address of the image disrupts an absorption in a homogeneous space of determined visual content.

A reaffirmation of the address requires a certain withdrawal by which what is inside the image enters into resonance with the image itself, with the image as an event of opening. When we look at an image, in Kenaan's words,

> we not only see what the eye has framed, but more importantly we encounter that which addresses or turns toward us as viewers. But the image's facing is anchored, as suggested, in the double root of *peniyya*. In turning toward us, the image is that which also takes its leave from us. The image's accessibility is made possible against the background of its uncontainability. To put this differently, in turning toward us, the image must be part of a space that allows this turning to take place. The image's *peniyya* can occur only on the condition that there is an outside to the frame of frontal vision, an exteriority from which the image could make its entry in turning to us.[97]

The reaffirmation of *peniyya*, as the imprinting of the trace of the ethical within the visual, involves a certain withdrawal of what the image gives from the visual content that the image nevertheless contains. Butler's formulation of the dynamic of betrayal and disruption is invaluable here. In her reading of the uneasy relation between the face and representation, Butler points out the ethical importance of failure with regard to presenting the human other – remarks reminiscent of what I referred to as a Levinasian reduction:

> For Levinas, then, the human is not represented by the face. Rather, the human is indirectly affirmed in that very disjunction that makes representation impossible, and this disjunction is conveyed in the impossible representation. For representation to convey the human, then, representation must not only fail, but it must show its failure. There is something unrepresentable that we nevertheless seek to represent, and that paradox must be retained in the representation we give ... In this sense, the human is not identified with what is represented but neither is it identified with the unrepresentable; it is, rather, that which limits the success of any representational practice. The face is not 'effaced' in this failure of representation, but is constituted in that very possibility. Something altogether different happens, however, when the face operates in the service of a personification that claims to 'capture' the human being in question. For Levinas, the human cannot be captured through the representation, and we can see that some loss of the human takes place when it is 'captured' by the image.[98]

The face breaks into the visual just as the saying needs the said to reveal itself. It is, however, through its very revelation that the saying of the face, its facing, disrupts the frontality and objectness of the visible face. The saying is characterised by its withdrawal from the said, yet also by the fact that it leaves a trace within the said. The trace is an effect of the withdrawal – it interrupts the rule of the said by its uncompromising uncontainability. Therefore, any attempt to represent the face is an impossibility. It is destined to fail from the outset.

Whereas failure is what is already taking place within any representation of the face, a *performative* failure sets up the image to demonstrate the withdrawal of the face from the image it leaves behind. It puts the failure to work, allowing it to do something to the visual, to exert a certain affirmative violence on vision. In a certain sense, a representation that fails ceases to be a representation of the face. It is not a representation of the impossibility of representing the other, but a testimony to the originary structure of exposure, to the non-frontal of the facing. Returning to *Close-Up* and *Still Life*, both Kiarostami and Shahid Saless seem to share the ethical conviction that the other must be said, but it cannot be properly said – the decision to bring the other into the image and tell the other's story bears the seeds of a failure from the outset. Kiarostami sees his performance of failure in his stepping back for the other to tell his own story to regain his status as someone who makes sense if given the channel to speak and as deserving redemption. According to Shahid Saless, however, the other is exposed to failure even before there is a subject to assume the failure. If the image is not only a necessary betrayal but also a necessary failure, if the other is to be said to be attested to in its distance, then the ethical image must reveal the failure to which it is exposed from the outset even prior to a self who is believed to authorise the formation of the image. It is not just because the image is intended to be merely a correction to existing images, or because it is simply intended to be inadequate to the other (the other overflowing existing images which in itself assumes a possible corrective containment). The violence of the image is subverted not simply when the privileged self steps back but when the image itself becomes anxious in the face of the other and the filmmaker/self exhibits this anxiety.

An image that captures the face leads to 'some loss of the human'. Most importantly, the 'more' that is lost is not simply a more that overflows representation. What is lost is not simply positive content that can be restored in a better, more adequate representation. What is effaced is the facing of the face. It is more precisely that something of the claim of the other's suffering is reaffirmed in a failure that stages the breakthrough and withdrawal of the other – a double movement that is already taking place within the visual. The face of the other breaks through the image, occupying the frontal visual field; yet precisely because of its appearing, the face troubles the domain of appearances. The facing image retains this troubling intrusion as what it gives is implicated within a certain withdrawal. It is therefore defined precisely by the way it is set up to perform its own anxiety before the face by staging its originary failure in capturing the face. What it delivers is not merely the singularity of the other but precisely the irreducibility of the event of facing.

Representing the face is an impossibility. However, that impossibility must be retained within the image of the face. The image evokes the invisibility of its address only if it fails to capture what it nevertheless presents within its frame. The ethical importance of performing this failure is a defence of the ethical relevance of the aesthetic as that which generates a testimony to the trace of the ethical. This line of argument can be mapped in Levinas's thought, even though he mostly seems determined to dismiss the ethicity of art without reservation. Reading Levinas 'both out of and through the gaps'[99] in his texts, a number of critics have focused on revisiting the Levinasian hostility to the aesthetic/poetic precisely by evoking the saying–said distinction.[100] Levinas himself is well aware of the need to struggle with philosophical language, which he deems to be dominated by the rule of being to bear witness to the trace of the ethical and to the otherwise than being. This endeavour involves a certain poetic approach to the language of the said, calling forth a certain conception of the poetic said that aims to resist the representational thrust of the said and imprint the trace of the ethical saying within language.[101] It is important to reconceive the aesthetic as the site in which a certain revelation of the ethical can take place precisely because this approach recognises the elusiveness of the ethical yet sees the aesthetic as the domain in which this elusiveness can be borne witness to – as opposed to being captured and reduced. Artistic activity, in this revised sense, is not violence *per se*. On the contrary, it is bound with a certain hope, promise and futurity from the outset.

The image is therefore a betrayal but a necessary one. The facing image is an aesthetic demonstration of how what appears in front of the beholder is not exhausted by its being offered within the frontal visual field. What is the uniqueness of film in this ethical revelation? It is pivotal to ask what it means to speak of cinematic images that are set up to perform their own failure in the face of the facing of the other. Equally imperative is an exploration of how the cinematic image can be transformed into a giving that provides the grounds for any givenness while remaining irreducible to what is given. To address these questions, I will take as my point of departure the proposition that the cinematic image has in its very structure a certain failure. The framed body of the other is always already withdrawing from its containment within the visual. This withdrawal will be demonstrated in the following chapters as the problem of the filmed body, as an originary actorlessness of the film medium that resides in a certain uneasy relation between the cinematic image and the body of the other. This uneasiness manifests itself in cinematic parallelism as a specific actualisation of the realisms of the body. A cinematic capacity, parallelism can make present a withdrawal essential to the reaffirmation of the ethical address.

Notes

1. The image, Levinas argues, fixes and stops 'the flow of time'. See Welten, 'Image and Oblivion', 60–3. The temporality of a work of art is not a 'living flux', nor towards an absolute future, but tends rather towards 'immobility'. See Crignon, 'Figuration', 114.
2. Downing, 'Re-viewing the Sexual Relation', 52.
3. Ibid., 52–3.
4. Ibid., 54.
5. Ibid., 58.
6. Ibid., 52. Also, see Levinas, *Ethics and Infinity*, 86–7.
7. Downing, 'Re-viewing the Sexual Relation', 52.
8. Hole, *Towards a Feminist Cinematic Ethics*, 9.

9 Levinas, 'Philosophy and the Idea of Infinity', 200.
10 Kenaan, *The Ethics of Visuality*, 36.
11 Ibid., 85.
12 Robbins, 'Aesthetic Totality and Ethical Infinity', 356.
13 As Simon Critchley argues, the saying is 'a nonthematizable ethical residue of language'. See Critchley, 'Introduction', *The Cambridge Companion to Levinas*, 17–18.
14 With the correlation that it establishes between the subject and the object, the said can be 'approximated to the symbolic order, to the provenance of the signifier and the abstractness of the linguistic code'. See Ziarek, 'The Ethical Passions', 80.
15 Dudiak, *The Intrigue of Ethics*, 194–5.
16 Ziarek, 'The Ethical Passions', 80. Also, see Levinas, *Otherwise Than Being*, 48.
17 Levinas, *Otherwise Than Being*, 45.
18 See Ziarek, 'The Ethical Passions', 80–1.
19 Ibid.
20 The said 'expresses a content', while the saying is 'expression without content'. See Riera, '"The Possibility of the Poetic Said"', 14–15.
21 Levinas, *Otherwise Than Being*, 5. My responsibility for the other 'signifies in saying before showing itself in the said'. See Levinas, *Otherwise Than Being*, 100.
22 Riera, '"The Possibility of the Poetic Said"', 22. Also, see Levinas, *Otherwise Than Being*, 43.
23 See Levinas, *Otherwise Than Being or Beyond Essence*, 85 and 180.
24 Levinas, *Otherwise Than Being*, 120.
25 Miller, 'Reply to Bernhard Waldenfels', 54. According to Levinas, the other 'skips the stage of consciousness'. Levinas, *Otherwise Than Being*, 119.
26 Ziarek, 'Semantics of Proximity', 213–14. Also, see Wyschogrod, 'Language and Alterity in the Thought of Levinas', 189 and Riera, '"The Possibility of the Poetic Said"', 14.
27 For Levinas, hospitality is 'not simply some region of ethics' – it is, rather, 'ethicity itself, the whole and the principle of ethics'. Derrida, *Adieu to Emmanuel Levinas*, 50. In *Of Hospitality*, Derrida describes the unconditional law of hospitality as a law without law: 'if I practice hospitality "*out of* duty" [and not only "*in conforming with* duty"] this hospitality of paying up is no longer an absolute hospitality, it is no longer graciously offered beyond debt and economy, offered to the other, a hospitality invented for the singularity of the new arrival, of the unexpected.' See Derrida and Dufourmantelle, *Of Hospitality*, 83. For a discussion of Derrida's relation to Levinasian ethical and political thought, see the third chapter of Beardsworth's *Derrida and the Political*.
28 Derrida, *Adieu to Emmanuel Levinas*, 25. For a discussion of Derrida's treatment of ethics after Levinas, see Bennington, 'Deconstruction and Ethics', 64–82.
29 Rosen, 'Emmanuel Levinas and the Hospitality of Images', 365. Also, see Levinas, *Otherwise Than Being*, 79 and 112. The guest, according to Derrida, 'becomes the host's host', as these 'substitutions make everyone into everyone else's hostage. Such are the laws of hospitality.' See Derrida and Dufourmantelle, *Of Hospitality*, 125.
30 Derrida, *Adieu to Emmanuel Levinas*, 24. See also Schroepfer, 'Hospitality and Hope', 353–69.
31 According to Derrida: 'The absolute guest [*hôte*] is this *arrivant* for whom there is not even a horizon of expectation, who bursts onto my horizon of expectations when

I am not even prepared to receive the one who I'll be receiving. That's hospitality.' See Derrida, 'A Certain Impossible Possibility of Saying the Event', 451.
32. Critchley, 'Introduction', *The Cambridge Companion to Levinas*, 20–1.
33. See Krueger, 'Levinasian Reflections on Somaticity and the Ethical Self', 610. Also, see Levinas, *Discovering Existence with Husserl*, 54.
34. Krueger, 'Levinasian Reflections on Somaticity and the Ethical Self', 608.
35. Critchley, 'Introduction', *The Cambridge Companion to Levinas*, 21.
36. Cited in Krueger, 'Levinasian Reflections on Somaticity and the Ethical Self', 605.
37. Levinas, *Otherwise Than Being*, 89.
38. Ziarek, 'The Ethical Passions', 82. Also, see Levinas, *Basic Philosophical Writings*, 80.
39. Crignon, 'Figuration', 105.
40. Ibid., 118.
41. Kenaan, *The Ethics of Visuality*, 32.
42. Levinas, *Meaning and Sense*, 95.
43. Kenaan, *The Ethics of Visuality*, 34.
44. The word '*panim* is derived from a verb: *panah*. The relation between the verb *panah* and the noun *panim* is in a certain respect similar to the way in which the word "face" relates to the verb "to face". And the noun *peniyya*, which is derived from the same root, can be translated as a "facing" or an "address" or a "turning". The face is, in other words, essentially, a facing.' See Kennan, 'Facing Images', 153–4.
45. See ibid., 154.
46. Kenaan, *The Ethics of Visuality*, 86.
47. See Kennan, 'Facing Images', 143–4.
48. Ibid., 144.
49. Ibid.
50. Ibid., 145.
51. Fried, *Why Photography Matters as Art as Never Before*, 153.
52. Fried, *Manet's Modernism*, 282–4.
53. The facingness of the image has not been investigated in the history of art criticism to the extent that it merits exploration. Cited by Kenaan, Michael Fried is one of the few thinkers who has specifically addressed this question in his discussions of painting and photography. See Fried, *Why Photography Matters as Art as Never Before*, 149–54.
54. Kennan, 'Facing Images', 157.
55. Ibid. My emphasis.
56. Kenaan, *The Ethics of Visuality*, 69.
57. Ibid., 44.
58. Finnegan, 'To See or Not to See', 23.
59. Ibid., 28.
60. Margulies, 'Exemplary Bodies', 239.
61. Manafi, 'The Ethics of the "Listening Eye"'.
62. Margulies, 'Exemplary Bodies', 238–9.
63. Finnegan, 'To See or Not to See', 34.
64. According to Joanna Zylinska, a Levinasian notion of the 'listening eye' is 'concerned about and listens to the other's story which always has to remain, to some extent, theirs'. See Zylinska, *The Ethics of Cultural Studies*, 58–9.

65 Vered Maimon, 'Beyond Representation', 336.
66 My argument is contrary to Margulies's contention that 'the efficiency of this confessing apparatus is purposefully lacking' and the film is 'void of redemption but also judgment'. Margulies, 'Exemplary Bodies', 240.
67 For a discussion of *Still Life*'s stylistic compositions, see Barzanji, 'A Still Cinema'. Barzanji interestingly sees an expressive yet subtle use of filmic elements in the film, one that appears to 'simultaneously negate and adhere to the [Robert] Bresson quote that "the crude real will not by itself yield truth"'.
68 See 'The Tragic Side of Cinema', uploaded to YouTube on *The Cinema Cartography* channel on 22 January 2021, <youtu.be/toQ1W_ILpBU> (last accessed 25 April 2022).
69 Naficy, 'Slow, Closed, Recessive, Formalist and Dark', 8.
70 Naficy, *A Social History of Iranian Cinema*, Vol. 2, 395.
71 Kenaan, *The Ethics of Visuality*, 131.
72 Blanchot, *The Infinite Conversation*, 160.
73 Dabashi, *Close Up*, 47.
74 I take this distinction between 'story proper' and 'some kind of story' from Sam Durrant's work on postcolonial narratives and work of mourning. Durrant distinguishes between, on the one hand, conventional narratives that digest the surplus of historical experience and, on the other, some kind of story that responds to this surplus without exhausting its ethical address. See Durrant, *Postcolonial Narrative and the Work of Mourning*, 8.
75 Dabashi, *Close Up*, 29.
76 Crignon, 'Figuration', 119.
77 Ibid.
78 Ibid., 121.
79 Ibid., 118.
80 Levinas, *Otherwise Than Being*, 7.
81 Ibid., 6.
82 Riera, '"The Possibility of the Poetic Said"', 25.
83 The reduction of the said to the saying is 'the continual disruption of the limit that separates the ethical from the ontological'. See Critchley, 'Introduction', *The Cambridge Companion to Levinas*, 18. Also, see Levinas, *Otherwise Than Being*, 43–5.
84 Levinas, *Otherwise Than Being*, 7. The unsaid would generate a 'saying saying saying itself'. See Levinas, *Otherwise Than Being*, 143. This dynamic is also echoed by Jacques Derrida's notion of 'countersignature' in his discussion of the ethics of reading: 'There is as it were a duel of singularities, a duel of writing and reading, in the course of which a countersignature comes both to confirm, repeat and respect the signature of the other, of the "original" work, and to *lead it off* elsewhere, so running the risk of *betraying* it, having to betray it in a certain way so as to respect it, through the invention of another signature just as singular. Thus redefined, the concept of countersignature gathers up the whole paradox: you have to give yourself over singularly to singularity, but singularity does then have to share itself out and so compromise itself, *promise to compromise itself*. See Derrida, *Acts of Literature*, 69.
85 Rather than being a matter of overthrowing ontology, ethics is instead reconceived as 'the persistent deconstruction of the limits of ontology and its claim to

conceptual mastery, while also recognizing the unavoidability of the Said'. See Critchley, 'Introduction', *The Cambridge Companion to Levinas*, 18–19.
86 Ibid.
87 Ziarek, 'The Ethical Passions', 80–1.
88 Wyschogrod, 'Language and Alterity in the Thought of Levinas', 201.
89 Ibid. Also, see Levinas, *Otherwise Than Being*, 190.
90 Wyschogrod, 'Language and Alterity in the Thought of Levinas', 201.
91 See Downing, 'Re-viewing the Sexual Relation', 58. The trace is 'witnessed but not thematized'. See Levinas, *Otherwise Than Being*, 148.
92 Butler, *Precarious Life*, 133–4.
93 Ibid.
94 Ibid., 34.
95 Butler, *Frames of War*, 14–15.
96 Kennan, 'Facing Images', 157.
97 Ibid.
98 Butler, *Precarious Life*, 144–5. Also, see Gies, 'Signifying Otherwise', 19. Also, for a discussion of the ethics of failure in Butler's previous works see Mills, 'Undoing Ethics'.
99 Downing, 'Re-viewing the Sexual Relation', 50.
100 As Seán Hand argues, it is 'through artistic or aesthetic practice ... that Levinas tries to work philosophical language and conceptualisation to the point where it can escape the closure of ontological finality and open up to ethical infinitude'. See Hand, 'Shadowing Ethics', 66. Trying to flesh out a version of Levinasian aesthetics, Gerald L. Burns asserts that both the aesthetic/poetic and the ethical are 'forms of saying (*le Dire*) on the hither side of thematization'. See Burns, 'The Concepts of Art and Poetry in Emmanuel Levinas's Writings', 228. As Wyschogrod claims, literary arts and ethics 'can be thought of as fields in which disclosures of formlessness occur'. See Wyschogrod, 'Language and Alterity in the Thought of Levinas", 138–9. Aaron Rose argues that the 'challenging, obscure style' that Levinas himself employs in writing his works demonstrates his tendency to employ 'flourishes of hyperbole and other literary devices' precisely to 'unsettle the domesticity of the said'. See Rosen, 'Emmanuel Levinas and the Hospitality of Images', 370.
101 Levinas himself alludes to this possibility when he writes: 'Language would exceed the limits of what is thought, by suggesting, letting be understood without ever making understandable ... an implication of meaning distinct from that which comes to signs from the simultaneity of systems or the logical definition of concepts. This possibility ... is laid bare in the poetic said.' Cited in Riera, '"The Possibility of the Poetic Said"', 14.

3

The Body and the Camera

Emmanuel Levinas's ethics envisages a self that is characterised by its immersion in the spectacle of the visual field yet is also affected by its incapacity before the other to exhaust what it sees in terms of content for consciousness.[1] According to his iconoclasm, the alterity of the other cannot stem from any visibility since the visible is what can be assimilated. The other does not appear within my horizon precisely because it is not, cannot become, an object. Levinas uses the face to describe this elusiveness but, as we have seen, he is indeed no less assertive in thinking the face away from the ordinary phenomenon that the self sees or perceives. The fact that the face, as a non-phenomenon, cannot be seen is rooted in its difficult relation to form – the face gives itself to my gaze without appearing to it as it defies every plastic form it leaves behind.

It is through the originary withdrawal of the other from every form that the non-frontal of ethical exposure is evoked within an otherwise frontal vision. The primary objective of this chapter is to propose that the non-frontal exists at the core of the cinematographic eye from the outset – a potential that the cinematic image can aesthetically earn through staging the withdrawal of the filmed body from the visual field. To substantiate this withdrawal, I take as my point of departure a reading of André Bazin's aesthetic theory of realism according to which there is an alterity inherent to fragments of reality that the camera automatically records. In Bazin's understanding of how the camera relates to the world and interacts with it, as I suggest, there is a decisive parallelism between a fragment of reality and the position of that fragment within the filmic structure as a whole. A film, however fictional or imaginary, is a documentary on the materials to be filmed and, by extension, a documentation of the filmed bodies. This parallelism places a certain withdrawal at the core of the filmic rendition of the body of the other, for the automatically affirmed body owes its cinematic presence to the camera, while preceding and remaining inexhaustible by narrative or signifying processes. Reviewing the automatism of the camera, the indexicality of the image and the temporal instabilities of the cinematic time, I contend that aesthetic realisms of the body neither shy away from the ontological indeterminacies of the filmed body nor uncritically submit to the mechanical determinations of automatism. At the intersections of the ethical and the aesthetic, realist practices of the body propose alternative responses by negotiating with the materiality of the body of the other and the duration of its persistence onscreen.

The otherness of fragments: bricks, stones and the body-too-much

The hospitality of the cinematic image resides in the manner in which it brings the automatically filmed thing into the visual field. It places the thing within the structure of the frame and issues a call to look at a presence affirmed prior to identification. The cinematic image encourages a certain appreciation of the thing captured by the camera, while harbouring the withdrawal of the thing from being reduced and rendered meaningful. In a certain sense, it utters the originary 'yes' by imposing the presence of the thing on the viewer prior to and beyond the latter's privilege to decide to embrace or reject the thing. This hospitality resides in the way the camera relates to and renders the thing that is submitted to its gaze.

In the second volume of *What is Cinema?*, Bazin evokes a metaphor of 'bricks' and 'rocks' to discuss why and how the neorealist film succeeds in breaking with what he brands classical aesthetics:

> A brick is the basic unit of a house ... One can apply the same argument to the stones of which a bridge is constructed. They fit together perfectly to form an arch. But the big rocks that lie scattered in a ford are now and ever will be no more than mere rocks. Their reality as rocks is not affected when, leaping from one to another, I use them to cross the river. If the service which they have rendered is the same as that of the bridge, it is because I have brought my share of ingenuity to bear on their chance arrangement; I have added the motion which, though it alters neither their nature nor their appearance, gives them a provisional meaning and utility. In the same way, the neorealist film has a meaning, but it is *a posteriori* ... whereas in the classical artistic composition the meaning is established *a priori*: the house is already there in the brick.[2]

The bricks are thoroughly justified by the function they fulfil in constructing the house. They are made according to an *a priori* scheme, and eventually absorbed when the house is built. In a sense, the bricks' existence is always already exhausted from the outset: the bricks have the house in them even before any house is built. On the other hand, however, the rock stands on its own terms even if it enters into an articulation. No *a priori* framework can fix and exhaust its existence. It precedes and persists beyond any utilisation. Bazin's reference to *a posteriori* meaning implies the alterity of the rock, the meaning of which cannot be exhaustively determined by recourse to its position within the whole. Classical artistic compositions, as Bazin phrases it, treat the fragments of reality as bricks.[3] These compositions are based on a certain mode of violence precisely because they force the fragments to fit into an *a priori* scheme, therefore working to deny the irreducible integrity of the fragments – the fact that they are found by the camera rather than merely produced by or for it.

It is with respect to this denial of otherness that Bazin regards neorealism as a form of resistance and alternative to established traditions of cinema. For him, film has the ability to treat each fragment of the real on its own terms. Discussing Roberto Rossellini's *Paisà* (1946), Bazin's use of the term 'ambiguity' emphasises the irreducible integrity of the profilmic fragment when he refers to a 'fragment of concrete reality in itself multiple and full of ambiguity, whose meaning emerges only after the fact', while applauding a direction that chooses the facts with some care while 'respecting their factual integrity'.[4] Bazin notes an inherent meaningfulness revealed in Rossellini's approach to reality:

> For Rossellini, facts take on a meaning, but not like a tool whose function has predetermined its form. The facts follow one another, and the mind is forced to observe their resemblance; and thus, by recalling one another, they end by meaning something which was inherent in each and which is, so to speak, the moral of the story – a moral the mind cannot fail to grasp since it was drawn from reality itself.[5]

Bazin similarly champions Vittorio De Sica's *Bicycle Thieves* (*Ladri di biciclette*, 1948) as a film that enacts a certain faithfulness to profilmic reality. In De Sica's film, according to Bazin, the 'events are not necessarily signs of something, of a truth of which we are to be convinced, they all carry their own weight, their complete uniqueness, that ambiguity that characterizes any fact'.[6] Bazin notably implies a parallelism between a fragment of reality and the position of that fragment within the whole film – between the rock and its being given a provisional meaning and application. It is as though the borderline that is supposed to keep separate from one another the fragment and its position within the film is already tenuous. A fragment of reality takes part in a bigger articulation. But it does not, strictly speaking, belong to the film. It is irreducible and its involvement is provisional and uncertain precisely because, in addition to its deployment, it is also foregrounded on its own terms. Fragments might be utilised to represent something other than themselves. But representation is already problematised from within because fragments overflow their containment.

Ivone Margulies speaks of the significance of '[i]mages that bear the marks of two heterogeneous realities, the filmmaking process and the filmed event'.[7] According to her, Bazin's insistence on an 'attentiveness to the density of the profilmic reality' resides in his interest in a *mis*-fit – the latter understood as 'the rough edges of representation, the moment of encounter and productive maladjustment between representation and the actuality of filmmaking'.[8] Similarly, Margulies speaks of the 'inherent heterogeneity of cinematic images', of their 'awkward amalgams of literal materiality and reference'.[9] There are always both representational and literal aspects to each cinematic image, implying an inherent polarity. This polarity is, as Serge Daney suggests, what defines modern cinema – the latter best characterised as 'being always more or less documentary on the state of the materials to be filmed'.[10] A film's literal aspect resides in its being a documentation of the found materials beyond any potential deployment of the materials in the service of representational ends. Furthermore, in fiction film, this documentation always already haunts the story on the way to being told. It is what provides the grounds for the story yet also for the withdrawal of the filmed fragment. A fragment is given, while, in the moment of its giving, it is not properly rendered as a given.

What Bazin argues with respect to fragments of reality is no less true in terms of profilmic bodies. As Jean-Louis Comolli argues, the body of the actor already precedes the body of the character as its condition of possibility:

> Imaginary characters have to be endowed with bodies, faces, looks and voices. Bodies which are quite real, since they are those of the actors: the ones we see. The body filmed is not an imaginary body, even if the fiction refers it to some purely invented character and whatever the phantasies for which it is the support ... The body of the imaginary character is the image of the real body of the actor.[11]

The real body of the actor is a requirement of the image. For the body to represent a character in a film, there must be a material body as a fragment of reality that pre-exists the film. Classical aesthetics is grounded in an attempt to deny this precedence of the material body. As Stephen Heath contends, it is often argued that 'professional actor is someone who possesses the technique of emptying his or her body to fill it with meaning'. The actor must absent themself so as to represent and ultimately become the character. There must be an exhaustion and conversion of the 'living body of the human being', so that there could be a possibility of filling this material body with meaning.[12] With its originary indifference to signifying processes, the filmed body must be reduced, tamed and contained. Aimed at exhausting the profilmic body, classical acting works to render the body readable. To appear as intelligible, it needs to conceal the precedence of the profilmic body. It is as if the body is brought into being only after it has been filled with meaning and rendered readable. This underlines the coded nature of classical notions of performance, their rootedness in certain conventions and their co-relation with other filmic techniques. The exhaustion of the filmed body through an embodiment of character is not granted in advance. On the contrary, it is dependent on stylistic decisions and conventions. Certain conditions have to be met so that the filmed body can be treated as an empty vessel to be filled with meaning. The filmed body is not readable in itself; its readability must be rendered through certain filmic practices. The fictional character is 'filmable only by proxy'.[13] But the two bodies are always in competition – they 'exclude one another while coinciding'.[14] The boundary between the two bodies is always already uncertain. First to emerge is the body, as Comolli contends, 'the body as an *empty mask*, and the character will only appear later and bit by bit as effects of this mask, effects in the plural, changing, unstable, never quite achieved, thwarted, incomplete'.[15]

An alternative approach resides in certain realisms of the body where this parallelism is emphasised rather than concealed. The profilmic body is not a unit that already bears the traces of the film as a whole. A found thing, it is not produced by or for the film. It takes part in its production. It is not produced as an object or enacted through signifying processes. It is, rather, found in the world and made available to the gaze of the camera. The filmed body might be associated with meanings and functions. But association is provisional and uncertain. While classical aesthetics endeavours to deny the profilmic presence of the body, parallelism draws on this primary uncertainty to further problematise the boundary between the two bodies. It attests to the fact that the borderline is always already tenuous. As Comolli argues, the body of the actor 'whose image we see' is 'too much'.[16] It bears an uncompromising existential thickness that resists readability. The body has to be rendered readable but such rendition is never complete. The appearance of the character as an abstraction from the materiality of the profilmic body is never an exhaustive translation. The filmed body not only precedes but also exceeds and overflows the body of the character and persists as that which haunts the latter.

Parallelism exposes to failure the attempt to reduce the profilmic body to the body of the character, interrupting and short-circuiting the translation of the body-thing. It can be said to make the 'surplus visible' by 'disturbing the spectator's look with a bodily supplement'.[17] The disturbing body interrupts the classical attempt at ensuring that the filmed body is forgotten. It disrupts the effort to cancel the body and keep it hidden. This alternative approach attests to a gap between the two bodies. This gap is itself a sort of productive maladjustment between character as representation and the actuality of the profilmic body. It is where 'the apparent naturalness, the familiarity of the body',[18] itself an effect of readability, is thwarted. This gap is a site in which a testimony to the alterity of the body resides.

Automatism: the thing comes into being

The cinematic image is that through which the world faces the viewer insofar as the giving of the image in duration is irreducible to what is rendered as given in abstraction from the actuality of this duration. The otherness of the other is less a property of the latter than the effect of an encounter where the body of the other faces the viewer and opens up as a being to be rewatched and borne witness to. Parallelism radicalises the encounter with the other. It theatricalises the breakthrough of the body of the other within the visual but also stages its withdrawal. What is pivotal in this dynamic of breakthrough and withdrawal is not only that the body is a found thing but also the way the cinematographic machine records and renders the body. The automatic recording of the profilmic and the cinematic image's physical bond with reality give film its distinctive capacities in staging encounters with the fragments of the real. They place a certain withdrawal of the fragments at the core of the medium.

Bazin's conception of the real, and his approach to the relation of the latter to the camera, resides in a certain understanding of the capturing of the world. According to Bazin, as Dudley Andrew observes, cinema 'more than any other art is naturally able to capture and suggest the sense of a world which flows around and beyond us'.[19] Regarding the real as a mass of changing and fluid matter, Bazin understands cinema as the medium that offers a certain capacity to retain the contingency of the real precisely because cinema like no other medium has the ability to capture time and space in chunks. This temporal and spatial richness of cinema puts it in close contact with *the actual*. On the one hand, there is an immediate quality to the way film makes the profilmic present. Images and sounds affirm the presence of the profilmic prior to mediation. Film is 'inescapably literal', Steven Shaviro argues, precisely because '[i]mages confront the viewer directly, without mediation. What we see is what we see; the figures that unroll before us cannot be regarded merely as arbitrary representations or conventional signs.'[20] Images affect the viewer before they find the leisure and privilege to regard them as signs and symbols and thus translate their literalness to meaningful constructs through representation. There is a witnessing to things as they appear in their literal presence. The way in which the viewer encounters the image of something is significantly different from the way in which they comprehend its signifier: the former cannot be reduced to the latter.[21] The viewer could retroactively reconstruct the experience and reduce otherness by rendering the image familiar. But there is always a gap that functions as a testimony to a presence that precedes and overflows comprehension.

Film affirms the contingent through automatic recording, bringing to life that its necessity is not determined and justified in advance. The fragments of reality are affirmed due to their presence before the camera and the mere act of recording. They may be utilised to represent; but the association of meaning and function is always secondary. Fragments do not bear the traces of the film from the outset. They are, in a certain sense, merely found by the camera, and their literal thereness is, strictly speaking, contingent as there is no *a priori* motivation. The cinematic image, therefore, has a unique capacity to screen material contingency.[22] Discussing Jean Epstein, Jacques Rancière conceives of this 'making present' as a 'coming into being' of things, which precedes a potential representation of them. To demonstrate this precedence, Rancière evokes the film's mechanical reproduction of the real as the basis for the film medium's inherently 'presentational' aspect:

> [C]inematographic automatism does not reproduce things as they offer themselves to the gaze. It records them as the human eye cannot see them, as they *come into being*, in a state of waves and vibrations, *before* they can be qualified as intelligible objects, people, or events due to their descriptive and narrative properties.[23]

Things come into being and are affirmed through mechanical reproduction before their rendition through representation. The camera as a machine captures what is before it with a certain indifference: that is, a mechanical, non-selective making-present that precedes the activity of representation. There is a certain thereness to the thing presented, a thrust of its existential thickness that precedes signification.[24]

Automatic recording implies a certain bypassing of human intervention. For the first time, Bazin argues, 'between the originating object and its reproduction there intervenes only the instrumentality of a non-living agent . . . an image of the world is formed automatically, without the creative intervention of man'.[25] Embracing the passivity of mechanical reproduction, Bazin claims for the fundamental realism of cinematic technology. His conviction is that film, more than any other art, is destined to realism. Kathleen Kelley contends that in automatisms 'something can go on that was not determined by us, that happens beyond our control'.[26] This, for Bazin, is a breakdown of the top-down semantics. Joseph Mai locates parallelism as fundamentally residing in what bypasses human intervention at the core of the filmic rendition of reality and, most remarkably, relates it to an encounter with the real as opposed to a mere offering of the real to consciousness:

> On the one hand, there is dramaturgy – the abstraction through which reality is filtered by a conscious subject, the artist, for another conscious subject, the viewer; on the other, there is Nature – the essence of reality, for the first time present independently of the artist's hand. Through realism, the cinema seems to lift faces and objects out of the ineluctable flow of time for us to encounter.[27]

More fundamental to this bypassing of human intervention is a recording of the physicality of human body enveloped in duration that is by essence contingent and thus in a state of incessant withdrawal. This withdrawal concerns traces that attest to the actuality of the profilmic.

Material traces: the cinematic presence

Another integral aspect to the camera's making-present that potentially undoes representation concerns material traces. Often referred to as the indexicality of the image, the existential bond between the image and the referent gives cinematography the power to bear witness to the irreducible presence of the profilmic. For Bazin, this existential bond resides in the automatism of the cinematographic machine, 'no matter how lacking in documentary value the image may be'.[28] As Laura Mulvey contends, the index as 'physical connection' primarily attests to the fact that 'something must leave, or have left, a mark or trace of its physical presence'.[29] The profilmic has left its trace on the celluloid due to its presence before the camera by way of a giving. It is only by refusing to account for this trace that Shaviro can say film's 'literalness is empty and entirely ungrounded; it does not correspond to any sort of presence. Nothing is there except the image.'³⁰ There exists nothing but the image, whereas the image itself is a bundle of traces owing to the physical link between the image and the thing. The image, of course, is not simply an image of or about the world – a mere secondary copy, a derivative. It is in the world as that which carries the traces within itself, doing something in the world beyond what it may (or may not) posit as meaning by testifying to a past presence. The image contributes to the production of the real by its testimony.

The bond between the image and the referent is what provides the material basis for film's 'privileged relation to reality'.³¹ It is with respect to this privilege that the making-present that the cinematic image does resists representation. A privileged relation to reality does not imply an accurate image of the thing (a matter of resemblance) or an aspiration to adequacy. As Mulvey observes, a 'return to the index and to the real of the photographic medium is not a return to realism's aspiration to certainty'. Rather, Mulvey continues, 'the trace of the past in the present is a document, or a fact, that is preserved in but also bears witness to the elusive nature of reality and its representations'.³² This privileged relation to reality implies that the thing has left its trace through automatic, material inscription. The witnessing that the making-present bears is irreducible to representation since it primarily attests to presence (a past presence) rather than rendering the latter determinate. The thing that has left its trace is suspended in a weird presentness, a ghostly state of presence/absence. According to Philip Rosen, the photograph provides the viewer with 'absolute brute knowledge that the objects visible in the frame *were at one time* in the spatial "presence" of the camera, that they appear from an irrefutable past existence'.³³ A filmed body, by the same token, is 'present in its absence, in the traces of an image', or one might say in a ghostly state.³⁴

Indexicality frustrates the abstraction and generalisation that are inherent to representation. It provides the premise for the withdrawal of what is giving within the image from what is rendered given as content within the frontal visual field. Even if understood as a sign, an index is not a sign that implies a lack. It does not unproblematically sit in the place of something absent. On the contrary, the index is a matter of testimony, not of signification. It implies a certain fullness. The cinematic image is always already too graphic (to be contained). This resides in the way the camera mechanically and indifferently opens up onto the world without interrogating the attributes of the things it captures. Its capturing of the world is not motivated by recourse to the value of what is offered to its gaze. Bazin locates the richness of the cinematic in the 'photographic mechanics of image production'. The cinematic image is 'inherently more graphic than other kinds of pictures' precisely because it is based on a 'physical relationship with the real'.[35] The photographic image resists generalisation precisely because, as Mulvey reminds us, its specificity resides in its indexicality: 'While written (symbolic) or graphic (iconic) representations can evoke a class of things, a photographic image is always of one specific and unique, although, of course, endlessly reproducible, thing.'[36] Representation needs to move beyond the concreteness of the thing and relate it to what is already known and familiar – to a class of objects. It is not simply a matter of reproducing an existing thing. It primarily produces an object as it needs to abstract from the concrete materiality of the thing. It is with regards to the inevitability of this abstraction that the indexicality of the image defies representation. It attests to the irreducible, too-much-presence of the thing in its radical concreteness, particularity and contingency, but also to its giving within a certain spatio-temporal juncture. Precisely because the camera automatically and 'faithfully' records the profilmic, the filmed thing is already detached from the question of verisimilitude. There is a certain making-unfamiliar at work when the profilmic thing is copied on to celluloid. The transference of reality that takes place is one that stages the withdrawal of the thing from the frameworks of familiarity. The profilmic thing offered to the camera transforms into a filmed thing that persists in its thingness and withdraws from evoking a class of objects, thus subtracting something from the frontal visual field.

Citing Cesare Zavattini's assertion that the camera 'sees things and not their concepts',[37] Margulies raises an important question by highlighting that there is an inevitable reduction implicit in any filmic representation: 'how is one to represent a general idea, collectivity, or moral through the always indexical and particularizing powers of image and sound?'[38] She contends that film has the potential to avoid 'making association and symbolic leaps, and to fend off an impulse toward allegory'.[39] An actualisation of this specifically cinematic potential can be used to 'fend off conceptualization'.[40] Due to its indexicality, film can 'guarantee the particularity of its object in time and space, its precise historicity'.[41] The same interest is evident in Mary Ann Doane's discussion of cinema's project in modernity as 'endowing the singular with significance without relinquishing singularity'.[42] Doane identifies particularity by describing photography as the 'culmination of a tendency in the history of art' and rejecting 'the general, the ideal, and the schematic' while privileging 'the particular, the singular, the unique, the contingent'. In short, photography is conceived to be 'allied with a "thisness"'.[43] By the same token and with regard to filmed bodies, as Nicholas Balaisis points out, presenting a character 'beyond both narrative function and political allegory' is an ethical treatment for Bazin.[44]

Connected with the individual (profilmic) thing, this particularity of the filmic presence is indebted to cinematic automatism. The 'here-ness'[45] of the referent that the camera has captured resides in a sort of stepping back, or a simple absence, on the side of human intervention. This opens up space for an inscription that is bound with the singular materiality of the thing captured. The index, as 'a material trace that can be left without human intervention',[46] implies an affirmation and making-present that the camera as a machine does prior to a potential human attempt at representation. This emphasis on the precedence of a non-human making-present and the resulting particularising effect is also shared by Roland Barthes in his contention that the photograph, 'in spite of all possible human interference', constitutes a certain immediacy. It 'always carries the referent within itself'[47] – that is, carrying traces that attest to the material, sheer, literal presence of the referent. It is the automatic relation between the camera and the profilmic that provides the image with contingency, a certain indifference and being unnecessary. As Karl Schoonover asserts, '[t]rue contingency cannot be implemented, repackaged, or lent. It perpetually dethrones semantic fixities and undoes the world as we know it.'[48] As Temenuga Trifonova observes, the index is essentially located 'on the threshold of semiosis: contingency, indexicality and intelligibility are understood in terms of photography's and cinema's capacity to record a plenitude of information irreducible to signification.'[49] At the core of the automatic recording, there is something necessarily contingent about the bodies and things giving themselves in their singular time and space.

Realisms: the filmed body and the aesthetic

Cinematic realism cannot be measured by a film's achievements in delivering reality as a recognisable image of a world the viewer is already familiar with. There is a transference of reality through the physical bond with the thing recorded that troubles the meaningfulness of the thing. Automatism makes the thing stand out in its singular actuality before the camera and subsequently as what faces the viewer through the image prior to positing any meaning. However, emphasising the openness and inclusiveness of the automatic making-present, that it automatically brings into being through the physical bond with the thing regardless of the readability or intelligibility of what is made present, does not mean that a sheer recording of the profilmic could be equated with ethical giving. Quite the opposite is the case since sheer recording nullifies the address of the image that resides in the double movement of breakthrough and withdrawal.

Andy Warhol's filmic experimentations can be considered among revealing examples where the blankness of surfaces that automatism brings forth is distinctly taken to its apotheosis. Consider his eight-hour stationary recording of the Empire State Building, or more particularly with respect to the face and the body, consider his silent film portraits – screen tests mainly shot from 1964 to 1966 in Warhol's studio where he regularly asked the visitors to his factory to sit before the camera against a neutral backdrop, and remain motionless for as long as a hundred-foot 16mm film reel would keep recording. To preserve the rawness of the automatic capturing of the body, the duration of each filming session was punctuated by the length of the reel and no subsequent editing was used to articulate and rationalise the crude time.

Orna Raviv approaches Warhol's film portraits through Levinas's ethical perspective and his annotations about the human face in particular. Raviv identifies in the status of the close-up in film theory an affiliation with Levinas's observations about the irreducibility of the human face. She cites Jean Mitry's contention that the close-up, unlike other shot sizes, provides the grounds for an alternative encounter with the human subject where the viewer is given the channel to experience and feel the face without the 'requirement for it to be understood'. The close-up shot stands out in its capacity to impact 'the viewer's feelings, arousing her emotions in a way that does not require understanding'.[50] This attention to the uniqueness of the close-up can be traced back to Béla Balázs's seminal work in film theory, according to which 'good close-ups' can be utilised to 'radiate a tender human attitude in the contemplation of hidden things, a delicate solicitude, a gentle bending over the intimacies of life-in-the-miniature, a warm sensibility'. Close-up shots are thus argued to be able to elevate the image to being 'lyrical' where perception is located in the heart, as the 'feeling organ', rather than in the eye, the latter as 'an organ of visible perception'.[51]

Drawing on Epstein's attention to facial expressions, Raviv associates the close-up with a certain registration of minimal, yet intense movements that are 'undetectable by the ordinary gaze', where 'almost unfelt movements generate a range of expressions that are noticed only in close-up'.[52] It is in this regard that Warhol's portraits, according to Raviv, show a resonance with the Levinasian 'meaning without context':

> Here we can see how Warhol's close-ups suggest an encounter with the Other's face without falling into routine acts of contextualization.

> Faces in the *Screen Tests* appear on the screen only in close-up without the other shots such as long or medium shots that could give them meaning within a certain context ... The whole burden of constructing meaning in the *Screen Tests* resides in the face in close-up. In this respect, Warhol's close-ups resonate with the face described by Levinas.[53]

While acknowledging the power of the cinematic image to sustain what defies meaning and intelligibility, Raviv's discussion remains tied to the prominence of frontal visuality. She locates the uniqueness of the cinematic image in relation to what can be perceived through the close-up and its micro-observation of nuanced facial expressions. The question of adequation remains primal, and the cinematic machine is celebrated as a tool that is an improvement in capturing what would otherwise go undetected. This is particularly evident when Raviv speaks of the effect of slow-motion projection. Warhol recorded the portraits in twenty-four frames per second and then projected them in sixteen frames per second for the faces to appear in slow motion. According to Raviv, the 'slow motion produced a unique effect: what was revealed on these faces went beyond the expectable detail of ordinary close-ups'.[54] Raviv sees the 'more' that the cinematic image brings forth reducible to a desire to be more adequate (slow motion as improvement in adequacy) in the rendition of visibility, while crucially overlooking the fact that the surplus that the other brings into vision is the promise of the image. The address that overflows the image does not, strictly speaking, belong to what is posited within the frontal visual field of the image, and an improvement in capturing the nuances of the face does not question the primacy of the visual. Raviv's approach reduces the invisible to the hiddenness of positive content and does not exactly move beyond a literal understanding of the face. As discussed in the previous chapters, the difficult and often contradictory connotations of the face remove it from merely visual understandings of the human face, and instead maps the face onto the body and its wordless vocalisation of precarity. A close-up, of course, does not guarantee the ethical epiphany. The originary exposure to the human other is reaffirmed only indirectly through the ethics of failure and not through a technologically improved capture of life-in-the-miniature or a mere decontextualisation of the face, for there would remain no context to evoke within the filmic whole from which the face and body of the other withdraw.

Shaviro's take on the hyperboles of Warhol's experimentation is more relevant in the framework of my study of realism and its relation to the body of the other. Warhol's film portraits, as Shaviro notes, are demonstrations of how it is possible to take literalism to its extremes so that images 'evacuate all other

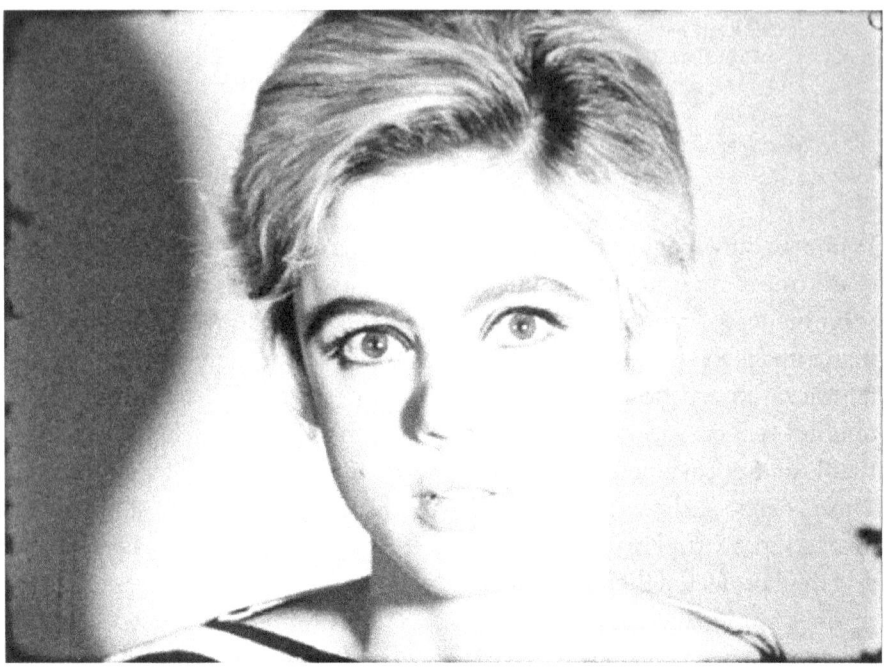

Figure 3.1 Edie Sedgwick in Andy Warhol's *Screen Tests* (Andy Warhol, 1965).

significance and content in order thereby to capture, record, and display the sheer, stupid, inert presence of bodies'.[55] The mechanical gaze of the camera does not offer any compensation as the 'appearance on screen doesn't point to anything beyond itself; specifically, it doesn't "stand for" (represent) the personality of the subject, as would be the case in traditional portraiture'.[56] The literalness of the image is unflinching as nothing is posited within or through the image beyond the immediately affirmed image of the body and the 'physical trace of bodily presence'.[57] The body of the other in Warhol film portraits is, as Raviv also observes, abstracted from any context that might render meaningful the appearance of the body within the visual field. More significantly, however, the body itself turns into its image prior to the image opening up within the visual, therefore undermining the ethical withdrawal of the body that the cinematic image could stage. As Shaviro contends,

> the body of the sitter, the object of the camera's gaze, has already become an image at the moment of the profilmic event. The body before the camera is a mute appearance, devoid of consciousness, will, or interiority. Warhol's 'subjects' are emptied out, distanced and absented from themselves, drained of their subjectivity, and reduced to a silent (yet insistent) spectacle of bodily presence.[58]

By taking the automatic recording to its extreme in their 'reductive literalism', Warhol's films mark a cinematic degree zero. Through what Shaviro notes as Warhol's 'excessive fidelity to the Bazinian project', his films derail the Bazinian venture by embracing the non-human 'passivity of mechanical production' in order to alter reality rather than faithfully reproduce it.[59] My argument diverges from Shaviro's in that I locate the significance of the altering of reality (against a presumably faithful production), not in a submission to the automatism of the camera (what Warhol attempts to stage), but in the tension that the resurfacing of the instability of sheer recording introduces within a filmic structure. Warhol's film portraits demonstrate an approach where the negotiation required to stage the heterogeneity of the filmic rendition of bodies, the awkward coexistence of literal and representational registers, is dismantled. Warhol's experiments aggressively evacuate the image of form – what results is not the withdrawal of the body of the other from the image (a process of formlessing the body) so much as an exhibition of the formlessness of the film medium itself at its degree zero. This aggression, of course, is not a reaffirmation of the Levinasian face, as Raviv suggests, but a necessary stage in an engagement with what realism of the body does to vision.

A sheer recording of the real, of giving it within the flow of the image, is a hyperbolic evacuation of givenness. By obliterating meaning, it effectively undermines a resistance to meaning. Resistance resides in a movement of withdrawal – there must be a meaning-making regime from which the withdrawal takes place. There exists a difficulty inherent to purist and essentialising approaches to automatism. When the story is forgotten, as Lisa Trahair observes,

> the Aristotelian legacy is thrown out the window. The arrangement of the plot, the structure of events, the protagonist's reversal of fortune, the alteration of his/her state of knowledge by the concatenation of events are all forgotten in favour of an interest in cinema's specific ability to passively record the brute materiality of the sensible world.[60]

This stance is to some extent reminiscent of the position of 'cinema purists' according to whom the mechanical function of the eye of the cinematograph in capturing the influx of the real must be celebrated and ultimately prioritised over storytelling and representational regimes that film has appropriated from other artforms over the course of its evolution. What is required, as Trahair contends, is an active dialectic and a tension between different regimes that govern the formation of the cinematic image and the parameters of its peculiar mode of opening up onto the viewer, between 'an aesthetic regime that celebrates aesthetic presence to the exclusion of everything else and the representative regime that subordinates the volubility of pure sensible presence by arranging aesthetic elements in the form of a good story'.[61]

Of course, one would be right in associating story with a certain will to bring the otherness of the world under form. To borrow from the Levinasian distinction between the saying and the said, story is in a certain way rooted in the structure of the said. The latter not only refers to the semantic content of an utterance in which signs are given by a sender to an addressee but also, as Gabriel Riera reminds us, brings about the 'different modalities by which a subject masters the world by assimilating it to the measure of consciousness (discourse, narration, history, manifestation, representation)'.[62] The saying, as the structure of exposure to the body of the other, is mediated by the said, the latter as a representation of this exposure. However, betraying the saying by putting it in a said is a necessity – it is through the failure of the said that the saying withdraws and imprints its trace within the said. Similarly, a facing image carries the other within itself, places it within a context of relations but also performs its own failure so that the withdrawal of the body of the other is theatricalised. Just as in Levinas's conception of reduction the said has to be unsaid so that the trace and residue of the saying can be heard, and the facing image has to stage the withdrawal of the body. What it involves is a negotiation with the medium that hosts the encounter with the other. This negotiation reintroduces the role of the aesthetic and resonates with the reading of ethics that this book is centred on. Realisms of the body must aesthetically earn what the film medium technologically achieves just as a facing image must earn the facingness that resides in the structure of the image. Facingness of the cinematic image requires retaining something of the inhumanity of the cinematographic machine. However, this is not a matter of the artist submitting themself to the rule of the machine so much as the artist showing an indebtedness to the automaticity of the latter and aesthetically negotiating with it. There is a debt that is affirmed through aesthetic intent.

Realism of the body is neither a sheer recording nor a closed set of norms and stylistic decisions that deliver transparent images of a world that is already familiar. As opposed to being a fixed noun, realism is a verb. It must earn what it has inherited owing to its debt to the cinematographic machine. Several contemporary film scholars defend the importance of rethinking realism away from the supposedly established equation of realism and essentialism to reflect upon the epistemological promise of referential images. The history of film theory especially in the 1970s and 1980s reflects an often taken-for-granted binary opposition between realism and modernism, a position that has been critically questioned over the past two decades. Opposing realism to modernism predominantly resides in an understanding of realism that reduces the latter to mimesis and transparency (therefore, is closely bound with the violence of representation). According to Clement Greenberg, realism is characterised by its tendency to use art to conceal art: 'It quickly emerged that the unique and proper area of competence of each art coincided with all that was unique in the nature of its medium.' He continues, '[R]ealistic, naturalistic art had dissembled the medium, using art to conceal art; modernist art used art to call attention to art.'[63] Kelley remarkably highlights this presumed opposition with respect to film by arguing that

> cinema, in fee to the real by the very nature of its photographic basis, could have no truck with modernism, which rejected cinema's transparent, mimetic omnivorousness in favor of a self-critical asceticism, attentive to medium and form and willing if not eager to let the represented world drop entirely.[64]

This binary opposition is problematic on at least two counts. Cinematic realism is irreducible to a question of mimesis. The automatic recording of the camera, unlike the popular belief, provides the premise for a radical refusal of mimesis.[65] Indeed, the realism that film achieves technologically bears the seeds of an interruption of mimesis because its automatic nature bypasses the mimetic impulses. As James Phillips argues:

> Technologically, in its recording of the real, [cinema] makes a mockery of the mimetic impulses of all animals, human and non-human. It does not so much copy as it is copied upon, with the objects it captures inscribing themselves in light and shade on its film stock ... the participation of the object in the production of its cinematic image overcomes the one-sidedness in the execution of an imitation ... Cinema colludes with its object rather than apes it.[66]

With the emergence of photography, as Trahair observes, aesthetics ceases to be a question of 'putting *human* spirit into matter' but becomes a matter of 'ensuring that it stays out of it'. This subversion is itself an alteration of the subject/object relation as 'nature now gives itself to be seen'.[67] Similarly, even though it is a human invention, cinema remains mechanical and thus devoid of human intervention at the degree zero of its automatic recording. This modesty implies a sort of receiving 'from above', an originary indifference but also a pre-reflective attentiveness to what is received, and a certain withdrawal of the latter from being contained as visual content.

Furthermore, there is a tension in Bazin's understanding between two different notions of realism. On the one hand, according to Phillips, there is the 'automatic realism of the mechanical reproduction of reality' as an affirmation of contingencies indebted to the automatic recording of the profilmic that bypasses human intervention. On the other, there is an aesthetic realism that 'finds itself still having to earn what it has been given'[68] – that is, having to confront its technological realism. Aesthetic realism is thus indebted to its '[entering] into dialogue with the objectivity that it achieves technologically'[69] – that is, resides in its tendency to reflect upon its own automatic recording of the profilmic. As Margulies tells us, Bazin himself was utterly aware of the fact that conventions can 'dull realism'.[70] A realist practice, however, is rather what is in an incessant struggle to earn what it has been given.[71]

Accounting for the complexity of filmic realism problematises the realist/modernist binary and opens up a new path for thinking the relation between the materiality of film and its aesthetic use. Conceiving of realism as something that is earned rather than merely rooted in film's technology, as not 'something given' but 'something achieved', Kelley contends that realism cannot be considered to take place automatically, merely as an inevitable outcome of the use of the medium. For Bazin, realism is 'something other than transparent access to the real', one that is presumed to be given when the medium is 'allowed to function at its most automatic'.[72] The question of artifice is therefore not a problem for Bazin to overcome, precisely because realism for him is neither a matter of mimesis nor a psychological need for appearances.[73] In other words, nothing is, strictly speaking, known or guaranteed in advance. Kelley introduces two new requirements for a medium to become art: intention and actuality. Intention 'saves us from the specter of absolute mechanization', while actuality, the fact that one must 'make something of the automatism', works through automatism to save us from the 'sense that the medium's possibilities are given in advance'.[74] A medium's potential is not entirely determined by its 'automatic nature', but only appears as a horizon of possibilities.[75] There should be a negotiation with what film as a medium achieves automatically, for an aesthetic use is not determined in advance. Rather than being a determinate entity, the constitutive element of a medium is not predefined but is instead 'to be capable of being called into play – not to always already be in it'.[76]

There is a necessity to speak of realism in plural terms. As Margulies reminds us, attention to 'the contingencies of reality and the film image' fleshes out 'the changeable nature of realism'.[77] Realism is a plural aesthetics.

Ever present is the possibility of inventing new forms of realism.[78] For a film to be realist, according to Daniel Morgan, it must account for the 'ontology of the photographic image'. Realism is thereby 'not a particular style, lack of style, or set of stylistic attributes, but a process, a mechanism – an achievement'.[79] The question of realism resides in a negotiation with what film achieves technologically, while the specific form that this negotiation takes is not determined in advance and is thus plural in nature. Cinematic realism is therefore open to the future as it is always incomplete. To retain the realist thrust, cinematic realism awaits the coincidence of automatism and aesthetic intent. This coincidence takes place in the face of an encounter with the otherness of the world and therefore is bound with the question of (un)familiarity.

Failure of recognition, temporal instabilities and bodily surplus

An uncritical conception of realism sees it as what delivers a recognisable image of reality, as what is identified by a return to the familiar. By contrast, the aesthetic thrust of realism is a failure in this reduction of the other. It is a making-unfamiliar that is central to this book's emphasis on film's rendition of the body of the other. Ethics is tied to realism as a critique of how the other breaks through the visual, and whether its breakthrough leaves an image that performs its failure in capturing the other.

Despite his condemnation of realism, Jean-Francois Lyotard's hostility towards the latter underlines the importance of aesthetic reworkings of realism and their problematic relation to familiarity. According to Lyotard, reality is not something that we know naturally. On the contrary, a sense of reality is a historical construct that is generated by different devices of a culture. Realist art is one of the things that is instrumentalised to assist us in creating a sense of reality. Lyotard associates realism as the 'mainstream' art of any culture, as 'the art of making reality, of knowing reality and knowing how to make reality',[80] with our familiar frameworks of representation and our 'good forms'.[81] The aim of realist art is to order the world 'from a point of view that would give it recognisable meaning', and thereby to 'protect consciousness from doubt'.[82] For Lyotard, as Simon Malpas notes, realist art is thus art that is recognised and grasped immediately, for it presents the world to us in familiar ways, refraining 'from challenging our beliefs about reality'. Protecting consciousness 'from doubts about the way things are', realism therefore 'serves to perpetuate narratives about the world'.[83] It captures the world through a decisive return to the familiar, leaving no room for the unrepresentability of the other.

This critique helps us to conceive of a different type of realism of the body – an experimental one that does not result in the solace and familiarity of good forms. Realism is self-critical, plural and changing precisely because openness towards the anterior other necessitates a constant reworking of what making-unfamiliar is and does. Phillips's approach to realism considers it as a making-unfamiliar and ultimately as a failure:

> The mark of success . . . of realist cinema lies not in the moment of recognition wherein the viewer acknowledges the faithful reproduction of something already familiar. The realist work exhibits its credentials when it surprises by what it shows, as though its reality is to be recognised in the failure of re-cognition, in the obviating of models.[84]

Realism as a performance of failure is always a work in progress while its incomplete nature puts it in close contact with ethics. In a certain sense, experimental realism is where the ethical and the aesthetic coincide. An image of the body of the other that is readily recognisable fails to address the viewer. It fails to stage the facing of the body of the other precisely because what it opens is already framed for the habituated eye. Moreover, the incompleteness of a realist image does not seek solace merely in a restoration of completion through an alternative image, which is equally determined by its givenness. Despite its seeming attentiveness to the other and its apparent commitment to bring the other onscreen to save it from oblivion, the pseudo-realist image manifests a problematic understanding of ethics that identifies the other based on a recognition of sameness and difference. By contrast, a truly realist image acknowledges that otherness primarily resides in the encounter with the other, that its own status as an image is destined to be incomplete, while its incompleteness is not rectifiable but resides in an originary failure in the presence of the facing of the other. To attest to this originary otherness, the inhuman eye of the cinematographic machine is required to bring forth an image of the other that, even though not framed for the eye of the viewer, visits the eye. Hospitality of the cinematic image is rooted in a negotiation with the fundamental fact that the viewer is exposed to a presence enveloped in duration that is affirmed prior to being identified and invited.

There is a promise in referential images – that is, as Margulies observes, 'what we see refers to an existing reality'.[85] In its degree zero, film's approach to bodies is a 'confrontation with real existing bodies'.[86] A reference to existing bodies of others is an integral aspect of a rewatching that the cinematic image offers. In this formulation, the too muchness of the material body is a question that helps to 'rethink, not to condemn, realism'.[87] To further the ethical implications of this position, I add that any critical notion of realism embraces some sort of openness, receptivity and exposure to that which is not constituted in advance – to what precedes, faces and thus is other. An alternative approach to the problem of the filmed body and its ontological instabilities is a response to this precedence at the heart of the film medium, and thus is a way for rethinking not only realism but film's originary bond with otherness and its potential hospitality.

I draw on this too muchness to demonstrate how realisms of the body facilitate the breakthrough but also the withdrawal of the body of the other. I consciously prefer to speak of the body in 'surplus' of narrative and signifying frameworks that work to situate the body, as opposed to conceiving the surplus as a demonstration of mere 'excess'. Angelos Koutsourakis's critical reading of the latter concept rightly points out the 'undertheorized' applications of the term in film theory. Revisiting Kristin Thompson's and Barthes's works on the notion of excess, Koutsourakis reminds us of the need

> [to] clarify some key points that can enable us to see how cinematic excess refers to those moments in a film that are not anti-narrative or cannot be simply reduced to a symbolic function; they work instead in a manner that produces an audio-visual surplus that exceeds esthetic functionalism.[88]

Stressing the fact that cinematic excess is not limited to avant-garde or anti-narrative cinema, Koutsourakis observes that 'a filmic sequence cannot exceed its narrative function within the film without a narrative in the first place'.[89] Furthermore, he elsewhere acknowledges that excess can indeed be appropriated for marketing purposes in mainstream cinema as well as in television productions and music videos, and therefore does not necessitate the ethical and political significance that is often associated with arthouse cinema.[90] The fundamental aspects of the formation of the body's image, as far as I am concerned here, provide the premise for a certain giving of bodies within narrative structures where the surplus of bodily presence is something not to shy away from but to utilise to ethical ends. Negotiating with bodily surplus, aesthetic reworkings of realism can potentially disrupt the return to the familiar and restage ethical exposure by putting failure to work.

Bodily surplus is not only bound with the materiality and existential density of the automatically formed image but also involves the question of cinematic time. Drawing on Doane's discussions of the emergence of time in cinema, Tiago de Luca traces the dilemma of automatism specifically in relation to filmic rendition of time:

> Carrying the promise of recording seemingly anything for unspecified periods of time, film enabled the potential irruption of the contingent into the image. Yet this ontological promiscuity posited the danger of a purely indeterminate and disembodied temporality that was subsequently countered with the emergence of narrative structures.[91]

In other words, the advent of narrative was to a great extent a response to frustrations with the indeterminacies of automatic recording that followed the initial fascination with the invention of the cinematograph. It was as though cinema required a certain negotiation between 'recording' and 'signification' at its core for it not only to be recognised as an emerging artform but also to retain its allure. According to Doane,

> [t]he inevitably historiographic tendency of cinema, its ability to record 'real' time and its duration, at first a source of endless fascination, poses critical difficulties for the early cinema. Cinema's time is surely referential; it is a record of time with the weight of indexicality. But its time is also characterized by a certain indeterminacy, an intolerable instability . . . The resulting cinema delicately negotiates the contradiction between recording and signification.[92]

In order to 'manufacture meaning' by containing the 'intolerable instability' of time, the history of cinema showcases narrative traditions that attempt to rationalise time by suppressing the *temps mort* (the 'dead', 'uneventful' or 'wasted' time). Yet, more significantly, it simultaneously hosts a certain resurfacing of 'anomalous temporalities' where empty time is foregrounded and the artifice of temporal processes that produce meaning is exposed.[93]

In my attention to the ways in which realisms of the body stage the withdrawal of the other, it is no coincidence that most of the films discussed in this book would fall under the rubric of 'slow cinema' – not least Chantal Akerman's *Jeanne Dielman, 23 quai du Commerce, 1080 Bruxelles* (1975), which is the focus of the next chapter and is inarguably considered as one of the prominent historical antecedents of modernist slow films. It is also important for me here to admit that my interest in these films in some respects diverges from the current discourses surrounding slow cinema's modes of production and reception. I tend to agree with May Adadol Ingawanij's observation that slow cinema, as a critical framework that encompasses 'a heterogeneous set of directors of disparate geographies and lineages, has the potential to obscure as much as it elucidates'.[94] Paul Schrader refers to a similar point when he acknowledges that, despite its usefulness, the term is problematic in itself as '[n]ot all directors use "slow" techniques for the same purposes' as even if they might 'employ similar stylistic devices, their intentions and films are in fact quite dissimilar'.[95] More importantly, as evident in my approach to the films in this book, I consciously focus on the ethical implications of the viewer's passivity as an alternative form of labour in watching the body of the other appear and persist onscreen, as a commitment to hosting the body's image opened up within the visual prior to and beyond an identification of the body. In so doing, I knowingly move away from an often taken-for-granted reduction of the viewing experience that slow films provide towards an active contemplation. Partly used to validate the cultural and aesthetic status of slow cinema and demonstrate that slowness is worth the labour, the latter view often assumes that slow films summon a viewer who takes part in the completion of the film, as though a deliberately incomplete aesthetics and the bodily surplus that results are to be domesticated through critical viewing practices that in the final analysis reinstate the viewing subject's authority over the body.

What intrigues me most is an account that regards slowness as a property exclusive to film and the role it can potentially play in practising realisms of the body, the latter as an ethical failure that traces the withdrawal of the other from the order of the frontal. In his discussion of what he terms 'the cinema of stasis', Justin Remes sees a demonstration of this cinematic quality in relation to other arts. Citing Walter Benjamin's contention that a 'painting invites the viewer to contemplation' and Barthes's stance that 'photographs create an opportunity for reflection', as opposed to the incessant interruptions of moving images, Remes argues that these notions are challenged particularly by films that 'arrest' moving images:

> After all, it is possible for an individual to visit a museum and glance at Salvador Dalí's painting *Sleep* (1937) for a few seconds before moving on to look at other works. The spectator could then honestly tell others, 'I saw Dalí's *Sleep*.' But compare this to Andy Warhol's film *Sleep*, which shows the poet John Giorno sleeping (and moving very little) for more than five hours. One could certainly watch just a few seconds of the film, but could one then say, 'I saw Warhol's *Sleep*'?[96]

Even though in my view Warhol's *Sleep* (1964) is an aggressive evacuation of meaning and cannot be equated with realisms of the body for reasons mentioned earlier in the chapter, and even though what slowness offers by

Figure 3.2 Restoring the variable of duration by the staging of a tableau in *Thérèse* (Alain Cavalier, 1986).

arresting moving images is beyond the question of reflection or contemplation, Remes's argument nevertheless demonstrates the fixed-time conditions of film viewing. Or consider Pauline Kael's reaction to Alain Cavalier's *Thérèse* (1986), which is revealing in approaching this cinematic imposition:

> Watching *Thérèse* is like looking at a book of photographs of respectfully staged tableaux and not being allowed to flip the pages at your own speed. You have to sit there while Cavalier turns them for you, evenly, monotonously, allowing their full morbid beauty to sink it. You're trapped inside his glass bubble.[97]

Thérèse was made with the assumption that any account of the life of Thérèse Martin, a nineteenth-century nun who managed to become Saint Thérèse of Lisieux, can be accessed mostly through her photographs, and any historical rendition of her story must account for the possibilities, but also the limitations, of 'a photographic take on the past'. Arresting the momentum of the progression of a historical narrative, as James Tweedie observes, *Thérèse* presents the past not through 'a string of facts emplotted into narrative but as a still image'.[98] More outstandingly with respect to my discussion here, Cavalier not only favours the stillness of photography over narrative progression, but he also reintroduces the duration of the documentation of the body by staging the process that produced the photographs. The photographic technology at the end of the nineteenth century required the sitter to remain motionless, bearing the intended pose for several seconds and avoiding extreme expressions of emotion. Cavalier reinstates duration into the still images by 'resembling the protracted process that produced them, imposing an unfamiliar way of seeing that restores the forgotten variable of duration'.[99] In addition to embodying a historical way of seeing, Cavalier's experiment demonstrates that, while a photograph or painting has an arbitrary viewing duration, a cinematic shot dictates the duration in which what is framed persists within the image even if this persistence reintroduces the instability of time into the image itself. Even if Cavalier radically reduces mobility within a shot to the point of almost turning it into a photograph or tableau, what differentiates his cinematic re-enactment of stillness from the latter is the obvious but crucial fact of the dictated duration of cinematic shots.

This imposition is a medium-specific property of film. It might be argued, indeed, that there are new and emergent viewing practices particularly due to new technologies that allow for more flexibility. However, the assumption in this book is that filmmakers intend films to be viewed in a theatre where film can enforce its own temporal composition. As de Luca rightly observes,

> [a]s far as the cinema is concerned, one of its fundamental properties is, of course, its ability to record time and impose duration. While the new spectatorial modes evinced by portable devices are defined by an ever-greater flexibility in terms of temporal manipulation, when watched under fixed-time conditions cinema strictly enforces its own temporality.[100]

Let me return to the opening shot of Pedro Costa's *Ossos* (1997), which I referred to at the beginning of the first chapter. One might rightly say that the shot of the woman is only the first shot of a film that runs for ninety-four minutes. The persistence of her offscreen stare may be resistant to meaning, but it is accentuated in its resistance just to be filled with significance later – it is a preparation for what is to come, an allusion to what is on its way to being materialised, a promise of an eventual fulfilment. Had I been holding a photograph of the same woman in my hand or encountered a frame grab of the same scene in a gallery, and the gloomy stare in the image demanded something of me as its viewer, then I would have been able to argue that what the image asks me is, in a certain sense, an impossibility. The composition of the still image makes a claim, but a claim that cannot be responded to because I cannot simply exhaust it by ascribing meaning to it, by decoding it or rendering it discursive. A photograph of the woman can refer to itself, to its self-presentingness, simply because its ambiguity and undecidability refer to a moment of a giving of a body that cannot be rendered given, to the event of its being opened to the viewer. Now that what I have before me is not a photograph but just the very first shot of a film, the initial shot is inevitably going to be followed by more shots and thus is inescapably going to be read through its juxtaposition with other shots, with what is not-yet and awaits articulation. It both registers a unique moment and introduces the moment-after, implicating the moment within a totality and forcing it to be meaningful and significant within a matrix of relations. Film, therefore, presumably destroys the purity of the indeterminate moment.

Beside the fact that it is difficult to define what a moment is and problematic to equate the resistance of a photograph to meaning with its being tied to a moment, this argument glosses over the essential detail that the initial shot of *Ossos* bears a certain difference from a photograph of the same shot, despite the fact that both have been automatically produced. Even if a shot is just a photograph projected on a cinema screen, it already embodies the fixed duration of its projection in advance. Holding a photograph in my hand, the photograph itself has a contingent temporality. It is impossible to say when and where the act of viewing the photograph must necessarily end. It is impossible to punctuate the end with respect to the beginning and thus calculate the necessary duration of its viewing. But the duration of the projection of the shot is an actuality and thus enforces a certain necessity. The viewer of the initial shot of *Ossos* has no choice but to look at this shot for almost a minute; unless they give up watching the film, turn away and perhaps exit the film theatre. The impossibility of reading into the woman's looking gloomily offscreen in the initial shot of *Ossos*, and thus the fact that the image refers to itself as an event of giving a body, are indissociable from the stubborn persistence of the filmed body onscreen within this particular shot and across other shots in the film, each of them characterised by a weightiness that owes to the automatic recording as much as to the preservation of this automatism in the way images are set up. A filmic shot is capable of a resistance to meaning beyond what a photograph is able to achieve owing to the imposing force of its duration, of the claim that its duration makes on the viewer, cultivating an attentiveness and a commitment beyond what a photograph can accomplish. The cinematic image can uniquely sustain (and appreciate) what defies explanation.

Moreover, speaking of temporality as an ethical compromise is inaccurate precisely because an integral part of the self-presentingness of cinematic images is a promise: a call to attend oneself to a story on its way to being told. A story has in itself a certain temporality, even a linearity (of film viewing rituals) despite all the possible temporal manipulations: a story that is recounted, that unfolds, that awaits, anticipates and thus calls into being a moment-after. Yet speaking of the promise as that which resides in the structure of the image, it does not follow that something given must be achieved and posited through the image so that the promise is kept. The promise is not exhaustively constituted by determinate content. It should not be equated with a triggering of curiosity or an evocation of cognitive activity that pays off. A story in cinema is anxious, as what it delivers is already haunted by cinematic parallelism. Heath articulates this parallel capacity through establishing a tense relation between the narrative and signifying aspects of film (what he considers as the unifying forces aimed at crystalising homogeneity) and the materiality of filmic practices:

> Just as narrative never exhausts the image, homogeneity is always an effect of the film . . . Homogeneity is haunted by the material practice it represses and the tropes of that repression, the forms of continuity, provoke within the texture of the film the figures – the edging, the margin – of the loss by which it moves; permanent battle for the resolution of that loss on which, however, it structurally depends, mediation between image and discourse, narrative can never contain the whole film which permanently exceeds its fictions . . . the film is the organisation of a homogeneity and the material outside inscribed in the operation of that organisation as its contradiction.[101]

Irreducible to technological determinism, the inclusion of the *temps mort* exploits parallelism to reintroduce ontological instabilities into the story to retain the promise of 'some kind of' story against a totalising story proper. Certain aesthetic inclusions of aberrant temporalities create an equivalence between what within the image appears to contribute to the filmic whole and what withdraws through its persistence. As we see in the next chapter, the inclusion of a time that does not pay off, as Margulies suggests, is an inclusion of 'images between images' as a means to shape 'a transformative realism'. The inclusion of the non-dramatic as that which 'resists direct representation in conventional cinema' is dependent upon a 'spatio-temporal expansion of cinema'. Margulies even goes further, to suggest that the inclusion of the non-dramatic is 'the signifier par excellence of the realistic impulse', of the 'realist desire'.[102] Indeed, there must be images between which the *temps mort* stands out as the force of interruption. Slowness is therefore not so much reducible to a set of recognisable stylistic norms, or merely an invitation for the viewer to actively contemplate, but is a demonstration of the intolerable instability of cinematic time and its rendition of the body of the other. Certain creative uses of slowness within specific filmic practices can result in a making-unfamiliar of not only the body of the other, but the relation of the body to the image. Through slowness, the cinematic image can stage the withdrawal of the other from the essential frontality of the screen by a return to the automatic affirmation of the body's image inside the camera – the body appears as facing precisely because, despite taking part in narrative composition, it appears to be sustained by the image itself beyond narrative exhaustion. This withdrawal takes place within the cinematic image and is tied to an originary refusal of the body of the other to merely produce a given image as the life that the camera–world interaction brings into being defies the necessities of intelligibility.

Notes

1. Visual perception is, prior to becoming knowledge, 'a spectacle in which I revel'. While an object is 'the assimilable;' it is 'the assimilated', the face of the other, strictly speaking, does not 'appear in my world;' it does not 'stand out on any of my horizons'. See Crignon, 'Figuration', 102.
2. Bazin, 'In Defense of Rossellini', 99.
3. As Dudley Andrew argues: 'Traditional literary realists like Zola or Verga . . . tend to shape their scenes to fit the narrative. Analogously, in its realist genres, Hollywood cinema moulds and bevels every shot into a brick that can be smoothly attached to neighbouring bricks in forming the bridge of the story.' Andrew, 'Foreword to 2004 Edition', xiv.
4. Bazin, 'An Aesthetic of Reality', 37.
5. Ibid., 36.
6. See Bazin, 'Bicycle Thief', 47–60. Cited in Grist, 'Whither Realism?', 22.
7. Margulies, 'Bodies Too Much', 3.
8. Ibid., 4.
9. Ibid., 17–18.
10. Daney, *La rampe*, 162. Cited in Margulies, 'Bodies Too Much', 17–18. Also, for a discussion of formalism in Bazin's realist theory see Wagner, 'Lost Aura'.
11. Comolli, 'Historical Fiction', 42–3.
12. Heath, 'Body, Voice', 180–1.
13. Comolli, 'Historical Fiction', 43.
14. Ibid., 47.
15. Ibid., 42–3.
16. Ibid., 49.
17. Ibid.
18. Ibid.
19. According to Andrew, Bazin considers film to be able to provide 'deep feeling for the integral unity of a universe in flux' and regards the realistic styles as 'approximations of visible [or perceptual] reality'. See Andrew, *André Bazin*, 21, and Andrew, *The Major Film Theories*, 139 and 157.

20 Shaviro, *The Cinematic Body*, 25.
21 Ibid., 28.
22 See George Kouvaros, '"We Do Not Die Twice"', 381.
23 Rancière also opposes human intelligence to the intelligence of the machine. See Rancière, *Film Fables*, 2. For a discussion of Rancière's relation to film theory, see Conley, 'Cinema and Its Discontents', and Ross, 'The Aesthetic Fable'.
24 The photograph, according to Roland Barthes, presents 'a kind of natural being-there of the object'. Cited in Wollen, *Signs and Meaning in Cinema*, 84.
25 Bazin, *What Is Cinema?, vol. 1*, 13. For a critique of automatism that understands the latter as a reduction of the complexity of film processes, see Ahern, 'Cinema's Automatisms and Industrial Automation'.
26 Kelley, 'Faithful Mechanisms', 30. Similarly, Wollen, in his semiological approach, reads this automatism as a lack of code between the object and the sign. See Wollen, *Signs and Meaning in Cinema*, 84. Also, see Wollen, '"Ontology" and "Materialism" in Film', 7. For a discussion of how the power of the image is bound with the bypassing of human intervention in Bazin's aesthetics, see Cardullo, 'Cinematic Realism and the Italian School of the Liberation', 4–5.
27 Mai, '*Lorna's Silence* and Levinas's Ethical Alternative', 439.
28 According to Bazin, 'The photographic image is the object itself, the object freed from the conditions of time and space that govern it. No matter how fuzzy, distorted, or discolored, no matter how lacking in documentary value the image may be, it shares, by virtue of the very process of its becoming, the being of the model of which it is the reproduction; it *is* the model.' Bazin, 'The Ontology of the Photographic Image', 14.
29 Mulvey, *Death 24x a Second*, 9 and 55.
30 Shaviro, *The Cinematic Body*, 25.
31 Mulvey, *Death 24x a Second*, 18.
32 Ibid., 9. For Morgan's formulation of the fundamental postulate of the index as that which is bound with the process of generation rather than resemblance, see Morgan, 'Rethinking Bazin', 450. Also, for Wollen's discussion of Bazinian realism's dependence on existential bond rather than mimesis, see Wollen, *Signs and Meaning in Cinema*, 92. Also, see Kelley, 'Faithful Mechanisms', 27.
33 Rosen, *Change Mummified*, 29. That is, 'everything that is filmed once *was* in reality'. See Cardullo, 'Defining the Real', 5.
34 Heath, 'Body, Voice', 188. According to Akira Mizuta Lippit at the heart of cinematic rendition of bodies there is a 'doubling of bodies'. See Lippit, *Ex-Cinema*, 123. Also see Eliaz, 'Acts of Erasure', 207–31.
35 Schoonover, *Brutal Vision*, 1.
36 Mulvey, *Death 24x a Second*, 9. According to George Kouvaros: 'Photography's unique relationship to the singular stems from its indexicality.' See Kouvaros, '"We Do Not Die Twice"'.
37 Zavattini, 'Some Ideas on the Cinema', 220.
38 Margulies, *Nothing Happens*, 22.
39 Ibid.
40 Ibid., 28.
41 Margulies, 'Bodies Too Much', 9.

42 Doane, *The Emergence of Cinematic Time*, 208. To re-engage the issue of indexicality, Mary Ann Doane sees the latter notion as 'anathema to film theory' while citing Bazin as an exception in this regard. See ibid., 25.
43 Ibid., 10. Doane refers to Charles Sanders Peirce, explaining how the indexical enacts a particular relation to the referent: 'Unlike icons and symbols, which rely upon association by resemblance or intellectual operations, the work of the index depends upon association by contiguity . . . the object is made "present" to the addressee.' Ibid., 92.
44 Balaisis, 'The Risk of Ambiguity', 44.
45 It is with respect to the particularising aspect of the index that Metz's reworking of the concept is focused on a *here-ness* of the referent. See Wollen, *Signs and Meaning in Cinema*, 84.
46 Mulvey, *Death 24x a Second*, 55.
47 Barthes, *Camera Lucida*, 5.
48 Schoonover, *Brutal Vision*, xxix.
49 Trifonova, *The Twilight of the Index*, 65.
50 Raviv, 'Andy Warhol's *Screen Tests*', 54. For Raviv's in depth discussion, see Raviv, *Ethics of Cinematic Experience*.
51 Cited in Raviv, 'Andy Warhol's *Screen Tests*', 54.
52 Raviv, 'Andy Warhol's *Screen Tests*', 55.
53 Ibid.
54 Ibid., 56.
55 Shaviro, *The Cinematic Body*, 209.
56 Ibid., 210.
57 Ibid.
58 Ibid., 211.
59 Ibid., 17–18. Margulies similarly identifies a mockery and subversion of 'all the basic values associated with neorealist "nothingness"'. See Margulies, *Nothing Happens*, 38.
60 Trahair, 'Godard and Rancière', 50–1.
61 Ibid.
62 Riera, '"The Possibility of the Poetic Said"', 14.
63 Greenberg, 'Modernist Painting', 103. Cited in Wollen, '"Ontology" and "Materialism" in Film', 11.
64 Kelley, 'Faithful Mechanisms', 23. From this understanding of realism, it follows that film as a medium, in its quest to be realist, strives for its own destruction, since 'in seeking realism as its perfection it seeks to efface itself more and more completely, erasing any unique characteristics it might have had in order to become a more perfect conduit. From a modernist point of view, [film] now appears as doubly heretical: already in love with mere representation, it is also ineluctably hostile to the very idea of a medium.' See Kelley, 'Faithful Mechanisms', 25–6.
65 Peter Wollen significantly emphasises this point when he contends that considering modernism as 'the drive to give works of art the integrity of objects, and to liberate them from the burden of human mimesis' implies that 'it is mimesis itself which is now associated with the burdensome intervention of the "human", the cultural, as the work of art is returned to the integral objecthood of nature, existing as pure being'. See Wollen, '"Ontology" and "Materialism" in Film', 10.

66 Phillips, 'The Fates of Flesh', 14. Wollen implies a similar conception by saying that, according to Bazin, '[b]y natural optical and photochemical processes, the being of the pro-filmic event (the objects within the camera's field of vision) was transferred to the being of the film itself'. See Wollen, '"Ontology" and "Materialism" in Film', 7. Also, for a discussion of thinking particularity away from the question of resemblance, see Morgan, 'Rethinking Bazin', 447–8.
67 Trahair, 'Being on the Outside', 132. According to Bazin, cinema 'retains a level of modesty before nature', it is 'in awe of nature'. See Schoonover, *Brutal Vision*, 24.
68 Phillips, 'The Fates of Flesh', 11.
69 Ibid., 12. Cinema, as Phillips argues elsewhere, 'makes an art out of looking' precisely because 'the agency of any individual filmmaker – if it is to find a place for itself at all – has to negotiate the passivity with which the apparatus records the profilmic'. The difference between a filmmaker and a painter is that, while 'the undeployed pigment represents only itself', the cinematic image from the outset is, 'in a very palpable sense, already fully there before the camera starts rolling: the art is to see it'. See Phillips, *Sternberg and Dietrich*, 91.
70 Margulies, 'Bodies Too Much', 2.
71 See Bazin, 'In Defense of Rossellini', 99–100. For readings of Bazin's realism as a set of stylistic decisions, see Carroll, *Philosophical Problems of Classical Film Theory*, 108–9, and Henderson, *A Critique of Film Theory*, 37. For discussions against essentialist understandings of the medium, see Rancière, *Film Fables*, 6 and Joret, *Studying Film with André Bazin*, 29.
72 Kelley, 'Faithful Mechanisms', 27.
73 Bazin's position on artifice is not a matter of 'surrender'. See also *André Bazin and Italian Neo-realism*, 6.
74 Kelley, 'Faithful Mechanisms', 30. Foregrounding the aesthetic aspect of Bazin's theory of realism, Kelley argues that Bazin has endeavoured to imagine 'a version of realism that, for all its commitment to the appearing world, can still keep pace with aesthetic and formal ambitions'. See ibid., 26–7.
75 Ibid., 32.
76 Ibid., 33. It is in the light of this dynamic dialogue with technological realism and the futurity of the medium that Bazin's claim for 'transference of reality from the thing to its reproduction' (see Bazin, 'The Evolution of the Language of Cinema', 14) seems irreducible to his somewhat dogmatic defence of certain cinematic techniques.
77 Margulies, 'Bodies Too Much', 5.
78 Ibid., 14. Bazin himself writes: 'The word "realism" as it is commonly used does not have an absolute and clear meaning, so much as it indicates a certain tendency toward the faithful rendering of reality on film.' See Bazin, *Jean Renoir*, 85.
79 Morgan, 'Rethinking Bazin', 445. For a discussion of similarities between Bazin's realism and Brecht's anti-illusionism, see Nagib and Mello, *Realism and the Audiovisual Media*, xix.
80 Lyotard, *Postmodern Fables*, 91.
81 Lyotard associates contesting good forms with a postmodern attentiveness to the unpresentable: 'The postmodern would be that which, in the modern, puts forward the unpresentable in presentation itself; that which denies itself the solace of good forms, the consensus of a taste which would make it possible to share collectively

the nostalgia for the unattainable; that which searches for new presentations, not in order to enjoy them but in order to impart a stronger sense of the unpresentable.' See Lyotard, *The Postmodern Condition*, 81. Lyotard sees the artist's function as no longer a production of 'good forms' but a systematic deconstruction of them. See Devismes, 'On Theory', 21.
82 Lyotard, *The Postmodern Explained*, 5–6.
83 Malpas, *Jean-Francois Lyotard*, 44.
84 Phillips, 'The Fates of Flesh', 12. In a sense, realism, if understood as dissociated from frameworks of familiarity, can be said to approach fulfilling the task that Lyotard assigns for avant-garde art – to 'bear witness to the indeterminate'. Lyotard, 'The Sublime and the Avant-Garde', 37.
85 Margulies, 'Bodies Too Much', 1.
86 Ibid., 9.
87 Ibid., 5.
88 Koutsourakis, 'A Modest Proposal for Rethinking Cinematic Excess', 703–4.
89 Ibid., 704.
90 See Koutsourakis, 'Cinema of the Body', 54–85.
91 De Luca, 'Slow Time, Visible Cinema', 30.
92 Doane, *The Emergence of Cinematic Time*, 163. Cited in De Luca, 'Slow Time, Visible Cinema', 30.
93 De Luca, 'Slow Time, Visible Cinema', 31.
94 Ingawanij, 'Philippine Noir: The Cinema of Lav Diaz', 54.
95 Schrader, *Transcendental Style in Film*, 11.
96 Remes, *Motion(less) Pictures*, 20. According to Karen Parna: 'What makes the strict separation between the fixed and the moving images even more complex is a consideration of images that are neither one or the other, yet have characteristics of both.' See Parna, 'Narrative, Time and the Fixed Image', 34. Cited in Law, 'Stasis and Statuary in Bazinian Cinema'. Also, see Catherine Russell's discussion of freeze-frame in Russell, *Narrative Mortality*, 187.
97 Pauline Kael, 'At Fifteen', 74. Cited in Schrader, *Transcendental Style in Film*, 17–18. Also see Grønstad, 'Slow Cinema and the Ethics of Duration'. As Angelos Koutsourakis argues, slowness is a cinematic quality that is not limited to the recent revival of slow cinema. See Koutsourakis, 'Modernist Belatedness in Contemporary Slow Cinema', 388.
98 Tweedie, 'The Afterlife of Art and Objects', 55–6.
99 Ibid., 57.
100 See de Luca and Jorge, 'Introduction: From Slow Cinema to Slow Cinemas', 5.
101 Heath, 'Film and System', 10. This understanding of reality has resonances with the distinction that Leo Braudy establishes between what he calls 'open' and 'closed' films, between 'finding a world and creating one: the difference between using the pre-existing materials of reality and organizing these materials into a totally formed vision'. An open film regards a fragment as that which has its own profilmic integrity. The precedence of the fragment is an actuality. See Eisaesser and Hagener, *Film Theory*, 30. Also, see Kelley, 'Faithful Mechanisms', 34 and 16–17.
102 Margulies, *Nothing Happens*, 22–4.

4

Literal Durations and Cinematic Parallelism

The kitchen scene mentioned at the beginning of the first chapter is one of many examples that characterise the stylistic arrangements of Chantal Akerman's *Jeanne Dielman, 23 Quai du Commerce, 1080 Bruxelles* – a Belgian-French film released in 1975. In the film, the viewer witnesses three days in the life of a lonely widowed housewife named Jeanne Dielman. With a running time that exceeds three hours, the film emphasises Jeanne's daily tasks, how she takes care of her apartment, where she lives with her teenage son, Sylvain, and how she makes a living by prostitution. From its early shots, the film proceeds by introducing the order that Jeanne imposes on her life and apartment and continues by developing and then rupturing this order, which concludes when Jeanne murders her client on the third day.

Jeanne Dielman is one of the most notable fiction films to demonstrate how bodies in cinema are in surplus of readability. While dominant forms of cinema conservatively rely on either a denial of this surplus as their condition of possibility or an often commercially motivated exploitation of aural and visual excesses, *Jeanne Dielman* opens up a different path by drawing on this unmotivated bodily presence to render explicit the impossibility of a total conversion of the filmed body – the latter as what might be associated with meanings and functions, but these associations are provisional and uncertain. Showing how Akerman couples the inhumanity of the automatic recording of the camera with aesthetic intent, my analysis in this chapter diverges from some of the existing psychoanalytical frameworks adopted to interpret the film. Despite their socio-political and epistemological significance, these interpretations are often inadequate in accounting for the surplus of bodily presence that *Jeanne Dielman* is predominantly concerned with. Whereas the film embraces too much bodily presence rather than shying away from it, interpretive attempts, mainly due to their apprehensive preoccupation with meaning, interiority and subjectivity, inevitably extinguish the anxiety that this surplus provokes and gloss over the unique mode of address that *Jeanne Dielman* calls forth and the responses that it encourages. A scholar preoccupied with interpretation and meaning-making is less interested in highlighting too much presence of the filmed body onscreen than in motivating and thus concealing this surplus by recourse to established pre-existing frameworks.[1] Interpretations of the film, despite their progressive attempt to show how *Jeanne Dielman* contests reification, nevertheless strive to digest and exhaust this surplus, thus reproducing the mechanisms of objectification. Engrossed by exhaustively making sense of what appears onscreen, they deny Akerman's achievements in hosting what breaks through the visual but also withdraws from containment to introduce a tension within the visual field. Whereas Akerman's realism of the body problematises the reduction of vision to visibility, interpretation quests for a world of sense unfolding in front of the viewer/critic. It forces the human other that breaks through the visual to make sense within frameworks of intelligibility and within an order of meaningful textual relations – as if the task of the viewer/critic is one of *completing* the film.

For *Jeanne Dielman*, however, respect for the human other requires retaining something of the thingness of its body welcomed first by the cinematographic machine. Distancing her work from interpretations that attempt to exhaust the images and their address, Ivone Margulies's remarks about realism in general and the hyperrealist practices of Akerman in particular open up a new path for critically engaging with the film and thinking the bodily surplus as a way to revisit realism.[2] By taking up Margulies's argument and following the ethical implications of her approach, I contend that *Jeanne Dielman*'s alternative aesthetics is a way of rethinking not only realism but also film's originary bond with otherness – the latter residing in the facingness of the cinematic image that evokes the look but complicates it by introducing the non-frontal aspect of vision. Accordingly, I demonstrate that *Jeanne Dielman*'s style redefines the role of the camera and turns it into a witness by assigning it a function irreducible to dramatic interests. The camera testifies to a surplus of presence that owes its existence primarily to a making-available of bodies to the gaze of the camera, and to an image that carries and sustains this debt to the machine within itself. *Jeanne Dielman* draws upon this too-muchness to highlight a space of alterity at the heart of the film medium's rendition of bodies. In so doing, the film enacts a parallelism between the body of the actor and that of the character in which the two bodies coexist so that the onscreen presence of one cannot cancel out that of the other.[3] The uncompromising persistence of the filmed body interrupts the attempt at ensuring that it is forgotten and kept hidden, thereby allowing it to resurface in its resistance to visibility.

The non-dramatic and extended duration in *Jeanne Dielman*

A housewife is within the frame, and is being looked at. She is, in a certain sense, displaced from the outset as the structure of the image harbours an address: the way the image opens up visually, by definition, already involves a call to look, an invitation to attend oneself to a story that is on the way to being told. Yet how is Jeanne's story to be told?

Jeanne Dielman carries a certain claim within its images by turning the camera into a witness, in part through an extended inclusion of non-dramatic elements. This inclusion of the mundane, evident from the initial shots of the film, is itself a way of demonstrating its worthiness – its justification to be filmed and included. It is a matter of challenging what is relevant and what is not, of contesting the normative frameworks that regulate the inclusion/exclusion of elements and what should be emphasised and what should be cut out. Whereas an economical method of constructing the scenes and actions excludes and minimises details unless their presence is motivated and rationalised by the progression of story, *Jeanne Dielman* foregrounds the *temps mort* and practises an obsessive emphasis on Jeanne's daily activities. Take an early sequence of shots where the film establishes that Jeanne welcomes Sylvain every evening and they eat dinner together. This is the information that the images are to convey. A conventional mode of storytelling would tend to choose the appropriate cinematic devices and techniques to manipulate the images so that they would represent this daily ritual and suggest its recurrent nature without the need to render the whole details in their complete duration. What *Jeanne Dielman* does instead is an extended accentuation of all the actions that constitute this daily ritual. The viewer sees multiple shots of Jeanne in the kitchen cooking, of her preparing the table in the living room, and of Jeanne and Sylvain eating dinner with all the details and duration that it contains. These shots do not advance the progression of the story or open up new developments. They neither shed light on what the viewer has seen to this point in the film, nor provide the ground for the next scenes by arousing anticipation or suspense. What is conventionally taken for granted and elided is overemphasised here.

Jeanne Dielman includes what Margulies calls the 'images between images', the latter understood as the '"leftovers" of conventional narrative'.[4] By this means, the film enacts 'a corrective thrust' – it is a 'setting straight' of what is normally taken for granted and regarded as too insignificant and mundane to be included.[5] As Song Hwee Lim argues,

> [i]f the films of Chantal Akerman can be summed up as . . . *Nothing Happens*, this phrase should not be taken merely as a descriptor of the property of supposedly slow films. Rather, it should lead us to pose a more fundamental question about what qualifies as a legitimate subject in film – the very notion of 'thing', and what counts as 'nothing' within a film's narrative.[6]

As one of the most passionate advocates of the introduction of the everyday in film, Cesare Zavattini would consider such an inclusion of the mundane as 'being able to observe reality, not to extract fictions from it'. It is resistance to a compulsion 'to insert a "story" in the reality to make it exciting and "spectacular"'.[7] This inclusion of the non-dramatic is accompanied and intensified by the film's spatial organisation, which breaks up Jeanne's apartment into demarcated blocks of space (the kitchen, the living room, the bedroom), yet at the same time refuses to break these places into smaller units as there are no insert shots or cut-ins within shots. This spatial organisation is further emphasised through Jeanne's obsessive tendency to turn the lights on and off when she enters or exits a room, the repetitive nature of the style, the limited number of the settings, the unchanging and uniform compositions and the extreme reduction of points of interest in each shot, all of which work to deprioritise attempts to scan the images for dramatic purposes.

Jeanne Dielman further attests to the worthiness of these elided aspects and transforms expectations by establishing an equivalence between the dramatic and the non-dramatic. Similar to what, according to Margulies, André Bazin identified in neorealism, the film introduces a balance between major and minor events, between the details usually considered significant and those that are regarded otherwise and thus perceived as unrepresentable. Adhering to a pattern in which the dramatic and the non-dramatic coexist in a de-hierarchised space and time often results in images that avoid presenting major events and thus refusing to arouse anticipation, curiosity, suspense or surprise – devices upon which a cinematic drama is conventionally founded. As Margulies asserts, there is 'a purposeful lack of hierarchy between the depiction of drama and the depiction of the surfaces of things'.[8] There is a blending of two modes of organisation: one 'geared toward plot' and the other 'a phenomenological approach to plot's "uneventful" background'[9] – an emphasis on 'dramatic equivalence between major and minor events' that works to 'equate the mundane and the dramatic'.[10] The dramatic and the non-dramatic are framed with similar camera angles and shot scales, similar lighting and colour, and ultimately similar duration, in which no event or action is stressed or accentuated through stylistic or narrative devices and manipulations. There is a 'temporal equality accorded to both significant and insignificant events'.[11] The inclusion of the non-dramatic is therefore irreducible to pauses that suspend the progression of the story. Rather, *Jeanne Dielman* is structured around this inclusion in a de-hierarchised narrative composition where dramatic progression is indissociable from the flow of non-dramatic durations.

This temporal equality brings the question of duration to the fore. The accentuation of the non-dramatic and the tension that results from it are amplified by the film's use of extended duration, long takes and real-time recordings. While a story proper would be essentially tied with a dramatic time that aims to suggest, one might say, the 'tediousness' of Jeanne's daily routine, Akerman's film radically performs tediousness, stretching the dramatic duration to a point that the image itself is turned into tediousness. Seven minutes into the film after Jeanne's first client leaves the apartment, the film cuts to Jeanne in the bathroom while she is taking a shower. The shot lasts more than three minutes as the viewer sees Jeanne sitting in the bathtub, washing her body in real time. Showing an action in its entirety is overemphasised here as the viewer is exposed to watching the scene through a camera that lingers on Jeanne's figure and her movements for minutes, even though the causally relevant information ('Jeanne takes a shower') could be and in fact is established and thoroughly exhausted in a few seconds.

Such an approach to a banal, everyday action, Zavattini would argue, stands out as a passage 'from an unconsciously rooted mistrust of reality, an illusory and equivocal evasion, to an unlimited trust in things, facts and people'.[12] Presenting an action within a literal flow of time that tends to contain the action in its entirety returns it to Delphine Seyrig doing the same task in the profilmic, a uniquely cinematic parallelism to which I return later in the chapter.

This hyperbolic emphasis on spatio-temporal continuity and the filming of the actions in real time in their 'dailiness' and 'longest and truest duration'[13] can be seen as what Bazin would call a process of transferring reality (as opposed to fragmenting) that offers significant defamiliarising effects.[14] Remaining in a scene and deploying extended durations that lack dramatic motivation transform the viewer's experience of the image and call forth a prolonged stare in which the figures and things remain onscreen far longer than an economical narrative would allow for.[15] As Kristin Thompson argues, every cinematic device exists through time. It is with respect to this temporal aspect that cinematic devices provide the premises for not only the progression of drama but also its interruption:

> We may notice a device immediately and understand its function, but it may then continue to be visible or audible for some time past this recognition. In this case, we may be inclined to study or contemplate it apart from its narrative or compositional function; such contemplation necessarily distracts from narrative progression.[16]

In *Jeanne Dielman*, long, unbroken shots exhaust narrative motivation. The sheer act of recording the profilmic constantly resurfaces to take the upper hand over dramatic development thanks to the camera's ability to capture blocks of space and time beyond a dramatically justified extent and to the images' tendency to preserve this extendedness.

The promise of the image is rooted in its very structure (what I referred to as the image's self-presentingness), but also in the attempt to bring a socially invisible figure onscreen. The power of *Jeanne Dielman*'s images resides in their allusion to Jeanne's story. More importantly, alluding to the story on the way to being told remains indeterminate. The flow of the everyday preserves an equivalence between a literal rendition of events and a more conventional dramatisation. According to Margulies, extended duration is a 'cinematic transformer' for a 'passage between abstraction and figuration'.[17] Long takes 'elicit a hyperacute perception, in which one recognizes both the image's literal and its representational aspects', precisely because a crucial quality of extended duration is the 'polarity of reception', an 'oscillation between (or rather coexistence of) representational and literal registers'.[18] This equivalence between the dramatic and the non-dramatic works to establish a tension within the film that reaffirms bodily surplus through a failure of exhaustive dramatic motivations. For the literal to be reaffirmed and indexicality to be intensified, and for the images to escape being exhausted by the drama, there should be an oscillation between the literal and what is otherwise. The sight of Jeanne making the bed after she wakes up in the morning contains the information to represent another daily ritual of her life and links the first and second days of the story. The use of extended duration and a compulsion to record all the details that a mere act of making the bed contains establish a tension that exposes to failure the progression of drama and thus the conversion of the filmed body into an embodiment of character. *Jeanne Dielman* does not refuse dramatisation altogether – what a sheer recording is supposedly about – but manipulates duration to avoid doing violence to the coming into being of the other's body (the initial welcoming of the body enacted by the camera). Margulies not only connects this structural tension to Akerman's attack on 'essentialist humanism' but equally remarkably notes an affirmative side in her non-canonical storytelling. Akerman's minimalist hyperrealism of the body, she argues, makes a positive claim to tell a story; her equation of drama and everydayness is made *from within* narrative. Moreover, it is in instituting another sort of hero(ine) that she mounts her blows on essentialist humanism. The singularity of Akerman's Jeanne defies the generic humanism . . . The historical grounding of this sort of heroine is represented at its best in Akerman's fusion of a minimalist hyperrealist sensibility with an acute awareness of 70's micropolitics, and of feminism in particular. And it is this awareness of the singularity of a woman's everydayness that forms the backbone of Akerman's corporeal cinema.[19]

Witnessing as exposure to expansive physicality

Jeanne Dielman's stylistic patterning results in a redefinition of the role of the camera, of what it is expected to do and how it is to shape the viewer's looking. The film not only avoids deploying point-of-view shots, eye-line matches and the shot/reverse shot structure but also forecloses emotional involvement through an excessive reduction of expressivity and psychologism, therefore frustrating the possibility of identification with the characters.[20] What the film encourages instead is an identification with the camera itself. With its relative autonomy over the onscreen action, the camera functions as something that is, in a certain sense, placed in the profilmic to bear witness to what is before it and make possible a radical exposure to bodies and things that moves beyond fictional or dramatic interests.

Exposing the viewer to the materiality of the profilmic, *Jeanne Dielman*'s camera is not implicit, as we might expect from a more classical rendition of the camera's role.[21] Its extreme fixity and stasis, as well as its emphatic frontality, which resembles early cinema's dominant compositions, render it visible and overt. This is more evident, particularly in cases where the viewer's expectations are unfulfilled by the camera's refusal to follow the action or the figures onscreen. The camera's stasis, in resonance with the editing, results in frames that truncate bodies or 'post-action lags' where frames are devoid of human presence.[22] The camera's lack of movement reminds the viewer of the mediating role to which the camera is assigned, its positionality and situatedness, and the presence of the offscreen space.[23] Akerman's camerawork therefore complicates the relation between the camera itself and Jeanne as the protagonist. While *Jeanne Dielman* is generous in offering the witness long extended durations, it is less inviting and more restricted when it comes to spatial organisation as the viewer is denied the privilege of following Jeanne and her actions in a way that an alternative rendition might encourage.

The camera as a witness is not only static but also exposed to recording a profilmic reality that most of the time lacks significance, thus further accentuating the materiality of the profilmic. As Margulies observes, *Jeanne Dielman*'s 'insistence on remaining with the scene even after its narrational or referential information has been decoded inevitably solicits an estranged experience of the image'.[24] The film's 'all-too-perfect equilibrium' and its 'emphasis on surface details intimates an estrangement, an excess', precisely because 'one sees more than one needs to in order to "read" the image'.[25] Although it is crucial to point out the defamiliarising effect of a fixed stare that results in 'the excess of detail', what Margulies does not discuss further is what it means to say that the viewer sees more. What merits further investigation is how this more is ethically significant in terms of an encounter with the body of the other that the images host. The material presence of Jeanne's body involved in doing the dishes or making the bed is enveloped in duration, and what the camera does, more than anything else, is to capture this duration through an automatic recording. The fixed camera that records the materiality of what is before it in its entire duration constitutes exposure to the persistence of the profilmic body within the image. This imposition on the viewer, who is sitting passively in the dark theatre, extends for more than three hours. The film's hyperbolic use of extended duration brings forth a filmic experience in which habitual ways of confronting the images are subordinated to attesting to the existence of an irreducible presence onscreen.

Tiago de Luca discusses the effects of the prolonged gaze accompanied by the camera's stasis by asserting that the stare of a fixed camera 'destabilizes the representational dimension of the image' so as to call attention to 'the film medium itself and the materiality of the profilmic event'.[26] In a realism characterised by its tendency to preserve 'spatial and temporal integrity' to hyperbolic extremes, the viewers are 'invited to adopt the point of view of the camera and protractedly study images as they appear on the screen in their unexplained literalness'. Temporal elongation overturns what proper storytelling dictates, therefore leaving viewers unguided in their attempt to read the image 'hermeneutically'.[27] Margulies refers to a similar point when she argues that through 'extended duration and fixed frame', the viewer is made to experience 'the profilmic event as an expansive materiality'.[28] The camera's extended gaze makes 'objects and spaces gain an effect of presence that is entirely devoid of metaphysical or symbolic significance', imposing instead 'a sense of gravity on both people and objects as they are anchored on screen'.[29] This calling attention to the physicality and materiality of onscreen presences, which is extended beyond the domestic

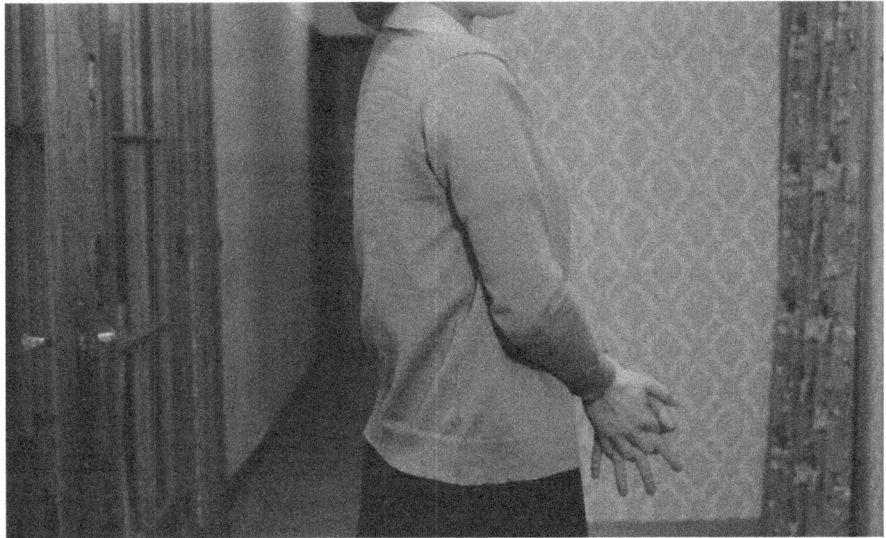

Figure 4.1 Camera as static witness truncating the body in *Jeanne Dielman, 23 quai du Commerce, 1080 Bruxelles* (Chantal Akerman, 1975).

scenes, is also indebted to Akerman's approach to sound. Although realistically motivated, *Jeanne Dielman*'s soundtrack is often a deliberate reduction of surrounding noises and an amplification of the sounds that stress Jeanne's bodily presence in space and her interactions and engagements with props and settings.

This foregrounding of the profilmic body as a summoning of expansive physicality further problematises meaning. It is particularly evident if we account for how *Jeanne Dielman*'s approach to the everyday and the mundane is not merely a matter of discovering or restoring unrepresented aspects of reality. Nor is this attention to the banal, unlike what Emre Çağlayan argues, 'an accurate representation of [the film's] character's state of mind, which is tainted by monotony and boredom'.[30] Of course, the film asks us to attend to what is often glossed over – Jeanne's bodily presence in her most ordinary moments and durations. The inclusion of elided aspects is an exposure to what is deemed unrepresentable because it is too insignificant and too tedious to be looked at. What the camera does, however, is not merely to represent what is overlooked but to expose the viewer to these durations that contain not much beyond what is being recorded. Speaking of unrepresented aspects and thus regarding an alternative or more inclusive representation as a correction remain tied to representation. Doing so implies that there exists something that is not yet meaningful and that remains to be rendered meaningful. In *Jeanne Dielman*, not only is reading the scenes made difficult but, to a large extent, the necessity of reading is put into question as the film demands responses other than the filling of bodies, actions and spaces with determinate meaning.

Consider how the film informs us about Jeanne's being a lonely widow. Jeanne talks to Sylvain about her marriage and her reluctance to remarry in a scene that, along with a similar scene to which I return in this chapter, stands out as an exception where dialogue is used to reveal something about the protagonist. Her tone is strangely similar to the times when she speaks about matters that are more ordinary, and there is no dramatic accentuation of this narrative exposition. The scene takes a form of a direct address – it is as if Akerman has staged this scene so that Jeanne could directly convey information to the viewer about herself. The scene de-dramatises Jeanne's decision to speak about herself by turning the dialogue into a staged, superficial act of revelation. Short-circuiting simplifying attempts to read Jeanne, the film disrupts the centrality of a recognition of otherness (that is, a return to the familiar through a transition from the indeterminate to the determinate), while instead foregrounding the density of the profilmic body and exposure to the impenetrability of the surfaces.

Parallelism and particularisation: hyperbolic cases of literal rendition

Bazin sees in realism an intrinsic obligation for the filmmaker to treat each event on its own terms: 'The events are not necessarily signs of something, of a truth of which we are to be convinced, they all carry their own weight, their complete uniqueness, that ambiguity that characterizes any fact.'[31] There is a wholeness to reality. To respect this wholeness, a film is destined to remain faithful to the profilmic that it automatically records by regarding it as pre-existing. There is an obligation to reality that, from a Bazinian view, resides in the degree zero of the cinematic, in its automatic recording of the profilmic, which preserves the fullness of the filmed event. Film should subordinate itself to the profilmic fragments rather than merely create them.[32] It is with regard to this pre-existence of the profilmic that Bazin opposes revelation to meaning: 'the cinema's ultimate aim should be not so much to mean as to reveal.'[33] As Lúcia Nagib points out, a 'basic faithfulness to the profilmic phenomenon, combined with the inherent honesty of the film medium, was indeed the main requirement of Bazin's realism.'[34] Yet faithfulness to the profilmic is not to be equated with a question of verisimilitude or mimesis. It is an affirmation of the contingent in its unintelligibility, of too much presence prior to activities of representation aimed at reducing and taming this surplus.

In *Jeanne Dielman*, the failure of dramatisation is the failure of an exhaustive abstraction from the images that would result in storytelling totalities. The breakdown of meaning-making helps the images to unsettle and ultimately blur the boundary between Jeanne Dielman (as the character) and Delphine Seyrig (as the actor playing her role). This blurring results in a parallelism that prevents the body–camera encounter from being compromised by a thorough translation of Seyrig's body to Jeanne's. Instead, the images reaffirm the body's literal presence, its thingness, and therefore bear witness to its past presence before the camera through the trace it has left on the celluloid. The filmed body persists because Seyrig's body is one that, prior to being an embodiment of Jeanne, has existed before the camera and has been found in the world. It has been filmed due to its material thereness before the lens of a camera that automatically records the body through its non-selectiveness but also through its indifference to the narrative or representational value of what is being recorded. Automatism therefore disrupts the givenness of the other for a conscious subject.

Remaining in a scene long after its narratively significant information has been absorbed and exhausted exploits parallelism to intensify the passive exposure to the materiality of physical presence onscreen. This exposure yields the most interesting results in extreme cases in which, as I have shown, the camera lingers on Jeanne's figure for several minutes to present unique instances of a gesture or event in its entirety and effectively frustrate the abstracting nature of representation. While representation works through coding, inference and suggestion, the extreme long takes of *Jeanne Dielman* that tend to show an action in its complete duration allow the literal to short-circuit abstracting processes. A literal rendition of an action that constructs its entirety replaces a representational suggestion of its entirety or recurrence. It establishes a one-to-one relation between what has once taken place before the camera and what is now shown on film (once during each projection). With respect to this one-to-one relation, the profilmic event regains its singularity.[35] Each event that is shown in its entirety is transformed into a self-sufficient, non-repeatable instance – something that is irreproducible – as it stands on its own because it happens (it has happened) once before the camera, leaving its trace on the celluloid. Its subsequent reproduction is a mere projection, and unnecessary to the formation of the image – it does not require reference to something other than itself to assert its entirety. The filmic event becomes something that is not necessarily inferred by codes and conventions, while its wholeness, in a certain sense, renders the viewer's cinematic literacy redundant. What the camera has recorded did happen (in the profilmic), while its happening is not inferred by combining bits and pieces, by combining broken shots into a whole by way of cinematic conventions and codes or by recourse to narrative context. The image no longer 'suggests' the event – it is stretched to a point that it stands in parallel with the profilmic event and gains a weight and truth of its own.

Lingering on bodies and things for a prolonged time allows the contingent details into the image, therefore enhancing the indexical effect of the formation of the image. However, speaking of the 'reality effect', what Roland Barthes attempts to conceptualise with regards to presentation of details, is inadequate in accounting for the radical potential of the cinematic image as it is brought forth in *Jeanne Dielman*. Arguing that 'when a text lavishes attention on nonnarrative detail, it endeavours to produce the effect of authenticity',[36] remains tied to the logic of representation. What is pivotal in such a formulation is the urge to exploit the details so that the text would look familiar and lifelike. An effect of 'authenticity' is produced once a text (filmic or otherwise) draws attention to details that are considered as non-narrative. It takes place once there is an introduction and inclusion of details that are indifferent to the progression of narrative. According to Barthes, this inclusion helps a text to achieve a proximity to the real. However, wherever there is a certain consumption of the detail by the whole, the withdrawal of the thing is denied. Genuine indifference does not simply exploit the camera's ability to capture details – it also demonstrates that the capture of the real is a capture in indifference, thus already bypassing frameworks that work to produce familiarity. Bazin's radical approach, by contrast, acknowledges a realism beyond frameworks of lifelikeness, beyond an exploitation of details that helps a text appear more lifelike. As Karl Schoonover remarks, 'an otherwise highly aesthetic (which is to say unrealistic) film redeems itself . . . through the inclusion of small non-stylised features'. These details, 'chosen precisely for their "indifference" to the action', function to 'guarantee its reality'.[37] Indifference to action, narrative or any other form of meaning-making is not simply to convey lifelikeness but to undermine any notion of familiarity.[38] This indifference is also a disregard for frameworks that identify bodies as objects based on their narrative and descriptive attributes and thus assign them a place within the frontal visual field as meaningful objects that can be pinned down. With his decisively unique attentiveness to details as effects of automatism, Bazin implies this withdrawal of the world from reduction to content by locating the true merit of the cinematic image in 'not betraying the essence of things' but in 'allowing them first of all to exist for their own sakes, freely'.[39]

What concerns me in my study is not so much the index but the indexicality of the image. Tom Gunning is right when he problematises the index argument on the account of its tendency to reduce Bazin's aesthetic theory to a question of signification. Bazin 'denies the photograph the chief characteristic of a sign, that of supplying a substitute for a referent', and it is problematic to reduce cinematographic automatism to the category of the index.[40] Indexicality is important here insofar as it reflects a quality of the image that attests to a past presence, which is made present by the automatic recording. More crucially, indexicality is what brings too much to life and is responsible for the image being too graphic, thus providing the conditions for the withdrawal of the fragments that are assigned with a new life within the image. As Sylvaine Agacinski contends, the photographic imprint 'touches us because it has been touched itself and because it speaks to us of presence and absence at the same time'.[41] The cinematic image is touching insofar as it carries its own being touched within itself; as, I argue, it performs its debt to its being touched. The index as a sign, however, belongs to signification and implies absence and lack. Due to its inherent abstracting nature, signification is incapable of representing the singular, since the latter is unrepresentable. By contrast, the referent that the indexicality of the image opens up to the viewer and bears witness to is a referent that defies signification insofar as it is presented through a short-circuiting. The immediacy of the image, as Steven Shaviro notes, 'short-circuits the processes of signification'.[42] The referentiality that this testimony is based on is bound with the singularity of the profilmic. The referent that is borne witness to is not merely produced by representation, for there is always a making-present already, which precedes and defies representation.

The augmented indexical quality of the images in *Jeanne Dielman* emphasises not only the irreplaceability of the profilmic but also the irreversibility of time. As George Kouvaros argues, the 'indexical nature of film reaffirms a notion of time as fleeting and unessential'.[43] The profilmic event happened only once, and what remains is a trace. This trace, even though mechanically reproduced through projection, testifies to a singularity that is irreproducible. The action took place at a certain moment before the lens and its entirety is justified by its own literal presence and the literal time devoted to it. It is there onscreen, referring to its happening before the camera. In a certain sense, there is no need to link it to other elements or events to make it complete. Margulies refers to the same point with respect to Akerman's style: 'By presenting unique instances of a gesture or event, and by stressing real-time representation, Akerman frustrates the abstracting nature of repetition – the suggestion of constant recurrences (every day, week, month).'[44] Furthermore, the singularity of profilmic time is not assumed *a priori*. It is not that what the image carries within itself is merely singular. Rather, singularity is indebted to the claim of the image. It is the image itself that claims the irreversibility of the onscreen action by presenting it in the entirety of its happening before the camera. In a certain sense, this mode of presentation of a filmic act is a demonstration of film's inherent capacity to repeat what is essentially irreversible. As Blandine Joret argues with regards to Bazinian realism,

> rather than concerning himself primarily with the specificity of photography, a theory that would lead to *a priori* accepting the authenticity of any filmed event, [Bazin] instead clearly valorizes the specificity of *reality*. In so doing, he implicitly supports his argument of cinema as the art of reality rather than that of the image or technology . . . Bazin here cleverly morphs an argument concerned with medium essentialism into his own valorization of the specificity of the event and cinema's fundamental capacity to repeat irreversibility.[45]

The capacity to repeat in its entirety that which is irreversible implies a certain redundancy of narrative ellipsis. For Bazin, ellipsis is abstract as it 'organizes the facts in accord with the general dramatic direction to which it forces them to submit'; whereas cinema, as he assumes and desires, is the exact opposite of the 'art of ellipsis'.[46] Ellipsis shapes the drama by bringing abstraction to the fore, whereas the 'ontological equality' between 'concrete moments of life' is an effect of rejecting ellipsis – it is that which 'destroys drama at its very basis'.[47] Furthermore, Bazin significantly relates the combination of broken shots to artificiality, to abstraction and ultimately to dramatisation: 'the breaking up of the scenes into shots and their assemblage is a reconstruction of the event according to an artificial and abstract duration: dramatic duration.'[48] In *Jeanne Dielman*, preserving the integrity of the profilmic action (by both hyperbolic use of the long take and equating the duration of actions with screen duration) disrupts the construction of a story in a dramatic sense. There is a resistance to elevating the sheer recording of what is happening before the camera and a resistance to establishing dramatic links that can exhaust the scenes. The dramatic duration in *Jeanne Dielman* is constantly interrupted by the film's use of extended duration and unbroken shots. This alternative emergence of duration sidelines the dramatic by giving the actions an integrity of their own that results in an accentuation of the profilmic. It turns the profilmic event into a singular instance.[49]

While irreplaceability and irreversibility of temporal presence are attributes inherent to the film medium, they are what a film technologically inherits but must earn by practising a certain faithfulness. The success of the realism of the body, as it is radically reworked and practised in *Jeanne Dielman*, is rooted in what Margulies suggests is an ungrounded yet powerful presence. Literal art, as she dubs it, rather than 'using language in a patently connotative way', tends to amplify 'what is implicit in any indexical language: its rendering of a first, "immediate" meaning – its referent'.[50] Accordingly, 'referentiality is the "natural" given of indexical representation'.[51] Margulies goes further by stating that Akerman's approach 'unbalances referentiality', providing the conditions for understanding referentiality with respect to the density of the profilmic.[52] The referentiality of *Jeanne Dielman* is not simply reducible to its tendency to represent the story of a housewife, the latter itself being a type that is an effect of representation. Referentiality is also, and more significantly, a matter of referring to what was before the camera (the profilmic body), to what was copied on the celluloid due to the physical contact carried within the image.

Preserving the integrity of the profilmic event through extended duration and real-time presentation, *Jeanne Dielman* blurs the borderline between the body of the character and that of the actor. Jeanne's bodily presence – as the fictional character – is indebted to the body of Seyrig. The latter body is a material whose density and singularity pre-exist any filmic event and overflow filmic patterning and manipulation. It is a debt that the film is neither denying nor concealing, but is accentuating. Patrick Kinsman refers to this blurring as a sort of parallelism: 'when Jeanne washes dishes, Delphine Seyrig washes dishes.'[53] *Jeanne Dielman* theatricalises the tenuousness of the conversion of the filmed body. It demonstrates how the borderline is always already uncertain and undecidable. By bringing the profilmic to the fore, the filmed body, not the character, gains prominence. Seyrig gives Jeanne a presence that is not dissociable from the presence of her body before the camera (during the filming process) – a body the trace of which has been recorded due to the automatism of the camera and the indexicality of the cinematic image. A middle zone is formed in which the body of Jeanne is indissociable from the body of Seyrig precisely because Jeanne's body is flattened out as a bodily presence, as a material figure whose presence on the screen is thoroughly indebted to the presence of Seyrig's body before the lens while the camera was recording. This debt is overtly emphasised by the film's unique stylisation, which bears witness to the inexhaustibility of Seyrig's body through a disruption of readability and a refusal to fill the body exhaustively with meaning.[54]

Interpretation is incessantly concerned with categorising the protagonist, Jeanne, making her represent an abstract category. Presented as a body committing gestures in real time, however, Jeanne as a character is bound with the filmed body and interrupts representation and its abstracting impulses. The film's radical referentiality extends beyond an evocation of any class or type. According to Margulies, the 'enhanced indexicality of Akerman's aesthetic encompasses ... an emphasis on the physical presence and performance of her actors and characters, suggesting an interest in a more concrete (less transcendent or ideal) human presence'.[55] Jeanne cannot stand for an abstract category in order to represent. The literalness of the cinematic image 'defies interpretation, inviting instead a descriptive impulse',[56] and *Jeanne Dielman*'s extensive use of literal time is an undoing of symbolic meaningfulness. Margulies therefore differentiates between Akerman's aesthetics (as well as Warhol's minimalist approach in her view) and what she argues a neorealist film would intend to achieve in terms of its social commitment:

> [T]here is a crucial difference between, on the one hand, Akerman's and Warhol's excesses, both a form of minimal hyperrealism, and, on the other, the expansive thrust of neorealist narrative, which, for example, may try to signify all unemployed Italians through a single character such as Umberto D. The minimal-hyperrealist rendition undoes any idea of symbolic transcendence. Besides injecting representation with the effect of a surplus of reality, literal time robs it of the possibility of standing for something other than that concrete instance.[57]

The filmed body, in its being too particular, defies representation and is not replaceable precisely because it is tied to, and cannot be abstracted from, the contingency and elsewhereness of the profilmic that has given birth to it. This enhanced indexicality is at the same time the reaffirmation of a non-anthropocentric deployment of the eye of the camera. Margulies pits this inhumanity against the dominance of the 'human perspective' in neorealism and its 'desire for totality:'

> In *Bicycle Thieves*, all of Rome (or rather all of Italy and of the postwar world) is meant to be represented by the syncretically woven neighborhoods and sites that Antonio traverses. The wanderings of the characters in *Umberto D* or *Bicycle Thieves* signify a solely 'physical' coverage of reality only superficially: here multiplicity – of spaces, of people – always reconvenes on a center, sucked back to it by a human perspective that is represented in the films by a human body, a hero. It is this

heroic body, the generic postwar individual, that Akerman's *Jeanne Dielman* takes to task.[58]

It is the one-to-one quality of literal presentation that demonstrates how a profilmic body can 'flicker in and out of character' but, most remarkably in the work of Akerman, still 'further a narrative'.[59] In so doing, it introduces a tension within the visual field, providing the conditions of the body's breakthrough but also its withdrawal through the bodily surplus that defies being sustained by anything other than the image itself.

Moreover, cinematic parallelism (as an 'oscillating perception') breaks down the intertextual associations that casting Seyrig could have brought forth as a well-known French actress, revered for her significant contribution to European arthouse cinema, particularly in the 1960s and 1970s. Akerman curiously turns Seyrig's presence in the film into a profilmic body found by the camera, and then found again in the extended duration of her images. Throughout the film, Seyrig's acting is underplayed and inexpressive. She does not appear as a performer acting out intentional meanings. She does not endeavour to make her bodily presence meaningful by filling it with subjectivity. Seyrig's embodiment of Jeanne is not based on a careful, rigorous reading of the script. She does not flesh out the character by adding dimensions and deep layers to appearances and surfaces. What Seyrig does is lend her body to the camera, making it available to the gaze of the cinematographic machine while controlling and minimising gestures and postures. Seyrig does not bring much to the role that she plays beyond a certain control over her bodily presence in space and time. The filmed body itself, and not an actor injecting consciousness into the character and the story, is the site in which the claim of the images resides.

The final scene

Seyrig's approach to her character is not simply 'realistic', if we understand the latter as easily conforming to our expectations of filmic performance. The way she is presenting Jeanne is deliberately restrained and underplayed. She does not tend to express herself and this lack of expression is amplified by the film's avoidance of close-ups or any expressive use of movement, colour, lighting or music. *Jeanne Dielman* contests the normative readability of acting and ultimately of character by denying the viewer access to psychological causes or determinate expressions that reveal interiority, flattening out the external gestures to render them inexpressive.

On the third day, the viewer notices that Jeanne is unable to keep the order that she herself has skilfully preserved throughout the film, a change that was gradually implied from the evening of the second day. This is most significant at the end of the film when the only dramatic climax, in the strict sense of the word, takes place as Jeanne murders her client after experiencing orgasm.[60] This scene might be considered to expose the presence of her interiority, indicating that there should be other aspects to the character beyond her physically recognisable traits and her bodily presence onscreen.[61] According to Margulies, the anti-psychological approach of the film that has rigorously worked to cleanse the narrative of 'psychological overtones' – accompanied by a performance that has 'a presentational quality that dispels dramatic development' – is troubled.[62] In short, the final scene appears to pose the question of interiority.

Predominantly concerned with what an image means rather than what it does, interpretations of *Jeanne Dielman* have often tended to read the whole film according to this final scene by assuming that the latter underlines the presence of an interiority that has been present throughout the film despite its concealment. These readings often reduce if not resolve the ambiguities of the film – an approach that certainly goes against the film's rigorous stylisation. *Jeanne Dielman* is less aimed at denying interiority for Jeanne than denying the viewer privileged access to it.[63] The film strategically focuses on the everyday, extends the duration of the shots, and refuses

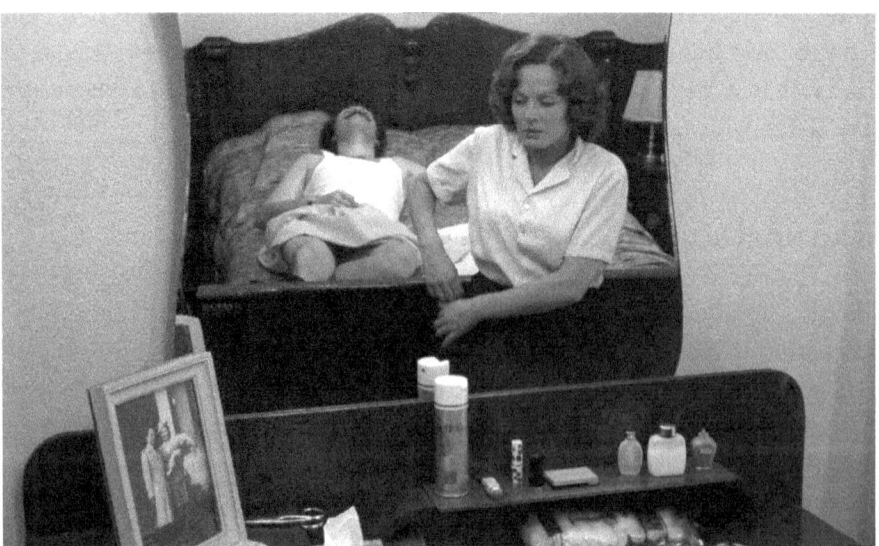

Figure 4.2 The final scene of *Jeanne Dielman, 23 quai du Commerce, 1080 Bruxelles* (Chantal Akerman, 1975).

to present psychological explanations primarily to introduce an alternative approach to its protagonist. In fact, the film's denial of access to interiority as a stylistic choice is significant insofar as the viewer assumes that there is an interiority that has been sidelined but not denied. This accentuation of materiality and denying access to interiority are responsible for the film's reflexivity insofar as it highlights the contingent nature of classical rendition according to which psychological explanations and the continuity between 'the internal' and 'the external' are falsely considered as optically necessary.

It is not a coincidence that Akerman herself redefines the sense of secrecy that the film might evoke by deliberately avoiding any speculation regarding Jeanne's interiority. She instead highlights the aforementioned parallelism: 'You will never know what is happening in her head and in her heart. I don't know. It's not Jeanne Dielman's secret, it's Delphine's secret.'[64] It is Delphine's secret but not because she knows more than Akerman does. Delphine is not acting out intentional meaning so much as making her body available to the gaze of the camera. The secret is hers precisely because what the film is most concerned with is the appearance and persistence of a body onscreen rather than a subjective state awaiting revelation.

There is a scene in *Jeanne Dielman* that evidently demonstrates Akerman's approach to potential interpretations of her film. Almost two hours into the film, the viewer is presented with a scene in the evening of the second day in which Sylvain, who is in bed, is talking to Jeanne, standing in the background. Without any discernible dramatic motivation, Sylvain starts speaking about his dead father, about hating him, about his father having sex with Jeanne, about penetration, orgasm and God. Without proper dramatic motivation, Sylvain's tone is impassive as though he is following the filmmaker's instructions and reading from a text. The scene's striking similarity to a previous scene discussed earlier, in which Jeanne was telling Sylvain about her reluctance to remarry in the evening of the first day, emphasises the directness of the film's mode of address. These two scenes clearly stand out from the rest of the film. Their tendency to 'convey' information in a concentrated way opposes the film's rarefied approach, while their directness is at odds with the focus on the flow of the everyday, which suggests rather than overtly reveals. Indeed, what Sylvain says in this scene can be easily used to justify interpretations. Problems arise precisely due to this easiness. What the film does is overtly provoke interpretations that are easily justified by recourse to this scene so as to render them redundant. The film calls for such interpretations but makes them seem too obvious and accessible and the interpreter's task too easy to be pivotal.

Furthermore, a gradual accentuation of the dramatic in the third day not only does not contradict the overall approach of the film, but effectively reinforces it. The explicit accentuation of the dramatic in the final part of the film works to amplify the tension between the dramatic and the non-dramatic without subverting the overall equivalence. The same is true about the murder scene, which is an event in a strictly dramatic sense. This scene aims to emphasise the recurrent, daily happening to which the viewer's access has been repeatedly denied throughout the film. For the first time, the viewer (with the camera as the witness) is allowed to enter Jeanne's bedroom while she is spending the afternoon with a client. This permission emphasises the previous times that the witness has not been trusted to enter the room, stressing that these scenes have been deliberately omitted. At the same time, the peculiar way in which the film stages the sex scene not only adheres to the dominance of extended duration throughout the film but also highlights the fact that the witness is, once again, not trustworthy enough to have access to an explicit and privileged view of what is going on. The only thing that the viewer sees is Jeanne and her client on the bed, both of them almost dressed, while the man is without any noticeable movement and Jeanne seems to be feeling what is unknowable even to herself.

The same style is preserved in the next shot when Jeanne murders the man with scissors – an event that functions as a shock to the viewer. Up to this point, the viewer is accustomed to the literalness of the images, to the fact that the images concern Jeanne/Delphine doing ordinary things in a manner the literalness of which is undeniable. But now the viewer is shocked precisely because they are aware of the overtly fictive nature of the murder, of the fact that this event is a deviation, since it cannot be literal. Abruptly shifting presentation into representation,[65] not only does the scene not disrupt the whole patterning of the film, but it stands out as an exception – as a constitutive outside – that reaffirms the literalness of the other scenes and events. More importantly, the murder scene works to punctuate the limitation of literalness. It intensifies the failure of dramatisation by taking this equivalence to a point of heightened tension. Margulies reminds us here of the film's equivalence by asserting that the final scenes extend this quality:

> Episodic, discrete events such as the orgasm, the murder, and even the disturbances in Jeanne's routine are dedramatized. Dramatic expectation is built up simultaneously with a distanciation created through the use of extended real-time shots. Illusion and fact are made equivalent . . . The murder scene makes clear the traversal of two distinct temporalities.[66]

The final shot of the film that follows the scene of the murder reintegrates the final part into the whole film. The viewer sees a shot of Jeanne sitting in the dark in the living room. She is at the centre of the frame, while the framing and the shot scale are similar to numerous other shots of the living room over the course of the film. The shot lasts for seven minutes, as the only thing that the viewer sees is Jeanne sitting in the living room without noticeable expression or even movement. Duration is felt here more intensely than ever since the seven-minute long take shows Jeanne doing nothing, reducing her performance to a degree zero. The scene encapsulates the whole tension of the film: on the one hand, the viewer sees blood on Jeanne's hands – as the fictive element – while the overextended duration of the scene returns the viewer to an exposure to a bodily presence that is made possible by the sheer recording. The scene attests to the coexistence of the two registers within a singular *mise en scène*.

Jeanne Dielman's promise is bound with its commitment to write the otherness of Jeanne. Yet it writes the otherness of the other so that the other can be faced, *not* read. The images theatricalise the anxiety of an author who does not allow herself to freely exercise authoritative power over the other. Paradoxically, it is by obsessively controlling everything that appears and persists within the *mise en scène* that Akerman undoes her authority and performs an ethical erasure of her subjective control. The images she sets up make a claim upon the viewer by sustaining a filmed body that opens up to the viewer but resists meaning. Subtracting the filmed body from a politics of the image that desires the visibility of the other, Akerman responds to the urgency of encountering in the other something that is not repeatable.

Notes

1 By reading Jeanne as a 'castrating mother', describing her daily routine as indicative of 'an unconscious awareness', identifying her son's inexpressive, unaffectionate interaction with Jeanne as his 'oedipal frustration', regarding the third client whom Jeanne murders as 'the surrogate father', and interpreting the narrative as a typical re-enactment of the 'primal scene', thereby regarding the film's specific stylistic qualities as representative of 'oral drives', 'incestuous longings' and 'anal fixation', such critical encounters with the film leave no room for the excess of presence that *Jeanne Dielman* is so evidently grounded upon. They are implicitly concerned with illustrating their own critical and theoretical positions rather than trying to address the film on its own terms. See Perlmutter, 'Feminine Absence', Loader, '*Jeanne Dielman*: Death in Installments' and Yervasi, 'Dislocating the Domestic in Chantal Akerman's *Jeanne Dielman*' as examples.

2 Margulies, 'Bodies Too Much', 5. For a reading of the ethics of Akerman's work that map out the consistencies of her cinematic and installation works, see Rennebohm, '"A Pedagogy of the Image"'.
3 See Comolli, 'Historical Fiction', 49.
4 Margulies, *Nothing Happens*, 4.
5 Ibid., 22. Eric Rohmer once wrote: 'The modern spectator . . . has been too long accustomed to *interpreting* the visual sign, and to working out *why* each image is there, to be able to appreciate the simple reality of these images . . . In learning to interpret, the modern spectator has forgotten how to see.' Cited in Leigh, 'Ontology, Film and the Case of Eric Rohmer', 3.
6 Lim, 'Temporal Aesthetics of Drifting', 89–90.
7 According to Zavattini: 'All we have to do is to discover and then show all the elements that go to create this adventure, in all their banal "dailiness", and it will become worthy of attention, it will even become "spectacular". But it will become spectacular not through its exceptional, but through its *normal* qualities; it will astonish us by showing so many things that happen every day under our eyes, things we have never noticed before.' See Zavattini, 'Some Ideas on the Cinema', 64–6. Also, see Balaisis, 'The Risk of Ambiguity', 42–3.
8 Margulies, *Nothing Happens*, 3.
9 Ibid.
10 Ibid., 23.
11 Ibid., 4.
12 Zavattini, 'Some Ideas on the Cinema', 64. Maurice Blanchot conceives of the everyday as that which is 'most important', even though it 'escapes every speculative formulation, perhaps all coherence, all regularity'. See Blanchot, *Everyday Speech*, 13.
13 Zavattini, 'Some Ideas on the Cinema', 65. For Zavattini, as Balaisis says: 'Cinema must not just turn towards the seemingly banal but it must *stay* there. In staying with the phenomenon for longer, more deliberate time, the phenomenon has "all the potential of being reborn".' See Balaisis, 'The Risk of Ambiguity', 43.
14 Bazin, *What Is Cinema?*, vol. 1, 14.
15 Zavattini's normative claim sees an intersection of the inclusion of the everyday and the duration accorded to it: 'No other medium of expression has the cinema's original and innate capacity for showing things that we believe worth showing, as they happen day by day – in what we might call their "dailiness", their longest and truest duration. The cinema has everything in front of it.' See Zavattini, 'Some Ideas on the Cinema', 65.
16 Thompson, 'The Concept of Cinematic Excess', 57–8. Also, see Noel Burch's concept of 'legibility' in Burch, *Theory of Film Practice*, 52.
17 Margulies, *Nothing Happens*, 4.
18 Ibid., 44–5. Also see Margulies, 'Bodies Too Much', 17–18.
19 Margulies, *Nothing Happens*, 41. My emphasis. This everydayness later was reformulated and extended beyond the domestic space in Akerman's *Les Rendezvous d'Anna* (1978).
20 What Annette Kuhn regards as the film's 'refusal to set up privileged point-of-view on the action by close-ups, cut-ins and point of view shots'. See Kuhn, *Women's Pictures*, 174.

21 Margulies argues that Akerman's style 'clearly departs from the transparency of classical realism according to the Hollywood formula', attaining an anti-illusionist quality. See Margulies, *Nothing Happens*, 7.
22 See Singer, 'Jeanne Dielman: Cinematic Interrogation and "Amplification"', 59. As Emre Çağlayan argues: 'Part of this aesthetic strategy is derived from modernist films, such as those found in the works of Robert Bresson, where the camera lingers on the space following the termination of narrative action.' See Çağlayan, *Poetics of Slow Cinema*, 58.
23 The camera's presence is felt almost as a body that occupies the diegetic space – as opposed to being a neutral window that, by definition, stays out of this space and is merely opened onto it. Of course, Akerman's camera is a body that is incapacitated. It passively observes as it does not freely move in space to explore or enjoy the privilege of different positions and multiple vantage points, or interact with the characters.
24 Margulies, *Nothing Happens*, 65–9.
25 Ibid., 46.
26 De Luca's discussion here mainly concerns the films of Tsai Min-liang, but he does refer to Chantal Akerman's *Jeanne Dielman*, whose radical emphasis on the everyday influenced the films he studies, as a prototype. See de Luca, 'Sensory Everyday', 157.
27 De Luca, *Realism of the Senses*, 193.
28 Margulies, *Nothing Happens*, 69.
29 Margulies, *Nothing Happens*, 69–70. As Pier Paolo Pasolini argues, the long take is less a matter of meaning-making than proposing 'All this is'. See Pasolini, *Heretical Empiricism*, 240.
30 See Çağlayan, *Poetics of Slow Cinema*, 57.
31 Bazin, 'Bicycle Thief', 47–60. There is 'a certain "wholeness" to reality' and the things 'embraced by a film . . . possess an ontological unity which film has to respect'. See Eisaesser and Hagener, 'Cinema as Window and Frame', 29–30. Also see Bazin, 'Will CinemaScope Save the Film Industry?'. Lúcia Nagib's reads Jean-Luc Godard's famous quotation 'The tracking shot is a question of morals' with regard to the integrity of the profilmic: 'The immediate attraction of [Godard's] formulation resides in the way it attaches ethical value to the index as elicited by the continuous, uninterrupted camera movement across objective reality.' See Nagib, *World Cinema and the Ethics of Realism*, 10.
32 Eisaesser and Hagener, *Film Theory*, 29–30.
33 Bazin, 'Will CinemaScope Save the Film Industry?', 91.
34 Lúcia Nagib, *World Cinema and the Ethics of Realism*, 11.
35 See Margulies *Nothing Happens*, 37.
36 Schoonover, *Brutal Vision*, 47.
37 Ibid.
38 Also, see Bazin's discussion of Jean Renoir's preoccupation with details in Bazin, *Jean Renoir*, 85.
39 Cited in Schoonover, *Brutal Vision*, 47.
40 Gunning, 'Moving Away from the Index', 33. For further criticism of index argument, see Gunning's 'What's the Point of an Index?', and Snyder and Allen, 'Photography, Vision, and Representation'. Bazin himself never game a sustained definition of the photograph. See Morgan, 'Rethinking Bazin', 445.
41 Agacinski, *Time Passing*, 101.

42 Shaviro, *The Cinematic Body*, 27.
43 Kouvaros, '"We Do Not Die Twice"', 381.
44 Margulies, *Nothing Happens*, 66.
45 Joret, *Studying Film with André Bazin*, 59. For a discussion of critiques of the co-relation between automatism and medium essentialism, see Costello and Phillips, 'Automatism, Causality and Realism'.
46 Bazin, *What Is Cinema?*, vol. 2, 81.
47 Ibid.
48 Ibid., 65.
49 Bazin's approach to performance as the 'once-only profilmic event' implies the same point. See Margulies, 'Bodies Too Much', 2.
50 Margulies, *Nothing Happens*, 72.
51 Ibid.
52 Ibid.
53 According to Patrick Kinsman: 'Everything that we see in the film – up to the murder scene – is, while fictional/symbolic – also naturalistic . . . The actress and the role are parallel, occupying the same space, committing the same gestures.' Kinsman, 'She's Come Undone', 218.
54 For a discussion of the fusion of modernist, anti-illusionist performance and the realist one in the film, see Jayamanne, 'Modes of Performance in Chantal Akerman's *Jeanne Dielman*', 153.
55 Margulies, *Nothing Happens*, 47.
56 Ibid., 6.
57 Ibid., 37.
58 Ibid., 40–1.
59 Ibid., 41.
60 For a discussion of Jeanne's ambiguous reaction in the scene, see Longfellow, 'Love Letters to the Mother', 84.
61 Kinsman, 'She's Come Undone', 219.
62 Margulies, *Nothing Happens*, 2. As Margulies argues, the murder as the fictive scene 'destroys the perfect homology between literalness and fiction in earlier domestic scenes'. See Margulies, *Nothing Happens*, 5.
63 Referring to the final scene, Sandy Flitterman-Lewis argues that Jeanne, 'who is only seen in surfaces, suddenly gains incredible depth by virtue of the viewer's attributions. We imagine "what she's thinking" . . . A depth of experience and feeling is attributed to this character whose interiority the film had worked so hard to deny.' Flitterman-Lewis furthers her argument by contending that Akerman's long takes 'invite the viewer's speculation about Jeanne's thoughts – she has to be thinking something – as she accomplishes each task'. See Flitterman-Lewis, 'What's Beneath Her Smile?', 33 and 38.
64 Cited in Kinsman, 'She's Come Undone', 219.
65 See Margulies, *Nothing Happens*, 122.
66 Ibid., 82–3.

5

The Inhuman Eye and the Formless Body

Emmanuel Levinas associates the image with form and violence. Significantly, he sees this violence already embedded within objecthood: 'the forms of objects call for the hand and the grasp. By the hand the object is in the end comprehended, touched, taken, borne and related to other objects.' Levinas continues: 'Beneath form, things conceal themselves.'[1] The object, insofar as it is nothing but the form it leaves and offers, has in its structure a call to grasp; perhaps somehow before there is a consciousness to assume the hand to grasp. The gaze is a hand that reaches out to grasp the object and, most importantly, is always already characterised by its eventual return to the same/familiar, by the solace of a return home. The gaze, as Hagi Kenaan remarks, 'zealously preserves closure as a condition of self-identity, without any possibility of opening up to a radical outside'.[2]

What if, however, the gaze is already altered when the cinematic image visits the eye; that there is a certain formlessing already at work before there is an eye that recognises and forms? Dziga Vertov eminently observes that the cinematographic camera, what he termed *kino-eye*, not only perceives more and better (than the human eye) but is also a potentiality, a capacity to be fostered: 'We cannot improve the making of our eyes, but we can endlessly perfect the camera.'[3] At the core of this machine resides a preoccupation with the filmed body. Through the automatic formation of the body's image, the camera says 'yes' to the body of the other and welcomes it before an identification of the body. Without discrimination, the camera hosts the body of the visitor. It receives the body and affirms its presence without expectation. The filmed body is therefore assumed before there is a subject to accept the body. In a certain sense, the body of the other has arrived in the absence of an authority to invite the body to be made present. What precedes is not a body that is readily recognisable as tied to intentional meanings. The inhuman eye of the camera transfers the body of the other without interrogating what the body is or signifies. The body being filmed is, at its degree zero, a thing made available to the gaze of the camera – as opposed to what is recognised based on an identification of its attributes and its embeddedness within a matrix of relations.

The body contaminates the image

The body is a fragment of the real made available to the camera, whereas its status is not like any other thing in André Bazin's theory. The body, as Karl Schoonover notes, is not just one aspect of the setting – it is 'a bridge within the image', blurring the line between 'the intentioned and the unintended', between 'the fictional and the documentary'. It provides a means of self-authentication (of the image). It is what 'permits the image to trace or track its own making'.[4] Realism respects what is in the setting through its capture of the flux of the real; yet it is the body that 'exposes what is valuable about respecting that realism of space'.[5]

According to Bazin's humanism, the body is not simply a vehicle for the filmic event. It is not what is to be exhausted so that the filmic event can emerge. The body is what stages the event, yet is also the event itself. It is what grants the image its singularity. The body is the premise of particularity but also of contingency:

> Bazin reads the details and excesses of the filmed body as the aesthetic activation of the real in the film image. They do not simply lend a realistic appearance to the *mise-en-scène*; they expose a dynamism of the image that other objects might not. Body detail grants the image singularity, the mark of a particular juncture in time and space. As such, the image is unrepeatable not only because humans age and bodies have histories . . ., but also because humans gesture in unexpected, unstaged, and inadvertent ways.[6]

The filmed body is that which contaminates the image. In its contingent duration, it breaks with the diegesis and evokes a body irreducible to semantic inscriptions. In its concreteness, however, the filmed body is not a general body – certainly not a universal one. Its break with the particularities of the diegetic body is paradoxically due to its being too particular. While the particularity of the former is pre-scripted and discursive, a text-bound production of sameness/difference, the radical particularity of the filmed body resides in its being produced by a machine that records regardless of the narrative or descriptive attributes of what is recorded.

There is a certain weightiness and density to the filmed body. Luchino Visconti echoes Bazin's reverence for the body when he says, 'the heft of a human being, his presence, is the only thing which really fills the frame'.[7] The image of this presence does not signify a lack. It is automatically produced and therefore is not yet formed. However, it is not a formlessness that calls for form. Rather, the body is, in a certain sense, characterised by its nudity.[8] As the 'preferred natural guarantor of the image's realism', the body is what 'evidences the physical transfer at the basis of the cinematic image'.[9] As Christian Keathley reminds us, Bazin considers the actor's body as irrepressible precisely because it is in the filmed body that 'film's privileged relationship to the profilmic reality it records registers with greatest force'.[10] The fullness of the image resides in its inscription of a profilmic body.

There is already a productive maladjustment in any filmic rendition of the body precisely because the documentary of actors and the fiction of characters are two heterogeneous realities that coincide but remain separate and irreducible. In a video essay on Vittorio De Sica's *Umberto D.* (1952) and Robert Bresson's *Mouchette* (1967), Jordan Schonig demonstrates the uniqueness of the body in the inscription of the profilmic reality by investigating examples of habitual gestures. Referring to the maid scene in *Umberto D.*, one of the most cited examples of realism in cinema, Schonig emphasises a realism that is born out of the maid's 'bodily habits' of striking the match or drowning the ants, the specificity of which is accentuated through a repetition of the gestures. In the next shots that show the maid sitting on the chair grinding coffee while closing the kitchen door with the tip of her foot, Schonig sees 'a display of bodily intelligence'. He goes further to point out resonances that scenes in Bresson's *Mouchette* bear where Mouchette performs her 'athletic gesture' in the kitchen, flipping a metal top onto the pot rather than simply placing it, or the way she playfully pours coffee into several cups. For Schonig, these gestures are exhibitions of 'immediate familiarity and ease' – they are 'smooth and measured', appearing to be 'ingrained in the body as habit'.[11]

In these examples, the body is not mediated through the power of the third – it does not stand out as a lack, requiring to be supplemented by narrative or signifying frameworks. The body is sustained by the image itself as the latter registers the body–camera encounter with the greatest force. This disruption of the rule of the third generates an immediacy that alters the viewing experience. Bazin sees in De Sica's film an attempt to establish a cinema concerned with a spectatorial engagement with the body that precisely counters the 'art of ellipsis'. The latter, according to Bazin, is 'a narrative process; it is logical in nature and so it is abstract as well; it presupposes analysis and choice; it organizes the facts in accord with the general dramatic direction to which it forces them to submit'. For De Sica, by contrast, the narrative is indissociable from 'the succession of concrete instants of life', while none of these instances can be perceived as more vital than another.[12] Heightening the attentiveness of the camera to 'a quotidian microevent', this alternative approach, as Schoonover notes, allows the body onscreen 'to amplify and expand the aesthetic registers of a slower spectating'.[13] The gesture, in a certain sense, becomes the thrust of a bodily inscription in a de-hierarchised space where the body does not await narrative articulation to become formally and visually significant, but persists in its density and indifference to narrative composition.

Additionally, Bazin's championing of the body is partly rooted in the unintended aspect of human gestures, the latter best realised in the long take that finds its spatial correlate in deep-focus cinematography.[14] Respecting the realism of time and space in the long take brings forth the contingent gestures. As Schoonover observes:

> The body makes visible how contingency productively contaminates the well-planed image. The inadvertent gesture, the blinking eye, the unplanned spasm, the random detail noticed only after the fact – these are the elements of the image the camera cannot help but record, and they remind us of how photographic media make images without the

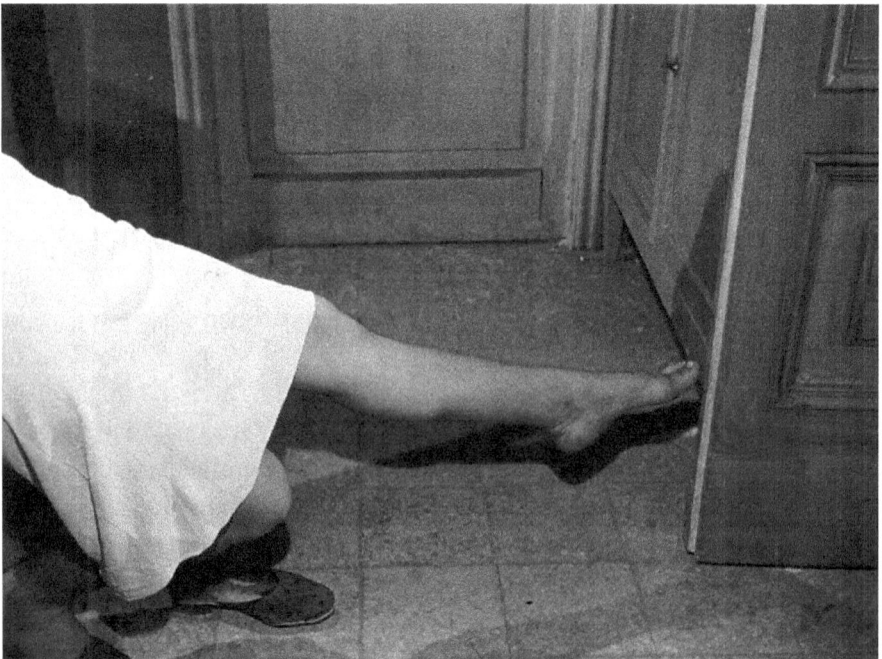

Figure 5.1 Inscription of bodily gesture in *Umberto D.* (Vittorio De Sica, 1952).

Figure 5.2 Capturing the habits as ingrained in the body in *Mouchette* (Robert Bresson, 1967).

> intervention of human psychology. Thus, sensitivity to contingency saves the image from reification, intentionality, and the concretization of any top-down semantics that might prevent the spectator from exercising her own democratic reading of the image.[15]

The uninterrupted shot gains an unrivalled regard in Bazanian film theory. The continuous flow that tends to show the action unfolding in its entirety 'allows the contingency of the profilmic event to unfold in real time and develop within the open field of the image'.[16] It is in this respect that Bazin tirelessly celebrates the achievements of neorealism. According to him, neorealism instrumentalises and amplifies contingency by 'foregrounding the accidental, flaunting the unintended, embracing the unstyled'. The diegetic fiction becomes no longer self-contained, but 'borrows from profilmic inadvertency: the consequential is made to parade as the incidental'.[17] The body, as the primary aspect of the profilmic, helps to locate 'the force of contingency in the image'.[18] The contingent nature of the filmic presence that Bazin honours is therefore indebted to the body as the latter fills the image with its weight without necessitating a call for meaningfulness.

It is important to acknowledge the need to instrumentalise the contingent as what withdraws from discursive containment. Yet, it is also worth noting that contingency is not limited to the unintended. It must be asked, what if the filmed body itself, in its being given within the image, foregrounds contingency, and what if the claim of the image resides in the unmotivated appearance and persistence of the filmed body? It is insufficient to tie the power of the body merely to its inadvertent gestures. This approach will overlook the founding stone of the cinematographic image – that is, its being an effect of the body-thing being offered to be automatically recorded. Merely speaking of the unintended feels inadequate to account for a more fundamental emergence of the contingent at the core of the camera: the body-thing captured not only in its physical appearance but also in its profilmic duration. If the long take offers a level of contingency to the image that is unavailable in shorter takes, then it could be validly argued that contingency also includes spatial and indeed temporal density. The duration of the profilmic body copied on the celluloid (and kept within the image) is an essential part of the contingency of the image and its temporal instabilities precisely because duration is automatically produced and can only subsequently be ascribed a secondary motivation. Contingency is always already emergent in cinema not only because it is rooted in a certain after-the-fact ontology (the unintended, the unplanned), but also because its emergence is bound with the duration of a certain becoming. This becoming is not a transformation that is necessarily visible (to the human eye). Rather, it is attested to by the cinematic image particularly when actions, gestures and postures are recorded in their entirety or presented within durations where the passing of time is felt in its nakedness.

Bazin's explicit celebrations of the long take clearly demonstrate his position towards the profilmic body. Indeed, the significance of the long take for Bazin owes less to the 'length' of the take than to a certain preoccupation with what takes place in the profilmic. This is partly because, as Ed Gallafent reminds us, the long take cannot be simply defined in quantitative terms. The length of a shot is first and foremost a perceived length. The perception of the shot depends on many factors from the 'length of shots in the rest of the film, the average shot length in the specific area of cinema and historical period of the film's production' to 'the content of the shot, how it draws our attention to its length or chooses not to do so'.[19] It therefore might be even argued that the extendedness of durations particularly with regard to the way time is felt in its passing is more significant for a particular rewatching of the body of the other, than a mere insistence on the application of the long take. In itself, the long take lacks aesthetic or ethical significance. As Emre Çağlayan discerns, the long take aesthetic is 'not entirely sufficient to warrant an aesthetic of reality insofar as its application in various sequences in mainstream escapist cinema displays contradictions to Bazinian realism'. He continues: 'While these films often deploy the long take accompanied by deep-focus cinematography, they hardly constitute the reality effect that Bazin has thoroughly explicated in his essays.'[20] The long take can be associated with a completely different temporal economy. The perseverance of the spatial and temporal unity can thus be 'in stark contrast to slow cinema and the earlier forms of realist cinema' that Bazin evidently championed throughout his theoretical endeavours.[21]

Bazin is most concerned with preserving something of the profilmic – a transformation taking place in the latter that the image preserves.[22] What fascinates him is an image that is set up to allow the spectator to bear witness to this transformation occurring in real time. Yet Bazin does not necessarily associate this transformation with a certain physical or bodily change that is deemed irreversible. More crucially with respect to the current image-saturated culture, it is inadequate to speak of cases in which the filmed body is 'in harm's way' and there is an imminent 'physical danger' in the profilmic, or of 'spaces hazardous for bodies', or 'the body in the midst or on the brink of suffering'[23] as the sole, necessary ways of evoking the reality and ethical claim of the profilmic. This understanding rightly assumes a culture in which the infinite circulation and recycling of images foreclose the possibility of the world facing the viewer through the image. It is right to assume a culture that is so desensitised that only graphically shocking images could minimally attest to the profilmic existing independently from filmic articulations. The senselessness of real graphic images can challenge the authority of the viewing subject over the world viewed through a withdrawal of the profilmic from meaning-making mechanisms. However, this approach effectively falls short of acknowledging the originary address of the image and takes the cultural degradation of the image as an ontological absolute. Recourse to visible bodily change (taking place within the profilmic) to shock the already desensitised viewer so that they could regain a sense of profilmic reality only reinstates cultural blindness.

What seems to concern Bazin most is not the irreversibility of a transformation necessarily visible onscreen in terms of bodily alteration, but the claim that an interrupted cinematic image of the body carries within itself. While in a photograph what is within the image appears to be indefinitely bound to a past moment, the imprinting of time in film creates an uncanny, virtual present tense that is troubling. The other is, in a sense, brought to life to be witnessed – they are virtually dragged into the flow of present tense. There is a certain dynamism to the cinematic image that fixes what is fleeting, but its historicity embodies a certain complex duality – the image is one that, Schoonover remarks, 'offers itself as recorded document and living testimony, a means of registration that fixes the past as a certainty while imbuing it with all the fragile and volatile ambiguities of the present'.[24] While a photograph fixes the world with an inflexible finality, cinema accounts for reality 'without arresting the fluidity of life midstream. The filmed image is more about transcending the limits of time's passage and maintaining time's shape than it is about concretizing the moment'.[25] The inhuman claim of the cinematographic eye resides in its preservation of a change in time that is not visible to the human eye but is sustained by the cinematic image. What evokes the irreversibility of time and change is an image that attests to the appearance and persistence of the filmed body recorded in real time. The image takes out a singular chunk of time and space and through its preservation attests to its irreversibility. The claim of the image accentuates an irreversibility that is *a posteriori* and thus is contingent. One could say that a prolonged documentation of filmed bodies and the images that are marginalised by the mainstream consumerist culture, yet are set up to make present a fundamental withdrawal at the core of the film medium resist a culture that equates looking with meaning, possessing and consumption. They heighten the physicality and significance of the profilmic body precisely by imposing duration (on the viewer), yet refusing to pay off. This imposition is a medium-specific property of film to repeat what is by essence unrepeatable.

This attention to a transformation that is not necessarily visible to the human eye but is preserved within the image further complicates the connection of the filmed body to intelligibility. In his explorations of the relation between film and theatre, Bazin argues for an unbridgeable gap between theatre and cinema in terms of the question of the body: a 'play requires the presence of at least two groups of humans in order to qualify as theatre: actors performing onstage and an audience watching from its seats'.[26] A film, by essence, involves different circumstances: it 'requires neither performers who enact the text nor an audience in attendance', precisely because 'a film can render a performance without a human agent being present'. For Bazin, as Schoonover observes, theatre is an 'anthropocentric medium in a way that cinema is not'.[27] Film offers an inhuman eye and could be argued to bring forth a certain (affirmative) violence through the image. At its degree zero, it opens up an image that is not tailored to the habituated viewing of the human eye yet nevertheless comes towards the viewer, making the latter host an image that has been automatically affirmed and whose duration imposes a certain passivity.

The possibility of the non-frontal of the image, discussed in the previous chapters, is premised upon this inhumanity. What the image offers is not simply in front of the viewer as formed objects, as contained forms of meaning. What is within the image is too much to be pre-framed and formed for the human eye and its quest for visibility and meaningfulness. What the cinematic image brings into being through its automatic reproduction are things presented to the inhuman gaze of the camera and thus persisting with a certain indifference to a human search for intelligibility. As Mary Ann Doane observes, in cinema the 'fidelity of the image to its referent was no longer dependent upon the skill or honesty of a particular artist. The imprint of the real was automatically guaranteed by the known capability of the machine.' Echoing Bazinian fascination with the invention of cinema, Doane continues: 'For the first time, an aesthetic representation – previously chained to the idea of human control – could be made by accident.'[28] The affirmative violence of the cinematic image rests upon its peculiar violence towards vision: the fact that it is a staging of real fragments of the world, first for a camera and then, but not necessarily, for a human viewing subject. What is offered is viewed, not by a viewer (whose existence is, in a certain sense, contingent on the formation of the image), but by a machine that copies the profilmic thing regardless of its descriptive or narrative attributes. Bazin's humanism resides in his paradoxical belief in an inhuman machine that appears to respect the human body precisely due to its own inhumanity.

Following Schoonover, I argue that Bazin locates a certain actorlessness at the core of filmic rendition of bodies. The persistence of the filmed body is rooted in cinema's privileged relationship to the profilmic reality, and actorlessness resides in the body being automatically generated. Bazin encourages us

> to think of the onscreen actor less as a performer and more as a filmed body. Bazin's film actor shares more with the human subject of documentary than she does with the stage actor . . . The cinema allows for an actorless drama that may include humans . . . an actorless cinema would bring us closer to a pure cinema. Cinema is able to tell stories freed from human agency and less dependent on the conscious expression of its performers. The viewer is given the sense that she is watching 'caught unawares.' The film actor's body is not tied to intentional meaning in the same way it must function on stage to make sense. Because on stage the actor is needed to give voice to the text, the function of his body is keyed to the intent of the script, tied to meaning in an *a priori* fashion . . . Because the body on film is automatically generated, the body neither speaks the text nor speaks for itself. Instead, it stands as an element of the cinematic experience.[29]

Actorlessness provides the grounds for a certain mode of fictionality that bears an interruption of intentional, meaning-oriented exploitation of the otherness of the world, resulting in a certain divergence between the filmed body and the body of the actor on stage. The filmed body is the site in which bodily surplus is staged while the body within the cinematic image embodies an originary indifference to the script.

The material bodies of Bruno Dumont

I turn here to Bruno Dumont who is arguably one of the contemporary filmmakers whose starkly materialist aesthetics is paradigmatic of an attempt to intensify the inscription of the profilmic body to achieve actorless dramas while remaining within the scope of fiction films. Equally austere and excessive, Dumont's films, particularly his earlier works before his 'comedic turn', manifest a tendency to restore the power of cinema by returning the man to the body. His films focus on ordinary people who, in his own words, 'don't speak a lot, but who experience an incredible intensity of joy, emotion, suffering, sympathy in death. They don't speak, speaking is not important.'[30] For Dumont, cinema seems to be a revelation of truth, but then through a return to what is common and ordinary. Often set in rural and rustic farm settings, Dumont's minimal plots may involve a gang of disaffected, unemployed teenagers whose leader is inarticulate and violent but epileptic and vulnerable (*La vie de Jésus*, 1997), an incompetent, unlikely policeman traumatised by a brutal child rape and murder case he is investigating in rural France (*L'humanité*, 1999), an impassive farmworker who goes to war in an unnamed country with undisclosed motives (*Flandres* 2006), a young novice who is expelled because her self-imposed suffering and self-abnegation are deemed to be indicative of her blind faith (*Hadewijch*, 2009), or a drifter who subsists on donated food and seems to possess healing powers and a troubled young woman (*Hors Satan*, 2011). The precariousness of the lives of Dumont's characters is compounded by his plots, which often involve bodies that are submitted to different forms of violence and regimes of subjugation, exposed to the violent acts of others, to bodily and sexual aggression, to the unforgiveness of nature, religion or war, to self-inflicted pain or emotional torment, or kept in hospitals or asylums and submitted to scientific, psychiatric and clinical gaze, all of which appear to desire a body that can be formed and contained.

Dumont's attention to the ordinary is predominantly reflected in his choice of actors, most of them non-actors recruited on location, picked from the chronically unemployed, disabled people, factory and farm workers. Dumont's iconoclastic choice of actors brings peculiar and uncanny bodies onscreen and, as Insook Webber argues, radically violates the 'sacrosanct codes of representation'. His bodies are 'bleak, mute, muddy, and devoid of bourgeois charm or comfort'.[31] Embodied by their physiognomies, Dumont's bodies carry their histories imprinted on them, and their bodies mirror their lives: 'worn, scarred, or deformed'.[32] As Michel Rubin also observes, Dumont's bodies are 'antithetical' to the dominant norms of bodies in narrative films, thus defying 'cultural legitimacy and aesthetic validation'.[33] For Dumont, the bodies of actors are the same as landscapes – they are found in the world and, in his own words, 'come readymade'.[34] Encompassed by nature and appearing to have been born out of it, the bodies demonstrate the originary being of the filmed body as a found thing in the material world. This originarity is literalised in Dumont's films, for the bodies are found in French Flanders, where most of his films are set, and the physicality of their profilmic existence is preserved in the images he sets up.

Dumont's specific form of presenting bodies is achieved partly through an intimacy that he establishes between his characters and the earth, with mud and soil, perhaps best exemplified by the opening scene in *L'humanité*, where the protagonist Pharaon collapses and takes solace in the mud following the witnessing of the violated and murdered corpse. Most of the filmic actions in Dumont's films unfold outdoors with rare exceptions: 'I film the earth and trees, the wind. Faces.'[35] Characters are presented in a raw and crude manner without offering any aestheticising filter that could mediate the presentation of the body onscreen, and the 'imperfect' body is often captured in 'unflattering postures'.[36] As several scholars have noted, this method is most evidently demonstrated in the way Dumont's films set up sex scenes – even 'the sex act, that most intimate of human activities, occurs mostly in open nature',[37] presented through 'clinically objective (and graphic) stagings',[38] where rawness is emphasised due to the 'reigning emotional illiteracy around sex'.[39]

In her reading of *Hors Satan*, Saige Walton notes a sensitivity in Dumont's style 'to the sensuality of bodies' being-*in*-the-world' to the extent that the human figure loses its dominance over the environment and instead turns into 'one element in a shifting array of worldly details'.[40] Dumont explains his interest in long shots in accordance with this reversal of dominance:

> Scope takes in so much that it brings the background to the fore; it makes it impossible for the figure to dominate. I wanted to shoot from far away, to minimise the characters as much as possible, and integrate them to the background.[41]

Figure 5.3 Staging of the sex act in open nature in *Flandres* (Bruno Dumont, 2006).

Figure 5.4 The human figure dwarfed by the landscape in an extreme long shot in *L'humanité* (Bruno Dumont, 1999).

Bodies engulfed by landscapes are accompanied by diegetic but dramatically insignificant sounds. The audience often hears clear and enhanced sounds of wind, pouring rain, feet moving across freshly wet grass or in the mud, or of farm animals, that prevail particularly in the absence of music, which could be utilised in expressing characters' moods and interiorities. As Martine Beugnet notes, the 'synchronous sound-track' as well as the 'audio close-ups' are crucial for Dumont in creating 'a supplement of materiality and a sense of weightiness to the image, evoking, in [Maurice] Merleau-Ponty's terms, the "stickiness" of the "world as flesh"'.[42] Despite the recurring lack of human conversation, Dumont's films are not silent, for sounds of 'worldly phenomena' fill and dominate space. As Walton observes, the sense of presence that Dumont creates, one that is 'non-verbal' and 'organic', resides in the audience's sonic immersion in the characters' inhalations and exhalations of breath; the shivering of bodies in the cold; sounds of the sea; cries of birds and other animals; barbed wire and iron sheets, lifted by the wind; the sound of boots crunching upon gravel or sinking into fresh mud.[43]

Despite the abundance of long shots in his films where the emptiness of the image is compounded by widescreen compositions, Dumont, like Bresson, also manifests a tendency to capture the body through often fragmented shots, even though Dumontian body parts do not sit in place of words to express characters but often to emphasise their physiognomic singularities. Shots of objects are accompanied by similar shots of bodies, resulting in topological parallelisms. There are recurring close-up shots where the camera lingers over a sweat-soaked neck, characters' teeth, wounds and bruises on their torso, scratches on shoulders and arms, dirt under nails, or emphasises the texture of sunburned or damaged skins, framed similarly to prolonged focus of the camera on objects. It is as if the inhuman is animated whereas the inanimate objects are given human qualities.[44] Close shots of objects, faces and body parts suspend plot progression. Removed from articulations of character psychology, they are instead part of a visual exploration and formlessing of the body. In what Beugnet terms 'cinema of sensation', the decontextualisation of the body-thing is partly operated through the tight framing, which

> does not operate as a narrative complement to the medium or long shot or as a means of objectifying and investigating the body. On the contrary, freed from the imperatives of plot developments and conventional fetishism ... the close-up creates a different space for the camera to linger, opening to the gaze the realm of the 'body-landscape'.[45]

As another stylistic parallel between Dumont and Bresson, the emphatic presentation of physiological attributes is compounded by non-psychological acting and a certain reduction of characters to mutism where human speech is rare and, when existent, limited to one-line exchanges that expose the characters' inability to meaningfully communicate.[46] Referring to his preference 'to use only the material found in the real', Dumont states that he sees characters not as 'mouthpieces, means of expression, but expression itself',[47] therefore locating the filmic event in the body. This radical reduction accentuates the markedness of the filmed body (by its real, material existence), and provides an encounter with alterity where the body is privileged over an easy access to interiority.

Figure 5.5 Lingering on body parts in *L'humanité* (Bruno Dumont, 1999).

Figure 5.6 Tight framing of the body in *Hors Satan* (Bruno Dumont, 2011).

The strangeness of the experience Dumont's that films offer is partly rooted in the filmic techniques he uses to evacuate subjectivity from the bodies. In addition to the mutism of characters, Dumont's style is characterised by elliptical editing, rare and inexpressive dialogues and non-committal, deadpan gestures despite the characters' torments. His 'ascetic images', as Raymond Watkins reminds us, often resonate with aversion to plot-driven narratives and in extreme cases a radical reduction of movement to 'painterly stasis'.[48] Dumont's aesthetics not only evacuates subjectivity from bodies and renders them opaque through his imagery but also gives his films an obscure quality – bodies gain extended screen time and emphatic visual interest, yet their persistence lacks definite meaning. There is a singularity to his bodies that is a consequence of images' unmotivated persistence, temporal indeterminacy and the surplus of bodily presence onscreen.

Despite his films' attention to the body–landscape affinity, Dumont does not use this intimacy to reintroduce interiority to his characters. Neither the bodies nor the deserted landscapes appear as contained forms of meaning. Frequent subjective shots of the sky or empty landscapes are emblematic of an approach where the meaningfulness that we often ascribe to the seer–seen dynamic is disrupted. Dumont's camera, according to Kent Jones, is often characterised by lingering on the profilmic bodies and things for 'an uncomfortable interval', which exhausts any 'mental or poetic correlative between the looker and the looked at'.[49] While Dumont often pairs bodies and surroundings, as Chelsea Birks and Lisa Coulthard observe, this pairing does not imply 'a psychogeography where landscapes and faces inform each other', but rather emphasises 'a pervasive sense of depthlessness or blankness' that characterise not only the human subjects but also the landscape they inhabit.[50] Contrary to romanticised conceptions of nature, bodies and landscapes are drawn together, whereas images resist meaning, instead exposing the audience to material and perceptual plenitude that emphasises the inscriptions of the profilmic contingencies. Landscapes surround the characters, yet their desolation does not mirror characters' interiorities. Rather, 'dwarfed by' the landscapes they inhabit (consider again the opening of *L'humanité* where the viewer sees a tiny figure running across the field in an extreme long shot), characters 'neither acquire significance from, nor confer meaning to, the environment or the community'.[51] Similarly, Dumont's signature editing, which constantly reverses the scales of bodies against the backdrop of landscapes as well as cutting long shots to close-ups as the opposite end of the scale, further emphasises the materiality of the bodies and frustrates meaning. This depthlessness accentuates the profilmic in its uncanny flow onscreen and returns the camera to the status of a machine that captures the body while displacing a viewing subject who desires the solace of form and familiarity. Despite the depthless surfaces, the unfolding of duration is real; it is happening to the viewer and carries a strong presentness. Yet, the viewer's relation to what they watch, to the images giving bodies in durations, is an uneasy one. It is as though the bodies cannot be properly located precisely because their persistence defies significance.

This exposure of the limits of seeing by aggravating the viewer's habituated search for meaning and form is evident in Dumont's several other aesthetic decisions. In the rare instances of two-shots, the bodies in the frame barely interact and their proximity often seems to be an effect of their being included within the frame despite the absence of meaningful connection, thus enhancing their isolation and disconnection. Exchanges of looks are sparse and, in the infrequent instances, the meaning of what is exchanged is often indeterminate and lacks enough context to be readable. This is also intensified by the offscreen gazes that problematise the meaningfulness of the shots by radically reducing the significance of what the bodies look at beyond the constraints of the frame. The faces are often blank and facial expressions are rare and decontextualised if they exist, granting characters a singularity that resonates with the uniqueness of their physiological appearance. Dumont seems to share Bazin's view that drawing the characters from the premises is a realist merit, that the 'ultimate merit of the amateur lies in his or her body and its history', applauding not the completeness of the image but the 'casting of nonprofessionals who share biographical features of their characters'.[52] Yet, even though non-actors' real lives resemble those of the characters they portray, the bodies are rather characterised by a formless weightiness that resides in their resistance to signification. The unique mode of exposure to the bodies that Dumont sets up resides in that the bodies are neither merely derivative of scripted characters nor of their real-life stories, for Dumont's direction and highly controlled compositions do not allow the non-actors to impart knowledge of their own existence to their characters.

Emphasising statis and the lack of actions that may reveal characters' interiorities is not to suggest that Dumont's films offer another example of an unequivocal aesthetics of stillness. Indeed, his characters move, yet their movements manifest a certain level of sterility. Neither Pharaon's wide-eyed gaze nor the way his body and arms move in *L'humanité* indicates his interiority but instead gives him a singularity that resides in his pre-script body. In *Hors Satan*, pan-shots (often the prevalent camera movement in Dumont's films) turn into a motif, following the languorous movements of its nameless protagonists (referred to as *Le gars* and *Elle*) as they walk towards the camera, pause, sit within the landscape to pray and reflect, and then move away from the camera. Framing the bodies as they gradually emerge into view or are absorbed into the distant horizon, the image punctuates the movements of the filmed bodies.[53] The repetition and insignificance of the movements take the form of a ritual that rhythmically resonates with the couple's prayer.[54] Or consider the occasional childlike playfulness of characters in *La vie de Jésus* and *Flandres* that are contrasted to their engagement in violent acts or unmotivated outbursts of aggression, which make it further difficult to read the images and tailor interiority for the bodies. These filmic rituals and gestures lack determinate meaning and instead turn the bodies into automatons staged to interact with the camera beyond narratively justified extents. In a sense, this repetitiveness of movements and gestures turns them into an exhibition of habits.⁵⁵ Inhabiting the diegetic space without being sustained by it, Dumont's non-actors are more to be identified with filmed bodies; with, one might say, subjects of a 'documentary', than with performers, even though Dumont's actorless dramas disregard a blurring of fiction–documentary distinction and remain stubbornly tied to the constraints of fiction films. For Dumont, it is not that there must be a breakdown of fiction so that the filmed body can emerge in its pre-discursive being. The fiction that recounts the lives of Dumont's characters is indistinguishable from their filmed bodies and can never be abstracted from their contingencies, thus problematising fiction–documentary binarism and evoking the body itself as the filmic event.

Depleted of dramatic charge yet replete with oddities, Dumont's images do not ask the viewer to read into the silent faces, to give them form by filling them with content. The viewing position he encourages is other than a desire for the meaningfulness of faces that unproblematically open within the frontal visual field. The image of the body exposes its own failure in containing the body as visual content, undermining an exhaustive readability of onscreen presences that assumes an association of body with context. The invisible of the image in Dumont's cinema is thus not the withheld and concealed interiority of bodies – it is the non-frontal aspect of the screen that hosts the persistence of bodies onscreen and sustains them. The body's resistance to expressivity is an aesthetic decision and not simply a demonstration of lack of affections. Birks and Coulthard see the fundamental problem being posed as

> the impossibility of accessing interiority, our own or that of another. This impossibility is crucial to . . . analysis of blankness in Dumont's cinema: rather than using [blankness] as surfaces on which to project meaning, . . . they do not conceal hidden internal truths (emotions, themes, motivations) but are rather a kind of truth in themselves.⁵⁶

Instead of encouraging reading into the images and translating emptiness, Dumont's aesthetic decisions effectively flatten the face: the 'human face – that conventional cinematic marker of human subjectivity and feeling – is in Dumont a flat surface'. Dumontian faces repudiate interiority to the extent that blankness is transformed into 'a truth in itself'.⁵⁷ Birks and Coulthard connect this to Jean-Luc Nancy's conceptualisation of the image, which bears a certain analogy with what was mentioned with regards to the Levinasian preoccupation with meaningfulness prior to meaning. According to Nancy, 'the image itself is only surface, and any meaning is created by the gaze that penetrates and is penetrated by the image: I the viewer become the "ground and depth" of the image, and "cogito becomes imago".[58] This analogy can be taken further to argue that even though both the viewer and the image lack determinate signification in this subversive setup, there nevertheless exists a meaningfulness that is 'nonsignifying but not insignificant'.[59]

Dumont's resistance to a reduction of bodies to intentional expressions of interiority and scripted meaning not only contests the dominant norms of mainstream cinema but also frustrates the expectations often associated with art house films. Dumont's viewers, as Hughes argues in his analysis of *La vie de Jésus* and *L'humanité*, even the ones 'trained to "read" the complex images of the art house' with 'intellectual rigor', often find themselves in a difficult situation. Prone to falling 'immediately into the trap of struggling to decode messages, unravel symbols, and impose order', even the trained viewer is disturbed by the 'impenetrable ambiguity' of images.[60] Indeed, emphasising impenetrability is not to suggest that what Dumont's camera does is merely observe the surfaces of the profilmic body. It is a repetition of the profilmic presences that takes the observational recording elsewhere, implicating it within the exasperation that specifies his films' mode of address. Observation *per se* has no inherent duration. It cannot be accurately decided where and when observation ends and something else begins. Yet film dictates the duration of its observational act by manipulating the time that the observed bodies and fragments appear, but also persist onscreen. In Dumont's films, while the camera observes bodies in their mundane and often profane moments rather than telling interiorities, this observation is supplemented by a certain degree of unproductive extendedness. A radical, emphatic recording of physical presence allows the latter to take part in but also to withdraw from the inscriptions of either the narrative or social context that informs the particularities of physical presences.

This return to the filmed body in its mundane moments seems inevitable in Dumont's cinematic world. As opposed to the abstractness of dramatic durations, to dominant conceptions of functionality and efficiency of time, his films offer an alternative temporal sensibility. In Dumont's words, 'the only truth is the duration of a shot, in other words the rhythm of the film itself: the exposure and the movement of bodies, faces, in time'.[61] This conception of duration returns the image to a making-present (film's technological realism) that makes bodies present prior to representation, therefore releasing them from the constraints of the knowable. Time resists being instrumentalised by representational ends, and bodily presence becomes a matter that is indifferent and grounded on a certain erasure of subjectivity.

The flow of meaning is often disrupted through Dumont's excessive inclusion of physicality and literal durations that accentuate the materiality of non-actors' figures and body movements in interaction with the settings. As Walton notes, this sense of 'groundedness' is revealed in Dumont films because, through experiential passage of time, they draw the viewer to a certain 'film-phenomenological participation in the materiality and temporality of filmic "nowness".'[62] Slow pacing, stillness, resistance to meaning and removing the psychological dimensions of the body create an intensified sense of existential presence that is not exhaustively motivated – it owes its existence to a material inscription (happening inside the camera). The distinction that Siegfried Kracauer sees between the images that further the story and those that 'retain a degree of independence' is instrumental in underlining how the latter images 'succeed in summoning a physical existence'.[63] As Miriam Bratu Hansen argues, Kracauer's claim that film has 'inherent affinity with the material world' highlights the possibility of a cinematic realism that defies our habits of perceiving images. The experience of viewing filmic practices that remain faithful to film's inherent affinity with the materiality of the world is thus far removed from 'cognitivist conceptions of film viewing' where an active 'scanning' of images in search of meaning is pivotal.[64] Exposed to a surplus of materiality and duration, the viewer revisits their own relation to the image and exposure to what appears and persists on the screen beyond a readymade rationalisation. What is within the cinematic image is no longer primarily framed for a human eye that searches for significance but is subject to several aesthetic decisions that renders the material presences formless. The claim of the cinematic image resides in its sustaining of a transformation (duration itself) that is not necessarily visible (to the human eye) but is nevertheless taking place in the profilmic (which the camera automatically records), and is preserved and carried within the cinematic image.

Dumont's recurrent theological themes of transcendence, the sacred and redemption, are treated with a same resistance to meaning and an emphasis on the material body. Except for *Twentynine Palms* (2003), none of Dumont's protagonists dies in the end – instead they are in differing ways 'reclaimed' by their landscape, while what appears to be sacred is rather found in the profane physicality of bodies.[65] Consider *Hors Satan*'s protagonist, who perpetrates violent acts yet also appears to work inexplicable miracles, like healing the sick or resurrecting from the dead. As Walton argues, what fascinates Dumont is not representing characters in devotional states; he rather 'solicits our own embodied encounter with film-as-devotion through his attention to time, body and landscape'.[66] Drawing on Nathaniel

Dorsky's notion of 'devotional cinema', Walton notes: 'Dumont's materialist aesthetic, together with his considered emphases on duration, stillness and the painterly tableau, incite our contemplation of and affective devotion to other bodies, selves, landscapes and objects, as well as to the sensuality of cinema itself.'[67] Or consider the final scene in *La vie de Jésus*. Following his arrest for a seeming racially motivated murder and his inexplicable escape, the viewer sees high-angle shots of the protagonist Freddy lying on tall grass under blinding sunlight. Dumont cuts to Freddy's skyward gaze and his point of view. With closed shots of an ant crawling across Freddy's skin and of his hands, as Hughes observes, Dumont returns to the raw material body, creating a 'heightened' cinematic experience of the body.[68] As Brett Bowles notes, the 'theological question of salvation or redemption' seems no longer central here as *La vie de Jésus*'s

> final pair of shots suggests that Freddy's potential redemption will consist not of religious conversion or spiritual ascension, but rather reintegration into earthly humanity . . . The ensuing long-range landscape shot [that follows] foregrounds the ditch against a farm in the distance, where we can just discern a farmhouse nestled between two freshly plowed fields.[69]

The finale of *Hadewijch* manifests a similar reworking of the redemption plot. The protagonist Céline decides to drown herself but is saved by David (David Dewaele, who later played the protagonist in *Hors Satan* before his sudden death) – by a peripheral character who appears in only a few scenes as an ex-convict and now a day-worker labouring at the church, and does not possess any narrative agency throughout the film. Céline's spiritual journey

Figure 5.7 The body reclaimed by the material world in the finale of *La vie de Jésus* (Bruno Dumont, 1997).

Figure 5.8 Following her spiritual journey, Céline is saved by David in the finale of *Hadewijch* (Bruno Dumont, 2009).

and torment ultimately bring her to be saved by a character who does not seem to help to confer religious or divine meanings on narrative or the image itself but whose visual charisma resides in his physique and withdrawn dispositions. Referring to the fact that the film including its final shots does not 'offer any meaningful insight', Tina Kendall argues that

> the value of the film lies in its refusal to make such an outcome *satisfying* for spectators. Indeed, the coda that follows resolutely refuses the kind of narrative resolution that might account for, and inform our reading of, the ultimate meaning of these images.[70]

Another curious example of formlessing the body is Dumont's retelling of the story of Joan of Arc in his *Jeannette, l'enfance de Jeanne d'Arc* (2017), arguably his most experimental film to date, made after Dumont's move from austere dramas to comedy. An adaptation of a play by Charles Péguy, *Jeannette*, brings Dumont's approach to non-actors and material bodies to a historical-biographical drama, also curiously enacted here as a musical. The plot deliberately ends before the war, and Dumont leaves out the trial of Joan of Arc and her accusation of heresy and avoids showing her fate at the stake – sections in her life that made her iconic as a revered martyr and have been the source of cinema's historical fascination with her story. Rather, Dumont focuses on minor events during the childhood and adolescence of the title character. This is particularly striking when we consider that Dumont decides to cast two non-professional actresses to evoke the historically and spiritually weighty figure of Joan of Arc. Drawing on Karen Lury's discussion of children's acting, Birks and Coulthard identify a flattening of the distinction between character and actor particularly manifested in the 'earnestness and apparent inexperience' of performance in equal measures. Similar to his *Li'l Quinquin* (2014) where Dumont disrupts the process of 'othering' children, onscreen performance in *Jeannette*, in a certain way, gains an unsimulated quality in which the actuality of the material body disrupts the seamlessness of good acting, resulting in a certain narrative 'dislocation' and ultimately blankness.[71] Dumont himself explains his iconoclastic approach to non-professional acting in *Jeannette*:

> I chose someone very ordinary, someone in her own idiosyncrasy, in its own particular being . . . So she has a body, she has a concreteness and that's serving the creation of Joan of Arc. I don't want professional actors, because they're a blank page, and they can do whatever you want them to do. But I need someone to be existing, physically-speaking, so that we can build this.[72]

Dumont observes in the shortcomings of her non-actor's performance, her inexperienced acting particularly evident in her untrained voice, a certain creation that is indebted to the 'miracle of cinema'.[73] Cinema, for Dumont, has always been 'a mystical art',[74] perhaps a Bataillean 're-mapping of theological concepts onto immanent reality'.[75] Also, consider Dumont's playful and perhaps most secular decision in the scenes where, speaking to God, Jeannette breaks the fourth wall by looking into the camera lens, relocating the religious into a cinematic interaction.

The story of Joan of Arc has always been associated in the history of cinema with a certain transcendence, whereas Dumont's flattened aesthetics emphasises 'immanence', while the viewer, as Birks and Coulthard observe, is 'encouraged to read the image as surface, and to receive the film world as it is presented rather than as hiding an internal truth or logic'. Dumont's attention to sacredness in *Jeannette* and his previous films manifests this ritual of bringing the sacred into the immanent materiality. 'Denied transcendence' in Dumont's cinema, material reality 'continually promises something that never quite arrives; the anticipation of deeper truths promised by religious themes and allegorical titles falls away to reveal a reality that seems flawed, ugly, stupid, or cruel.'[76]

Jeannette is set in rural landscape that, far from being merely faithful to a historical period, seems to evoke the landscapes in Dumont's earlier films where nature and rustiness are an essential part of his material aesthetics. Dumont deliberately reduces historical chronology and specificity of setting to bring the timelessness of nature into his recounting of Jeanette's story. Moreover, immanence is also created against the sonic landscape of generic musicals where sound is created, augmented and added in post-production. Dumont, by contrast, refuses lip-synching and insists on direct sound where the non-actors are singing in the actual profilmic, while deliberately allowing other unwanted sounds of wind, sea and sheep to be recorded and heard.[77] Singing as an expression of Jeannette's interiorities paradoxically helps to flatten and render formless her bodily presence, not by denying access to interiority, but by de-prioritising it through its over-expressions. Or consider the bizarre and absurdist upside-down movements of adolescent Jeannette's friend across the field, or her uncle's whirl-and-dab dance style performed by a local rapper – bodily movements that are unproductive, and the excess they create is not generically motivated, nor is it exactly attractive. Or the deliberate disruptions of continuity between shots or minor unscripted incidents (Jeannette's reaction when her uncle stumbles off the horse) that grant the images an enhanced level of contingency. These maladjustments that lie at the heart of filmic rendition of bodies and performances are rendered explicit within the image as Dumont's camera registers stylised movements and gestures yet also allows for the unplanned, startling moments. While still representing the characters at the surface, the filmed bodies remain heavily tied to the sheer recording of imperfectly choreographed performances. The characters are thus too tied to the particularities of the filmed bodies and durations to be properly representative.

Dumont's Jeannette is evidently different from the characters in his earlier films – she is athletic, with an ardent, childish playfulness, dancing, singing, jumping and spinning around. We see in *Jeannette* the same choreographed relation of the body to the camera prevalent in musical genre. Through the use of non-actors, however, the body–camera interaction is often turned into a depiction of bodies at the feats of endurance. The difficulty the non-actors bear is made visible by demanding non-professionals to perform tasks of dancing, head-banging, swaying, hair-whipping, all of which are choreographed by the professional mime Philippe Decouflé, while singing to the music of French experimental musician Igorrr. There is an accentuation of this endurance, compounded by the 1.55:1 aspect ratio that provides a boxier frame than Dumont's use of cinemascope in his previous films, permitting a closer and more emphatic focus on bodies. Not simply a sign of failure in acting 'professionally', bad acting becomes a formal constituent in *Jeannette*. It creates a parallelism – a productive maladjustment that not

Figure 5.9 Returning the body to formless precarity released from mediation and sustained by the image in *Jeannette, l'enfance de Jeanne d'Arc* (Bruno Dumont, 2017).

only emphasises the profilmic contingencies but goes on to stress the eventualities of the production of images in which the profilmic bodies take part. Bad acting therefore counters the largely accepted belief that acting should be oriented towards looking more familiar. It bears a heightened level of contingency that overshadows the fit and the adequacy of a pre-scripted, controlled acting that would work to create the impressions of familiarity.

The same Dumontian austere seriousness and stasis frequently resurfaces in between musical set-pieces, in some cases resulting in raw, degree zero body–camera interactions where there is a radical reduction of artifice, soundtrack and performance. Staging the withdrawal of the filmed body, this relation to the body is best demonstrated towards the end of the film when, following shots of intense dancing, the music abruptly stops, Jeannette falls to one knee and her body becomes static. Heavily breathing and her heartbeat audible, Jeannette looks directly at the camera, with an evident expression of exhaustion. There is a momentary suspension of all that sustained her fictional body – what remains is a body in its formless precarity, released from mediation and sustained only by the image.

What Webber argues with regards to Dumont's previous biographical drama *Camille Claudel 1915* (2013) would equally hold true here where dominant traditional notions of 'the beautiful, the true and the good' seem no longer to be tenable in the context of Dumont's aesthetics despite their inevitable evocations.[78] Returning to what is common and profane, Dumont's aesthetics works as a demonstration that film is a dual operation in that it oscillates between the particular concreteness of the profilmic body before the camera and the body of the character as an effect of abstraction from this uncompromising materiality. The camera, as the only device that can provide the film with a proxy to represent Joan of Arc onscreen, is radicalised in *Jeannette* as the material body disrupts intertextual associations, conspicuously considering in particular that the story of Joan of Arc has been repeatedly interpreted and told in the history of cinema – most notably by Carl Theodor Dreyer, Robert Bresson and Jacques Rivette. Dumont's Jeannette troubles identity – she does not exactly become Joan of Arc.

The formless body

Averse to representational logic and focused on physiognomic peculiarities, Dumont's aesthetics renders the bodies formless. Formlessness enacts a resistance to meaning. Persisting onscreen within literal durations, the formless body does not seem to lack or call for form. Its image implies that there is a certain fullness, a weighty presence prior to consciousness. Dumontian images can be said to return the body into a 'base matter', one that Georges Bataille would describe as 'external and foreign to ideal human aspirations', as what 'refuses to allow itself to be reduced to the great ontological machines resulting from these aspirations'.[79] In Dumont's cinema, the formless body is a capacity (residing in the inhuman automatism of the camera) that should be fostered through failure (of forms). The world of forms should be traversed so that it will be exposed to failure. The formless body, in this sense, is not to be confused with the profilmic body. It is not that there is a pre-form body that the camera captures in a faithful way – that is, so that formlessness is preserved. Formlessing is rooted in the way the image is set up aesthetically so that the fiction that the filmed body is to host remains tied to the materiality and the duration in which the profilmic body is made available to the camera. Formlessness does not precede the event of the image, just as otherness does not precede the encounter with the other.

The formless body becomes a theatricalisation of the fact that the body of the other is in surplus of referential regimes of meaning. It undermines the viewer's illusion of having control over the bodies onscreen (dependent on forming the latter into meaningful entities), dismantling the subject/object dynamic. While the latter assumes a distance responsible for a violent subsumption of alterity, the formless body emerges from the withdrawal of the filmed body from the domain of the visible. It can be said to evoke an ethics of hospitality that is associated more with touch than vision – an ethics that, to borrow from Joanna Zylinska, 'implies the possibility, and danger, of the intrusion of the unpresentable, of what we cannot yet know or name, into the confined territory of the self'.[80] Through the formlessing of the body of the other, the viewing self becomes already persecuted – denoting less the activity of viewing than the receptivity of being touched.[81]

The metaphor of touch in Levinasian thought signifies not 'the mastering spontaneity of vision' but, as Ewa Ziarek notes, 'contiguity, contact, and exposure to the outside'.[82] As Levinas asserts in *Totality and Infinity*, the exposure to the other manifests itself in the immediacy of proximity as 'caress'; the latter as that in which 'the body already denudes itself of its very form, offering itself as erotic nudity'.[83] As opposed to the hand that grasps and possesses, the caress

> consists in seizing upon nothing, in soliciting what ceaselessly escapes its form toward a future never future enough, in soliciting what slips away as though it *were not yet*. It searches, it forages. It is not an intentionality of disclosure but of search: a movement unto the invisible.[84]

The caress, according to Philippe Crignon, is not a seizure as it is 'a hand that seeks without ever finding'. A radically alternative mode of approaching the other, the caress is a 'self-sufficient way of relating to the other's flesh'; a flesh that is not a presence but is always to come.[85] Evoking the non-frontal within the visual, the caress 'grasps nothing' and, most crucially, 'does not expect anything from the thing'. It is, in a certain sense, a 'contact that holds back, for what it touches . . . is no less scarcely a phenomenon than the face itself'.[86] Levinas underlines this power of the carnal by establishing a link between a caress, formlessness and aversion to the dominance of 'content'.[87] The caress in this sense is not what is represented within the diegetic world but what is evoked when vision, by formlessing, is exposed to fail in exhausting what breaks through the frontal visual field. Nor should the caress be taken literally and outside the hyperboles of Levinasian thought. More precisely, the caress is an originary affectability that resides in the structure of ethical exposure – it is that to which the image bears witness through the process of formlessing. The proximity to the formless body is intimately linked to pre-reflective sensibility, while implying not a closeness in terms of geometrical space (contained forms of meaning appearing at hand within the frontal) but an immersion in a lived and affectively charged one.[88]

The formless body ceases to be a sturdy anchor of subjectivity. The thingness of the human body is captured by the cinematographic machine and Dumont, like Bazin, seems to find something authentic in this inhumanity. There is something obscene yet profound in the way the other submits its body to the camera – to a machine that does not interrogate the body by recourse to an identification of its descriptive and narrative attributes. Something of that submission must be retained if the gaze is to be altered and the other is to be appreciated. Dumont's elusive images exhibit this contradictory play of obscenity and ethicity. His static shots that linger on things, pan-shots that track the movements of the body, long shots that dwarf human figures or tight framings that fragment the body offer a certain appreciation of the human others, despite the strangeness or reprehensibility that their bodies or violent actions induce.

In Dumont's cinema, stressing the peculiarities of the profilmic body to resist an eye that desires form culminates in a certain enhanced indexicality – yet one detached from notions of familiarity that are often associated with the index. Indexicality is not tied with realisms of the body (as where the ethical and the aesthetic intersect) if it is to be understood and practised as a production of familiarity and a return to the same – the latter as a consciousness that is constituted through a certain recognition of for-consciousness. The physical inscription as the result of the existential bond between the image and the profilmic body acts as a certain making-unfamiliar. Indeed, the thrust of Dumont's images is not to be reduced to the questions of verisimilitude, resemblance or plausibility (consider Pharaon as the never credible detective in *L'Humanité*, the wandering miracle worker in *Hors Satan* or the head-banging Joan of Arc in *Jeannette*). Instead of yearning familiarity or faithful observation, Dumont's realism is mainly indebted to his focus on the body of the other while his camera provides the premises for a rewatching of the body not to render it meaningful but to theatricalise its urgent but inaccessible materiality.

Formlessing is facilitated by Dumont's choice of non-professionals but also by the settings he picks. He appears to be interested not in the social context so much as in what it enables in terms of bodily presentation. As Morrey contends, Dumont's approach to filmmaking is only 'deceptively social',[89] as his 'scrupulously materialist *mise en scéne*' centres the body at the core of the 'dramatic arc and narrative meaning' of his films.[90] Setting his films in Bailleul in northern France does not necessarily indicate Dumont's concern with unemployment as a social problem but, as David Vasse observes in *La vie de Jésus*, it demonstrates his interest in 'inactivity as an idea for *mise en scéne*, the largely goalless trajectories of these young men on their mopeds giving the shape and rhythm to the film'.[91] Dumont, according to Jean-Michel Frodon, 'invented for himself a position from which he can show everything', where shots of the body are 'born from a necessity of *mise en scéne* rather than a narrative obligation'.[92] Indeed, Dumont's actor-less aesthetics and his focus on the common human are a return to the fact that everything is filmable. Most crucially, returning to a radical equality of filmability where the image of any actuality is automatically affirmed by the thing's sheer thereness before the camera is a return that provides the conditions for the claim of the image. With a return to an infinite filmability, it is the image that decides that this filmed body (nothing else) must appear but must also persist onscreen. After all, out of an infinity of filmable fragments of the real, this particular thing (body) is/ has been before the camera and sustained by the image. That said, the filmed body does not appear as readily meaningful, and persists in its weird density. There is a purpose in giving the body. Giving is not just purposeful but also meaningful – but a meaningfulness prior to form because it is not supplemented (by frameworks of intelligibility). Giving is the event of meaning.

Notes

1. Levinas, *Totality and Infinity*, 191–2. Form 'offers a surface that covers a depth, a front hiding what lies behind'. See Crignon, 'Figuration', 104–5.
2. Kenaan, *The Ethics of Visuality*, 30.
3. Dziga Vertov, *Kino-Eye*, 14–15. See also Shaviro, *The Cinematic Body*, 31 and Benjamin, *Illuminations*, 233–4.
4. Schoonover, *Brutal Vision*, xxix.
5. Ibid., 43. Also see Bazin, *What Is Cinema?, vol. 1*, 37–8.
6. Schoonover, *Brutal Vision*, 43.
7. Cited in Overbey, *Springtime in Italy*, 84–5.
8. To demonstrate the uncompromising resistance of the face, Levinas envisions the absence of form by using the term 'nudity' instead of 'formlessness'. Formlessness implies a 'deficiency' or 'privation', whereas the absence of form, 'not having a form' is, 'for the face as for the flesh, a positive determination'. See Crignon, 'Figuration', 104.
9. Schoonover, *Brutal Vision*, 3.
10. Keathley, *Cinephilia and History*, 48. Cited in Schoonover, *Brutal Vision*, 42.
11. Schonig, 'Italian Neorealism and Gesture', uploaded to YouTube by *Film & Media Studies with Jordan Schonig* channel on December 6, 2020, <youtu.be/A3tdDdKDCv8> (last accessed 25 April 2022).
12. Cardullo, *André Bazin and Italian Neorealism*, 116.
13. Schoonover, 'Wastrels of Time', 70.

14 Bazin, 'The French Renoir', 90. 'Essential cinema', for Bazin, can be found in 'straightforward photographic respect for the unity of space'. See Bazin, 'The Virtues and Limitations of Montage', 47.
15 Schoonover, *Brutal Vision*, xxvii.
16 Ibid.
17 Ibid., xxviii–xxix.
18 Ibid., xxvii.
19 Gallafent, 'The Dandy and the Magdalen', 68. Cited in Çağlayan, *Poetics of Slow Cinema*, 44. Also as Matilda Mroz argues: 'What for one viewer might seem too long for another might offer a moment of elongated rapture.' Mroz, *Temporality and Film Analysis*, 41. Also see Henderson, 'The Long Take', 314–24.
20 Çağlayan, *Poetics of Slow Cinema*, 51.
21 Ibid.
22 According to Bazin, 'cinema is objectivity in time. The film is no longer content to preserve the object, enshrouded as it were in an instant . . . Now, for the first time, the image of things is likewise the image of their duration, change mummified as it were.' See Bazin, 'The Ontology of the Photographic Image', 14–15.
23 See Schoonover, *Brutal Vision*, 29–31. Also see Daney, 'The Screen of Fantasy (Bazin and Animals)'.
24 Schoonover, *Brutal Vision*, 43.
25 Ibid., 53.
26 Ibid., 33.
27 Ibid.
28 Doane, *The Emergence of Cinematic Time*, 22.
29 Schoonover, *Brutal Vision*, 40–1.
30 Cited in Hughes, 'Bruno Dumont's Bodies'.
31 Webber, 'Dumont, Bataille, and the Materialist Sacred', 73–4.
32 Ibid., 74.
33 Rubin, 'Corporeal Affects and Fleshy Vulnerability'.
34 Cited in Webber, 'Dumont, Bataille, and the Materialist Sacred', 76.
35 Cited in Walton, 'Film and/as Devotion', 195. For a discussion of space in Dumont's cinema, see Williams, 'Topographies of Being'.
36 Morrey, *The Legacy of the New Wave in French Cinema*, 112. Also, see Alligier, *Bruno Dumont: L'animalité et la grâce*, 30.
37 Webber, 'Dumont, Bataille, and the Materialist Sacred', 75.
38 Hughes, 'Bruno Dumont's Bodies'.
39 Douglas Morrey, *The Legacy of the New Wave in French Cinema*, 114.
40 Walton, 'Film and/as Devotion', 192.
41 Cited in Beugnet, *Cinema and Sensation*, 105.
42 Ibid., 104.
43 Walton, 'Film and/as Devotion', 195.
44 See Watkins, 'Robert Bresson's Heirs', 769.
45 Beugnet, *Cinema and Sensation*, 94–5.
46 See Webber, 'Dumont, Bataille, and the Materialist Sacred', 76.
47 Cited in Beugnet, *Cinema and Sensation*, 60.
48 Watkins, 'Robert Bresson's Heirs', 769.

49 Jones, 'L'Humanité', 73.
50 Birks and Coulthard, 'Divine Comedies', 247.
51 Ibid., 253.
52 Schoonover, *Brutal Vision*, 44.
53 See Walton, 'Film and/as Devotion', 192.
54 See ibid., 190.
55 This can be seen to be reminiscent of Bresson's famous quote that 'Nine-tenths of our movements obey habit and automatism. It is anti-nature to subordinate them to will and to thought.' See Bresson, *Notes on Cinematography*, 11.
56 Birks and Coulthard, 'Divine Comedies', 261.
57 Ibid., 254.
58 Ibid.
59 Ibid.
60 Hughes, 'Bruno Dumont's Bodies'.
61 Cited in Walton. 'Film and/as Devotion', 191. See Tancelin, Ors and Jouve, *Bruno Dumont*.
62 Walton. 'Film and/as Devotion', 191–2.
63 Margulies, 'Bodies Too Much', 3.
64 Hansen, 'Introduction', xxi. Overall, Kracauer's as well as Bazin's insistence on the affinity of the film with the material world is in conformity with their shared belief in 'cinema's unique ability to provide us with access to a profilmic event'. See Kouvaros, '"We Do Not Die Twice"', 376.
65 See Webber, 'Dumont, Bataille, and the Materialist Sacred', 83.
66 Walton, 'Film and/as Devotion', 190–1.
67 Ibid., 189.
68 Hughes, 'Bruno Dumont's Bodies'.
69 Bowles, 'The Life of Jesus (La Vie de Jésus)', 52.
70 Kendall, 'No God But Cinema', 411.
71 Birks and Coulthard, 'Divine Comedies', 258. See Keohane, 'Dismembering and Remembering Childhood in Bruno Dumont's *P'tit Quinquin*'.
72 Kasman and Walker, 'On the Verge of Heaven'. A conversation in Cannes Film Festival uploaded to YouTube on 26 May 2017, <youtu.be/PBYlxdIomPc> (last accessed 20 June 2022).
73 Ibid.
74 See Douglas Morrey, *The Legacy of the New Wave in French Cinema*, 117.
75 Birks and Coulthard, 'Divine Comedies', 259.
76 Ibid.
77 See Kasman and Walker, 'On the Verge of Heaven'. Also, see González, 'Interview (with Bruno Dumont)'.
78 Webber, 'Dumont, Bataille, and the Materialist Sacred', 85.
79 See Bataille, 'Base Materialism and Gnosticism'. Also, see Crowley, Hegarty, 'The Interminable Detour of Form', 186. For both Bataille and Levinas, the beyond is 'the beyond thought, beyond the idea, beyond form: it is the singular, what Bataille calls *l'informe*, the formless'. See Horowitz, 'Bringing Bataille to Justice', 129. Also, see Noys, 'Georges Bataille's Base Materialism'.
80 Zylinska, 'The Future . . . Is Monstrous', 223.

81 A receptivity that can be translated as 'here I am'. See Levinas, *Otherwise Than Being*, 114.
82 Ziarek, 'The Ethical Passions', 82.
83 Levinas, *Totality and Infinity*, 258.
84 Ibid., 257–8. This conception of caress is closely relation to Levinas's account of Eros (and love) as the latter consists in avoiding fusion, possession and knowledge. See ibid., 261. According to Crignon, 'Eros does not put me in relation with anything that is a presence, an existent, but, on the contrary, with something that always eludes me in a 'later', that is always to come'. See Crignon, 'Figuration', 110.
85 Crignon, 'Figuration', 110. In a caress, Levinas writes in *Otherwise Than Being*, 'what is there is sought as though it were not there'. See Levinas, *Otherwise Than Being*, 90.
86 Crignon, 'Figuration', 105.
87 According to Levinas, 'the caress does not know what it seeks . . . [It is a] not knowing, a game with something slipping away, a game absolutely without project or plan, not with what can become ours or us but with something other, always other, always inaccessible, and always still to come. The caress is the anticipation of this pure future without content.' See Levinas, *Time and the Other*, 89. Cited in Downing, 'Re-viewing the Sexual Relation', 62.
88 See Krueger, 'Levinasian Reflections on Somaticity and the Ethical Self', 612–13. Also, see Levinas, *Otherwise Than Being*, 75.
89 Douglas Morrey, *The Legacy of the New Wave in French Cinema*, 111.
90 Ibid., 113–14.
91 See Vasse, *Le Nouvel Âge du cinema d'auteur français*, 157. Cited in Morrey, *The Legacy of the New Wave in French Cinema*, 111
92 Frodon, 'À bras le corps dans l'enfer du Nord', *Le Monde*, 5 June 1997. Cited in Morrey, *The Legacy of the New Wave in French Cinema*, 115.

6

Re-enactment, Proxies and the Facing Image

'Loosely based' on the Columbine massacre – almost every text on Gus Van Sant's *Elephant* (2003) starts with this. Critics and commentators appear to unanimously share the contention that, despite being inspired by the real massacre, the film also takes a path of its own, or at least allows itself more freedom in the path it takes in narrating the event. But what does it exactly mean to say that a fictional film is loosely based on a real event? What is considered loose in such a description? And what fictionality and reality are at stake when we point out looseness as what characterises the connection? Being based loosely on a real event is less a matter of emphasising the 'looseness' of a connection than an indication of the existence and persistence of the connection despite all the looseness. It is not that first there is a connection and only then a loosening takes place as an extension, modification or failure of the connection. On the contrary, the connection is that which is posited by the looseness. It is what persists and is thus reaffirmed despite the originary looseness. In addition, the latter, if taken in a broad sense, fails to add anything meaningful to the fiction–reality connection. It is so true that it fails to make any sense. Even if we accept the suspicious assumption that there exists something called 'reality' as an independent, pre-existing entity, a fictional film that is based on real events cannot be identical to the reality it claims to portray. It is a re-presentation and, by extension, a fictionalisation. The question of fiction–reality connection is better formulated as a matter of adequation, rather than identity. Adequation is a making adequate – making stories, images and aesthetic devices and decisions adequate to the reality that the film represents. Adequation is an implicit acknowledgement of a gap, of a looseness that should be bridged, but only through the work of bridging and making-adequate.

Adequation sees its success in an annihilation of looseness, itself a matter of wishful thinking than of factuality. By contrast, being loosely based on a real event, as that which seems to characterise *Elephant*'s cinematic take on the shootings, implies a deliberate failure in making adequate. Looseness is not simply an explanation regarding a connection; it is more a matter of delineating an orientation. It implies a certain performative failure. The film puts the failure to work to highlight an originary ungraspability, the denial of which is the basis for any (false) claim to the adequacy of realism. *Elephant* enacts a break with the cliché-laden conception of being (firmly) based on a real event to problematise the authenticity that such a conception presupposes and promotes. Being authentic is no longer a matter of providing an identifiable, familiar image of reality. It does not involve a consensus that affirms the faithfulness of the fiction to the reality of the event. Rather, it primarily concerns a certain problematisation of such an image, its givenness and ultimately its impotence in addressing the viewer beyond predefined frameworks.

What is this address that the familiarity of a given image of reality fails to maintain? How is it significant in terms of the tension between the ethical and the visual? What are the ethical implications and risks of bringing the shooting event into the viewer's visual field by re-enactment? And why is it crucial to evoke ethics as a critique of 'making adequate' in the face of a tragic event? It is my contention here that Van Sant acknowledges the violence inherent in portraying an event whose ethical claim is disproportionate to figuration. Yet he does not shy away from the image. Van Sant's approach to the event resides in a commitment: the real death of the other has to be retold, not through a proper retelling but a certain 'untelling' – a performative failure that disrupts the adequacy of the image to the claim of the horror. Van Sant's commitment resonates with the Levinasian 'reduction' – the said is a necessary betrayal that has to be unsaid so that the saying, as the ethical exposure to the other, can be reaffirmed.

To do justice to the bodies involved in the shooting, Van Sant gives himself a certain freedom. It is not the freedom of an artist who is playful with 'historical facts'. He frees himself from the limitations of a mainstream re-enactment of the event precisely to achieve what goes missing in canonised responses to such tragic events. Van Sant is inclined to find something alternative in this virtual encounter with the bodies involved in the shooting by negotiating with the technological realism of cinema. He stages a peculiar encounter between the cinematographic machine and the proxies – real high schoolers as non-actors brought onscreen to embody the real bodies of the victims, perpetrators and eyewitnesses involved in the Columbine shooting. Van Sant turns the image into an exhibition of high school bodies that, rather than make sense of the senselessness of the event, attests to its otherness and reaffirms its claim on the viewer.

Elephant uses the high schoolers of a real high school and is shot on location where they study. In a certain way, the film bypasses the need to transform the profilmic bodies to deliver readability. The bodies, as found things on location, evoke the high school life and short-circuit the conversion of the profilmic body. Moreover, Van Sant gives the body-proxies freedom in terms of moving in space. The non-actors are even given room for improvisation while unintended and accidental gestures are foregrounded. What results is a defamiliarisation: it is precisely by evoking the familiar image of high school life that the filmed bodies turn the image into something incomplete – into a failure. In *Elephant*, as we shall see, the familiar image of high school life is fragmented, displaced and ultimately contaminated with unmotivated durations.

Spatialisation and the failure of drama in *Elephant*

Elephant is committed to writing the other through the said. It is equally committed to preserving the thrust of the saying, as the ethical exposure to the other that interrupts the adequacy of the said. Vans Sant's intervention as performative failure is significant against the backdrop of dominant approaches to the Columbine school shootings. Presumably self-evident claims to the truth are mostly informed by the gravity of the event: two ordinary students killing thirteen people including students and staff members of the school at which they studied before killing themselves. It is a tragic event that causes anxiety and attracts a great deal of curiosity. Most importantly, it leads to a desire for a restoration of order – or at least the solace of an impression of such a restoration. News coverage of the shootings claims access to the truth by an inclusion of real-time coverage of the event and its aftermath, by providing footage from CCTV cameras, and presenting interviews with actual eyewitnesses and analyses from a group of sociologists, psychologists and criminologists who evoke certain discourses to shape the truth by making the event meaningful. Even if the experts express their shock by asserting that the crime did not make any sense or the massacre was senseless, their preoccupation with meaning remains untouched. What remains the primary concern is a certain conception of realism that regards it as a matter of adequation. Pivotal is a hunt for images, words, analyses and discursive propositions that are considered adequate to the event – a making-adequate that is more a matter of making the event adequate to pre-existing discursive formulations, and of containing the horror by explaining it away. Even though the media and the experts initially acknowledge the otherness of the event – the fact that it brings forth a certain shock that demands response – the realism as adequation that they defend turns out to be an annihilation of this otherness. It ends up being a working through, a successful work of mourning that aims to contain the trauma. It moves beyond not only the bodies of the irreversibly lost others but also the ethical claim that such losses call forth.

Van Sant himself gestures towards his cinematic intervention as a response in the face of this hypersensitivity.[1] However, his intervention seems, from the outset, a frustrating one simply because his response to the event seems to stubbornly downplay the largely accepted requirements of a responsible approach. Writing a review on the film in *Variety* while aiming to address the public, who have the shootings still lingering in their collective memory, Todd McCarthy opens his attack on the film with an unreserved condemnation: making 'a film about something like the Columbine student shootings incident and provid[ing] no insight or enlightenment would seem to be pointless at best and irresponsible at worst, and that is what Gus Van Sant has done in "Elephant"'.[2] He continues by describing the film as a 'failed attempt to find a fresh method to deal dramatically with a traumatic topic'.[3] McCarthy's remarks are emblematic of an understanding of the film common to many film viewers and critics, summarising what is normally expected from a preformulated and thus largely accepted response to the shooting event. Most significantly, these remarks condemn the film on account of its irresponsibility and its failure. McCarthy is unambiguous in his use of the terms as he clearly associates responsibility with a commitment to providing insight and enlightenment and he understands failure as opposed to success in dealing dramatically with the event. It is as if a responsible response to the event should have resulted in a better, more adequate understanding of it, and of its conditions of possibility; apparently more adequate than what has been presented to the viewer mainly through the news and media coverage. Moreover, it is presumed that a responsible response would have found its best cinematic actualisation in a dramatisation of the event. *Elephant* frustrates McCarthy and those who share his stance, as it offers no new insight into the nature of the event. What it does is rearticulate all the presumed causes and motivations assumed to be responsible for the event, which have been repeatedly recycled by the media and its accompanying discourses. It also avoids a presentation of these elements within a dramatically justified whole where all bits and pieces simply fit in and make sense. In short, *Elephant,* as a cinematic take on the shootings, is unsurprisingly deemed uncommitted and immoral.[4]

The conception of responsibility that is assumed in these accounts is one that is blind to its own irresponsible foundations and assumptions. William G. Little deconstructs this normatively conservative notion by spotlighting the ethical risks that inhere in a cinematic re-enactment of the shooting event:

> Why respond to a traumatizing event of this kind by re-creating it? How is the viewer to respond to such a text? More broadly, is it possible for cinema to offer a responsible response to acts of violence such as this one?[5]

Little moves further to couple the question of re-enactment with otherness: 'How does a filmmaker produce a fictional narrative that makes real death's incalculability count? What would a film look like that strove, responsibly, to plot death's "pure contingency", its radical drift'?[6] By associating the question of responsibility with the risks of representation (Little is most concerned with the representation of death onscreen), he decouples responsibility from its pathological undertones. Responsibility, understood in this alternative way, is less a matter of diagnosis and cure, a matter of providing 'fresh' ways of comprehending the event to tackle it, than a matter of reflecting upon the risks that inhere in this apparently benevolent decision of narrating the shootings. Rather than consider an adequate representation of the event as the benchmark of responsibility, Little's approach, if followed to its fullest potential, is aimed at highlighting the ethical implications of representation in general and of a conventional dramatisation in particular. The critical practice of *Elephant* that resides in its being 'loosely based on' the Columbine massacre is not simply critical of the society it depicts (it certainly is). It is critical of a way of looking that fails to expose itself to, also fails to allow itself to be affected by, the otherness of the event beyond its discursive formulation. Rather than turn the Columbine massacre into a theme and subsequently trying to be adequate to it, the film takes itself, and ultimately the devices traditionally associated with realism, as a theme to open up room for reflecting upon the violence intrinsic to certain established forms of looking and storytelling. This alternative way of addressing the event primarily resides in a certain concern with the body of the other, with how it is enacted and put on the screen and how it persists and withdraws. For Van Sant, the question of re-enactment is bound up with the withdrawal of the filmed bodies.

Elephant's alternative engagement with the human others involved in the Columbine shooting is predominantly evident in its approach to story time.

By narrating the diegetic events in a simultaneous manner and by forgoing the sequentialism of a more conventional rendition, *Elephant* grounds its mode of narration in the form of a spatialisation. *Elephant* spatialises time to avoid the simplification that resides in a linear recounting of the story. Rather than proceed from a fully articulated beginning to a fully designated narrative tension and then continue towards a determinate resolution, the film instead focuses mostly on the final ten minutes prior to the shooting incident and expands this segment into the whole running time of the film.[7] Expanding the time of the narrative, *Elephant* turns its story into a sort of expanded present that comprises multiple spaces, perspectives and durations.[8]

Elephant refuses to focus merely on specific characters, as protagonists or otherwise, who might act as the main agents that progress the story by their dramatic actions and decisions. It instead aims to open up space so as to include a multiplicity of perspectives of numerous students within the school who, in one way or another, are involved in the shootings, as perpetrators, victims or passive witnesses and observers. A linear rendition of the events would have emphasised the trajectory of the two perpetrators towards their violent act, leaving the other students and staff members within the school as mere secondary characters who are supposed to supplement the main two characters' plans. By contrast, *Elephant* uses title cards to introduce characters (or group of characters), each evoking certain archetypes of high school life. Starting with John and his drunken father, whom John is apparently taking care of, the film proceeds to recount the seemingly banal daily activities of a number of other students including Elias, the calm, compassionate and devoted photographer who is taking random pictures to develop his portfolio; Nathan and Carrie, the couple, who seem to attract a considerable deal of attention and envy from other students; Acadia, who seems to have an attentive, generous attitude towards the others; Michelle, the marginalised 'geek' whose appearance and behaviour are often criticised and mocked by others; Brittany, Jordan and Nicole, the 'popular girls' who manifest a constant inclination to bully and gossip; and Eric and Alex, the bullied, isolated and marginalised students who execute the shooting.

This emphasis on simultaneity and downplaying single causes for the tragedy has understandably prompted discussions according to which this spatialisation is read to be an acknowledgement of the complexity of the event and its underlying situation. By deploying 'a non-linear and looping narrative structure that fragments a seemingly ordinary day at school',[9] Tiago de Luca argues, *Elephant* subverts a linear progression that assumes a causal, unidirectional movement to be captured instead a broader context of

160 The Eye of the Cinematograph

Figure 6.1 Introducing multiple characters through title cards and extended screen time in *Elephant* (Gus Van Sant, 2003).

events that inform the tragedy. Spatialisation opens room for a presentation of multiple social, cultural and psychological factors that shape the situation. It forms a constellation of clues and reasons, one hardly imaginable in a linear unfolding of events and thus often excluded by the latter as a narrative impossibility. De Luca emphasises that this formal presentation should not be read as mere aestheticism,[10] but, I would add, as the way in which *Elephant* provides a responsible response to the event through a recognition of complexity. *Elephant*'s 'political power derives from the way it averts a representational logic, opting instead to "present" a problem that cannot be accommodated into a neat problem-solving narrative but which instead demands a formal treatment that acknowledges its intricate complexity'.[11] This acknowledgement of complexity is often accompanied by a similar stress on the freedom that the film grants the viewer in interpreting the events that unfold onscreen. Spatialisation is read as a certain opening up of a multiplicity of interpretations and a democratisation of meaning-making. Associating an uncritical emphasis on forced interpretations with a receiving of 'information', Van Sant regards his filmmaking practice in *Elephant* as an attempt to call forth a viewer who has the space to formulate their own take on the event, thus escaping the otherwise undemocratic, top-down flow of information. However, it is essential to ask here whether what *Elephant* achieves in terms of doing justice to the otherness of the event is irreducible to a granting of freedom to the audience to interpret.

Reworking realist aesthetics: the long take, fragmentation and resistance to meaning

Elephant's spatialising structure problematises a didactic and pathological understanding of responsibility in favour of an alternative notion of the latter. A genuinely responsible approach seems to concern itself, first, with a recognition of the irreducibility of the bigger picture to simplified causes and, second, with an obligation to grant the viewer the freedom and privilege to bring into play their own share of opinions and time to reflect.[12] However, regarding *Elephant* as an acknowledgement of complexity and a promotion of spectatorial democratisation only constitutes a first step towards understanding Van Sant's realism of the body. It is insufficient as it fails to enact a radical break with the normative force of adequation. Speaking of complexity not only presupposes that the whole is graspable (acknowledging the difficulty to grasp leaves the question of graspability untouched), but also uncritically assumes that the will to grasp and capture is in itself righteous and justified. Responsibility understood in this way is a matter of modesty and caution while it effectively anticipates the possible or future grasp (the event might not be grasped through a simple dramatisation, but certain formal experiments can equip us with the necessary means to achieve it).

This approach calls forth a specific correlation between responsibility and realism that is problematic. Contending that a film is realist precisely because it attests to the complexity of the situation it aims to portray reduces realism to model/copy binarism. According to this paradigm, a realist work is a derivative that gains its value from its faithfulness to what is conceived of, or is presumed to be, the original: the real event. What this paradigm keeps untold and concealed is that the original is never the 'real' event itself but its given, established image. Faithfulness is not automatically achieved and simply evaluated based on a detailed, loyal attention to what happened and took place. Rather, it is affirmed through a recognition of the familiarity of an image. In this formulation, realism stands out as adequation and images are forced to conform to the givenness of a pre-existing image of reality, while the latter is already detached from any significant negotiation with reality and the gravity of its address due to the automatised responses it provokes.

Elephant's intervention gains its significance by taking issue with this notion of realist practice.[13] What *Elephant* does is not to be more adequate to a given image that appears as realistic. Rather, it problematises the question of adequation as a constitutive factor of realism. The film does not treat the real shootings as an original of which it is a copy – a paradigm that, by definition, evaluates the copy based on its adequacy and regards a progressive realist endeavour as an attempt at being 'more' adequate. The model as the given image of reality is already displaced within the film. Being loosely based on as performative failure is the first and most essential step that *Elephant* takes towards problematising the model/copy paradigm. Rather than reduce itself to a derivative that is ultimately aimed at capturing the 'essential truth' of the original, *Elephant* treats the real event as a call for response. The tragic event is evoked not as that which is merely too complex and sophisticated and is thus in need of a more rigorous investigation. It is that which addresses, and whose address must be reaffirmed.

Elephant's reworking of realism is therefore enacted with a certain orientation: to attest to the otherness of the event and the bodies involved in it, executed through a certain making-available of bodies, gestures, fragments and durations. The film brings forth a specific form of resistance through a de-hierarchisation and a dismantling of the given image of the event, a radical exhaustion of interpretation and a critical reworking of realist aesthetics that render meaning-making redundant and instead heighten a specifically cinematic exposure to the filmed bodies. Spatialisation recognises complexity, but only to dismantle it and thereby attest to an otherness that escapes the questions of complexity and the accompanying politics of adequation. *Elephant* provides a different mode of address and form of engagement with images. It calls forth the event of the image – *Elephant*'s images not only bear the promise of a story on the way to being told but also harbour a certain incompleteness that stages the withdrawal of the filmed bodies. For Van Sant, doing justice to the human other requires a retelling of their death by bringing it to the visual field. But it is equally crucial for him to account for what this breakthrough of the body of the other does to the visual. While re-enactment involves a certain referentiality (referring to a real event), *Elephant*'s referentiality is of a peculiar kind as it is bound up with a certain concern with the bodies in the profilmic.

Both in its production methods and in the ways in which it sets up images, *Elephant* adopts a certain cinematic style in which aesthetic devices and strategies traditionally associated with realism are identifiable. Deploying non-actors, and giving them room for improvisation, location shooting and inclusion of unbroken shots and long takes place *Elephant* within realist traditions. With an explicit Zavattinian tone, Van Sant's own words demonstrate his inclination towards realist aesthetics and the implication of his film within the latter:

> Hollywood busies itself with ultra-scene changing, getting quickly in and out of places. But a lot of stories happen in our lives when we park six blocks away and walk. If we can show walking slowly to a mailbox and back, it can be a brilliant, brilliant film.[14]

Elephant does not however show an uncritical adherence to normative understandings of realism according to which a deployment of certain devices and techniques qualify a film as realist. Its fragmentation of the bigger picture and incessant problematisation of the dominant calls for making-adequate are already far removed from realism as a predefined set of aesthetic decisions. Rather, *Elephant*'s radical critique of adequation finds its most challenging manifestations where it redefines realist devices and strategies. It revisits uncritical, conservative conceptions of realist aesthetics according to which aesthetic decisions are regarded as realist insofar as they conform to the requirements of adequation. For André Bazin, as Lisa Trahair observes, there is a critical distinction 'between the true realism that derives from the aesthetic dimension of art and the pseudo-realism that is driven purely by psychological need and eventually satisfied with illusory appearances'.[15] *Elephant*, aligned with this Bazinian notion, sees realism not as a production of familiarity through recognisable aesthetic devices but as what must be reinvented for alternative ethical possibilities to emerge.

An account of *Elephant* that reduces the realist thrust of the film to the question of adequation regards the coupling of the long take and spatialisation in the film as a multiplication of perspectives that is presumed to facilitate the grasp of the bigger picture and the domestication of profilmic bodies. A closer investigation of the film's spatialisation clearly reveals how *Elephant* frustrates what is habitually expected from a multiplicity of perspectives – that is, an expanded access to the story world through a presentation of multiple vantage points. *Elephant* evokes and deploys multiple perspectives just to expose them to failure. The tracking shots of the film work to establish a peculiar interaction between the camera and the profilmic body where an appreciation of the body of the other is prioritised over an adequate investigation of the shooting event. They problematise the privilege that a vantage point assumes. The camera makes journeys across the whole school and sometimes its independent movements heighten its embodied curiosity. On almost every occasion, however, extended durations deliberately fail to progress the narrative by lingering on bodies and fragments beyond a dramatically justified extent. The camera contaminates this curiosity with a level of contingency and undecidability that resists the meaningfulness and productivity that we might associate with curiosity. *Elephant* shows the scene in which John poses for Elias's camera in the hallway of the school three times; each time presented in a tracking shot following John, Elias and Michelle. Watching the same actions from multiple perspectives, especially when characters seemingly meet each other by chance while wandering around, is not in the service of providing fresh and in-depth insights into what is going on in the school. On the contrary, it effectively frustrates the function that a multiplicity of perspective is often associated with. Rather than create suspense, or parallel and in-depth information, the simultaneity that results from spatialisation brings time to the fore not to highlight dramatically significant moments but to arrest the rhythm and rationalisation inherent in dramatisation. *Elephant*'s peculiar manipulation of time fragments the high school life through a multiplication of perspectives while highlighting the sterility of cognitive exploration. There is no build-up, and the promise of in-depth portrayal of the bigger picture is evoked so that it can be frustrated.

The bigger picture is also dismantled and deferred through a deliberate allusion to the impossibility of the multiplication of perspectives. *Elephant* not only multiplies perspectives but also, more critically, reveals how this multiplication must be further developed to an extent that is uncontainable. To adequately capture the reality of the shootings, multiplicity must be extended to every student and their every non-dramatic moment. The expansion of the present tense must therefore overflow the boundaries of any cinematic narrative. One of the scenes in which this formal strategy is made evident is where the camera makes autonomous journeys through the school cafeteria. While, to this point, the film has followed its own structuralist, intrinsic norm (introducing characters by title cards and devoting time to their daily routines) the scene presents a deliberate break with the latter. Whereas the camera is supposed to merely follow Brittany, Jordan and Nicole in the section devoted to them,[16] the camera gains a floating quality by leaving the girls and making independent journeys through the cafeteria and the kitchen. It briefly presents other characters within the school (including kitchen staff and other students) who, each in their own right, allude to a perspective that could have been included within the film's spatialised screen duration. It is as if each student who is present at this specific high school has a singular perspective of their own and thus deserves a title card. This implies that accounting for all these perspectives for the bigger picture to be constructed is an impossibility. The open-endedness of perspectives is also emphasised by the manner in which this scene overtly stages and choreographs the introduction of characters in a reflexive way. The camera repeatedly shifts its focus to different people in the cafeteria while each of them reacts to the camera's floating attention by acting, improvising or spelling out the lines predefined for them. The scene further attests to the sterility of an inclusion of multiple perspectives by showing how arbitrary the inclusion of perspectives is. It also demonstrates how contingent the inclusion is upon the floating movements of the camera and upon what is staged for it. Emblematic of the whole film, the scene demonstrates that the camera is neither following the characters nor simply operating autonomously in relation to the action onscreen. Every action and movement is staged for it. This contingency, impossibility and deliberate failure gain another considerable manifestation in the film through the title card and introduction of Benny. Introducing him in the final minutes of the film and during the shootings, the film devotes a title card to him just a couple of seconds before he gets killed by one of the shooters. While up to this point each title card has been accompanied by an extended screen time, Benny's late introduction and his short life onscreen attest to how open-ended the spatialisation could potentially be simply because any other student within the high school could similarly gain a title card.

The spatialisation of *Elephant* embodies a certain open-endedness also because the ones who gain screen duration and visual attention are not necessarily more significant than those who do not. Nor do they possess significant narrative agency throughout the film. Spatialisation is a sort of de-hierarchisation that refers to the deliberate arbitrariness of the filmic structure. It demonstrates that *Elephant* could have included other characters and still fulfilled and achieved the same dramatic ends. The bigger picture is further fragmented due to the alternative economy of inclusion/exclusion on which the film is based – a disruption of a rationalised, economical narrative that would be selective in choosing which students should gain screen time to make the narrative more adequate to the event.[17]

It can be argued that by evoking archetypes the film aims to select characters that can effectively represent the bigger picture of high school life. Instead of 'an overarching story line', according to Jennifer A. Rich, *Elephant* 'introduces a succession of students who evoke archetypes – the jock, the sensitive boy, the alienated loners, the plain girl and the cold beauty queens – while being barely distinguished as victims and perpetrators'.[18] This argument, despite its initial intrigue, fails to account for the specific ways in which *Elephant* presents the archetypes. The film evokes the archetypes as givens – as the unit that shapes the given image of a high school life 'reality' – just to dismantle this picture. Giving each archetype an extended duration of their own, granting each a screen time that frustrates exhaustive narrative or dramatic signification, *Elephant* alludes to the archetypes but at the same time gives them an unusual, heightened life of their own onscreen which is too much to be reducible to a simple constituent within the bigger picture. Each of the durations devoted to John, Michelle, Elias and others gains a singularity and irreducibility. It is as though the bricks that are supposed to make possible the edifice of the bigger picture resist being exhaustively exploited in the service of its creation. The students are not only not fashioned into a proper plot, they are also presented such that their belonging to student high school life, to what would be considered as a collective life or a community, is problematised. It is not simply because their interactions with one another are most of the time limited, cold and emotionless in nature. Each of them is implicated within an extended duration that equips the images with an inexhaustible particularity and thus disrupts the representation that an archetype is assumed to facilitate.

Fragments overflow their potential instrumentalisation precisely because *Elephant* is predominantly based on a forced juxtaposition of fragments. It is not that fragments already bear the traces of the bigger picture and what the film does is merely actualise their potential fitting together. Fragments are indissociable from the durations attached to them. More importantly, durations carry and impose their own claim – the viewer can never deny the actuality of the durations, the way they sustain the bodies and things onscreen. The walking and wandering bodies are too immersed in the duration of the profilmic as their initial context that they stubbornly resist exhaustion by any additional or secondary context. The filmed bodies do not unproblematically fall into their presumably predefined places in the bigger picture, despite their obvious belonging to high school life and their evocation of archetypes. They are too implicated within the time of their being made available to the camera such that a possible further re-contextualisation is exposed to failure from the outset. *Elephant* therefore creates its own *a posteriori* claim by turning itself into a manifestation of a given image of the community that is already tenuous.

Consider references to gun culture, bullying, marginalisation, broken homes, violent video games and social segregation. The camerawork in the scene in which the viewer sees Eric and Alex at home, the former playing the piano and the latter playing a violent, first-person shooter video game, introduces the clues and reasons precisely to disrupt their explanatory function. The 360-degree pan that scans the whole room dislocates the elements from their predefined place, turning them into mere clues to which the camera is simply referring. Just as the filmed bodies are unsustained, these clues are fragments within a de-hierarchised whole. They do not enjoy a special treatment but are merely included and are just simply there within the image rather than deployed and mobilised to justify the way in which *Elephant* grants its characters an irreducible life onscreen. The film presents an emphatic persistence of the image, thus prompting the viewer to pose questions about their relation to images. What is given and ready-at-hand – the bodies, fragments, archetypes and the insights into the conditions that breed such acts of violence and destruction – are evoked and staged not to reiterate and reclaim the given image of high school life and the event but precisely to displace them. The formal structure of the film renders redundant exhaustive attempts at reading the film precisely because the film is not based on reading clues and reasons but on their mere recycling. Speaking of the film as if it is a puzzle to solve,[19] and insisting exclusively on the freedom of the viewer in doing so, reappropriates the evidently de-hierarchised structure of the film in favour of the given image.

Little's reading of the tracking shots as an appreciation of otherness, as opposed to a comprehension of the latter, is revealing here. By deciding to 'track' the characters while 'refusing to plot them conventionally', the camera is transformed into a device that 'registers appreciation for the mysterious otherness of others, calling attention to its own limitations'.[20] Exposing its own limitation and thus failure in grasping the other, *Elephant* testifies to the otherness of the event and the bodies involved in it.

The reel-time: the giving of the profilmic

With the Columbine school shootings having been televised in real-time and the abundance of CCTV footage of the incident and its aftermath, and the circulation and availability of the footage,[21] *Elephant* as a realist cinematic take on the event is from the outset implicated within a complicated position. As de Luca rightly reminds us, *Elephant* is based on 'a radical assertion of the film medium's recording ability'.[22] However, what does automatic recording have to offer in *Elephant* as a re-enactment of the events? If realism is equated with an extended capture of what has happened in real time, then how would it be possible to demonstrate the realist thrust of *Elephant* while realism – as a capture of real time – is already achieved by other media to a great extent? It is as though *Elephant* is a derivative of the original televised event and gains its realism only through its secondary relation to what has been instantly affirmed and achieved by surveillance cameras. This notion can effectively disguise Van Sant's *Elephant* as a desperate, doomed effort to make the impression of real-time presentation and the instantaneity that results. In short, the film appears to be a belated, sterile effort.

Elephant introduces the everyday as one of the main devices to counter the hegemony of dramatisation in mainstream filmmaking (and in a more conventional rendition of the same story). According to Ira Jaffe, *Elephant* 'deploys techniques commonly associated with both realist cinema and slow movies. Not the least of these are long takes, which Bazin argued preserve the natural continuity of the time and space of everyday life.'[23] Similarly, Anna Backman Rogers associates the everyday with, once again, notions of complexity and the bigger picture:

> the reasons for this violence are far more socially complex and embedded in what we may overlook in the everyday. *Elephant* forces us to re-establish a link with our quotidian reality that has been broken due to our need to distance ourselves from, and thus morally 'explain away', any tragic event such as 'Columbine'.[24]

Rogers further contends that 'Van Sant's characteristic long takes serve here to emphasise the impression of real time and existence as duration . . . Van Sant forces the viewer to experience the sheer banality of their routines and idle chatter'.[25] By opposing the act of explaining away to an attentiveness to the banal and the quotidian, Rogers exposes the irresponsibility of a mere dramatisation in the face of the tragic event. However, her understanding of the everyday gains a normative stance in her assertion that the film restores what is often overlooked. Speaking of the everyday remains tied to the logic of representation despite the blatant fact that the long takes and extended durations of *Elephant* are detached from their traditional function, the latter regulated by the frameworks that govern our understanding of familiarity and givenness.

Most approaches to *Elephant* tend to describe its specific stylistic and formal presentations, and in particular the certain qualities that the film achieves mainly owing to its camerawork, with regard to an observational model. Bill Nichols defines observational filmmaking as a mode of approaching reality in which 'a direct engagement with the everyday life of subjects as observed by an unobtrusive camera' is emphasised.[26] Reading *Elephant* according to the observational model inevitably turns the focus from the filmic to the profilmic. It also brings to attention unobtrusiveness as a certain requirement. Highlighting *Elephant*'s preoccupation with the profilmic, de Luca emphasises the observational approach of the film by arguing that '[i]n order to highlight profilmic event at the expense of the fictional world, *Elephant* further appropriates techniques traditionally associated with the observational tradition of American documentary'.[27] According to de Luca, *Elephant* emulates 'fly-on-the-wall style, as in the shots whose framing composition conveys the impression that the camera simply happened to be there, recording whatever happened to be passing in front of it', while the viewer is left with 'the impression that the camera has captured these ordinary occurrences by chance'.[28] Along similar lines, Little regards this observational style as an impression of being unscripted: 'Throughout this uncut stretch, the camera drifts from figure to figure, making the filmic operation appear unscripted, improvisational.'[29]

These elaborations embody a certain contradiction. Speaking of the primacy of the profilmic presupposes that the latter has a reality in itself that the film borrows to provide itself with the realist thrust of observation. On the other hand, however, these accounts always assume or even explicitly refer to an impression of reality that *Elephant* provides through its observations. It is as though what the film is concerned with is primarily the creation of an impression of realness – a position that effectively undermines any claim regarding the genuine reality of the profilmic. *Elephant*'s style is a matter of staging bodies and fragments for the camera rather than a longing for impressions – including the impression that the camera 'happened' to be there to capture an 'unscripted' reality.[30] It is precisely in its preoccupation with the profilmic that *Elephant* succeeds in problematising the normative sense of observation that assumes the reality of the profilmic as a given.

Moreover, as Little reminds us, Van Sant's desire 'to create a pure index of high school experience' can be traced in 'his decisions to recruit non-professional actors and to shoot the film on location at a real high school'.[31] This attempt is accompanied by a certain enhancement of indexicality, which foregrounds the profilmic by emphasising the debt of the images to what has been before the camera. Images explicitly reflect the fact that their formation is a result of the interaction between what has been offered to the camera and its automatic recording. The profilmic participates in the re-enacting project and equally goes on to take on a quality that is not exhaustively justified or sustained. *Elephant* undermines the assumption that there is a pre-existing reality that the camera merely steps into and faithfully records. Van Sant makes evident how the reality of the profilmic is always already contaminated by the camera's presence. It is not that the characters are simply doing their daily stuff and the camera is merely following and observing them by tracking shots so much as that the filmed bodies are submitting themselves to the camera and are moving in somewhat choreographed ways for it. What is before the camera is staged. The filmed bodies are gesturing and moving for the camera.

There is a corporeal contingency inherent to employing non-actors and allowing them the room to improvise in their movements. *Elephant* not only deploys non-actors, it preserves this non-professionalism in the way that images are set up. These inadvertencies are, of course, primarily rooted in the originary manner in which the camera encounters the world before it. As Karl Schoonover observes with regards to film's capacity to screen contingencies:

> The inadvertent gesture, the blinking eye, the unplanned spasm, the random detail noticed only after the fact – these are elements of the image that the camera cannot help but record, and they remind us of how photographic media make images without and even in spite of conscious intent. For Bazin, the realist strength of photographic media derives from their ability to create an image without the intervention of human psychology.[32]

Elephant intensifies this degree zero relation to the real and exploits the non-professionalism of the non-actors and their discomfort before the camera to reveal how the real, profilmic bodies of students are affected by the conditions in which they are made available to the camera. The filmed bodies therefore carry this 'being made available' on them. Throughout the whole film, the non-actors implicitly but constantly reflect the presence of the camera through their often obvious expressions of discomfort and their clumsy performances. More importantly, this discomfort is inscribed within the images of *Elephant* and preserved. The non-actors most explicitly reflect the camera's presence in cases where they break the fourth wall by accidentally looking into the lens of the camera.[33] As Van Sant asserts, *Elephant* was 'designed so that whatever [was] shot was what was going to end up in the film'.[34] Preserving the first take at the expense of more takes, which would have resulted in a presumably desired actualisation of a pre-existing script, grants the images a peculiar quality. It is not that each long take of the film is forced into conformity with a pre-scripted, predefined 'model'. Including the first take in the final cut of the film destabilises the normativity of the model. The contingencies of the first take are prioritised over an obsession with fitting the shots into a pre-planned model. They allow the automaticity of the camera to have its say. What is crucial is not what a scene is supposed to convey – a quest for a certain aesthetic effect, impression or significance

Figure 6.2 The breaking of the fourth wall does not necessitate second takes in *Elephant* (Gus Van Sant, 2003).

that would necessitate going for multiple takes to achieve the highest impact. It is more a matter of allowing the contingencies of the first take (including bad acting) to stand out as the image's debt to the profilmic. More decisively, it is with respect to this debt that the images of the film are given the space to have a certain claim of their own. By subverting the primacy of the model and giving priority to the first take, *Elephant*'s images are provided with the capacity to attest to the irreplaceability and irreversibility of the reel-time. In the absence of the authority of the model, what is real is the bodies and fragments of high school life presented to the camera, while having inscribed on their surface the imprints of this giving.

Similarly, speaking of documentary style as a way of demonstrating the realist practice of *Elephant* neglects the essential hybridity of fiction film.[35] According to such a view, the film's parallelism (an oscillation between the fiction of characters and the documentary of the filmed bodies) is reduced to an approach that informs the audience of an independent, pre-existing reality in a truthful way (or in a way the truth content of which can be validated). Yet, in a parallel formulation, the documentary on the filmed bodies is contaminated by the fiction of characters, and thereby its truth content cannot be simply conceived as pure documentation. There is a filmic if not a thoroughly fictional purpose in making the students' bodies available to the camera and prompting them to move in space. In an early scene, the viewer is introduced to several students who are taking part in a group discussion about sexual preferences. In a single, unbroken shot, the camera pans to scan the faces of all the students present in the discussion. While the scene evidently adopts a documentary mode (overtly improvised and unscripted), it nevertheless belongs to the film's spatialising structure and is thus motivated by the aesthetic effects the film aims to achieve. It is a documentary of the students' group discussion staged for the camera while the camera's presence is rendered overt through manifestations of inadvertent expressions of discomfort and amateur performances before the camera. It is true that, as de Luca argues, 'Elephant gives real voices and bodies to these adolescents'.[36] This is not, however, simply a question of embodiment, of representing the subjectivity of the unremarked, marginalised adolescent. Bodies carry their social and cultural inscriptions imprinted on them. Yet, at the same time, they embody the failure of such inscriptions through their implication within the actuality of the profilmic and their stubbornly irreducible physical appearance and persistence onscreen. Consider the tracking shots that follow and observe Nathan and Carrie. The extended use of shallow focus detaches their bodies from the surroundings and isolates them. Filming their back while they walk through the corridors, what the camera prompts the viewer to observe is no longer two bodies embodying articulated characters or representing determinate social traits but two faceless bodies with rarefied features characterised only by their surfaces and immediate physical features – for instance, by the texture of Carrie's hair and the way it moves.

The facing images

Elephant is not a work of mourning the success of which would be the reappropriation and digestion of the bodies of the irreversibly lost others. It is melancholic, as it forecloses the possibility of actively working through and moving beyond the too-muchness of material bodies.[37] The images of *Elephant* address the viewer, making them responsible insofar as this giving of bodies as fragments, the compulsion to record, track and repeat, is too much to be contained as visual content, disrupting the solace of a familiar image or a restored sense of sensible reality.

The event of the image in *Elephant*, its capacity to face the viewer and have a claim of its own, involves a persistence within the image that is primarily indebted to duration. Little's reading of *Elephant*'s deployment of the long take and its radical relation to temporality underlines the crucial importance of recording the other over time. According to Little: 'One explanation for the film's frequently slow pace is that it foregrounds cinema's capacity to represent the passing of time. The pace allows the camera to entertain, and perhaps sustain, that which seems to resist explanation.'[38] Recording the other over time equips the images with a certain power. Affirmed by the camera and retained within the image, the body-thing precedes the body-object – the latter as the effect of an identification of the body. More crucially, the body-thing's 'coming into being' as a fragment always fragments given realities, whether the latter are conceived as what is preformulated in objective reality to be faithfully recorded ('The camera happened to be there') or as what has already attained an image ('The image looks familiar'). The image exposes its failure by revealing its debt to the reel-time, reaffirming what is invisible (its uncontainable address) beyond the visible that it contains.

The tracking shots of *Elephant* structurally lack a proper introduction or a meaningful progression. The way the camera follows the body presents a certain arbitrariness. It is the image, not a properly pre-scripted justification, that claims for the worthiness of this display of the body. The progression of the shots that last for minutes is indissociable from the movements of the body within the corridors of the high school and from the randomness of what appears within the frame, while the camera tracks and automatically records. Sustained merely by the image, the filmed body no longer unproblematically belongs to a frontal world of givens. It cannot be located and referred to as this or that in the visual field. A body as frontal and given requires a certain fixedness, while the durations of the images and the peculiar re-enactment of the bodies in *Elephant*'s durations are, in a certain sense, flooding. The address of the image resides in the breakdown of meaning in the wake of this too muchness. It is rooted in the time when the physical world, copied and preserved by the automatic recording, presses itself without necessarily making sense. The viewer is visited by images that make a claim, yet is unarmed by the latter in the task of domesticating the projected bodily presences.

Consider how Van Sant's camera sustains the bodies of Michelle and Elias till their eventual fate. What the tracking shot does is an appreciation of their bodily presence in their empty, literal durations in the face of the senselessness of their tragic fate. It is not that Van Sant is indifferent to the loss of the other. What he does in *Elephant* is problematise what it means to give a responsible account of the death of the other without falling prey to limited understandings of what committed art is and does. The claim of the image in *Elephant* is an interruption of meaning-making, not by a refusal to tell a story, as the lost other must break through the image so that it can be faced, but precisely through a failure of story proper in exhausting the body.

Notes

1. Gus Van Sant interview about *Elephant* uploaded to YouTube on 19 March 2010, <youtu.be/nyyCOR3kL_g> (last accessed 25 April 2022).
2. McCarthy, 'Elephant', <variety.com/2003/film/awards/elephant-2-1200541588> (last accessed 25 April 2022).
3. Ibid.
4. See Rich, 'Shock Corridors', 1311. Also see de Luca, 'Gus Van Sant and Visionary Realism', 207.
5. Little, 'Plotting Dead Time in Gus Van Sant's *Elephant*', 115.
6. Ibid., 118.
7. See Backman Rogers, 'Realism and Gus Van Sant's *Elephant*', 86–7 and Jaffe, *Slow Movies*, 52.
8. As de Luca puts it: 'Rather than evolving in a linear and chronological fashion, time in *Elephant* is constantly circling back on itself, as if in an endless loop, replaying situations from different vantage points.' See de Luca, 'Gus Van Sant and Visionary Realism', 193.
9. De Luca, 'Gus Van Sant and Visionary Realism', 188.
10. According to de Luca, *Elephant* has been condemned on account of its aestheticism: '*Elephant* does not explain the massacre through a morally edifying and revisionary glass . . . This was in fact the main accusation it received on its release: that its highly aestheticized re-enactment provided no answers about this event.' See de Luca, 'Gus Van Sant and Visionary Realism', 202–5.
11. De Luca, 'Gus Van Sant and Visionary Realism', 202–5.
12. Rogers regards this democratisation as emblematic of the film's *responsible* response, which eschews a conventional approach to avoid dictating what a viewer must think. See Backman Rogers, 'Realism and Gus Van Sant's *Elephant*', 86. Randolph Jordan also points out reflection in relation to sonic composition in the film. He identifies an experimental approach to sound in Van Sant's film in addition to his preoccupation with visual and spatial organisation. According to Jordan, *Elephant*'s 'soundtrack floats between the registers of immediacy and distance, documentary and formalism', allowing us to 'think about film sound through the processes of reflective listening engendered by soundscape composition', which in itself 'can lead us to a higher level of engagement with the film's audiovisual ecology'. See Jordan, 'The Ecology of Listening while Looking in the Cinema', 253.
13. A preoccupation with the question of meaning and interpretation, and ultimately an implicit understanding of realism as a matter of adequation, does not do justice to the specificities of *Elephant*'s alternative re-enactment. The same holds true with

respect to Van Sant himself who surprisingly conceals the radical potential of his film by adopting a seemingly democratic position towards the viewers of his film through his 'poetic' approach that includes 'the audience's thoughts', without elaborating the connection between being poetic and resistance to meaning-making. See Jaffe, *Slow Movies*, 47.
14 Cited in ibid., 45.
15 Trahair, 'Being on the Outside', 130.
16 See Backman Rogers, 'Realism and Gus Van Sant's *Elephant*', 93–4.
17 See Jaffe, *Slow Movies*, 57.
18 See Rich, 'Shock Corridors', 1324.
19 De Luca regards the film's formal presentation as a 'conceptual montage' in which 'chronology is shattered and perspectives shuffled, which highlights as a result the structural relation between images' like the 'completion of a puzzle' in which 'the spectator must reconstruct this event by putting together pieces of information which the film's form renders disconnected'. See de Luca, 'Gus Van Sant and Visionary Realism', 195.
20 Little, 'Plotting Dead Time in Gus Van Sant's *Elephant*', 118–19. Also, see Jordan Schonig's article ('The Chained Camera') on the ethics and aesthetics of follow-shot in Gus Van Sant's *Elephant* and Alan Clarke's short film of the same title (1989) set in Northern Ireland during the Troubles – a film that influenced the minimalist style of Van Sant's film. Schonig discusses the follow-shot as a peculiar mode of seeing particularly with regards to human agency in acts of violence where the viewer's access to interiorities via the face is denied.
21 De Luca, 'Gus Van Sant and Visionary Realism', 186.
22 Ibid., 160.
23 Jaffe, *Slow Movies*, 57. Of course, this is not to suggest that slow cinema, particularly with its recent revival, is reducible to a closed set of pre-established norms. As Çağlayan argues, 'Bazinian realism is invested in the objective and unfiltered representation of reality in cinema, while slow cinema recasts this mode of realism as a different, exaggerated, mannerist and quite often distorted subjective perception of reality'. Çağlayan, *Poetics of Slow Cinema*, 12.
24 Backman Rogers, 'Realism and Gus Van Sant's *Elephant*', 94–5.
25 Ibid., 85.
26 Nichols, *Introduction to Documentary*, 33.
27 De Luca, 'Gus Van Sant and Visionary Realism', 190.
28 Ibid., 191.
29 Little, 'Plotting Dead Time in Gus Van Sant's *Elephant*', 118.
30 Jaffe recognises this aspect, even though he does not follow its implications, arguing: 'Of course, Van Sant in *Elephant*, which might be considered a docudrama, does not just sit back and let things occur.' See Jaffe, *Slow Movies*, 57.
31 Little, 'Plotting Dead Time in Gus Van Sant's *Elephant*', 118.
32 Schoonover, *Brutal Vision*, xxvii.
33 Jaffe refers to Michelle's interaction with the camera: Jaffe, 'though she does not look directly into the camera, she seems to be aware of it, even to pose for it, to acknowledge its presence more than any other character has'. See Jaffe, *Slow Movies*, 51. See Jaffe, *Slow Movies*, 51.
34 Cited in de Luca, 'Gus Van Sant and Visionary Realism', 190.

35 See ibid., 192. Amy Taubin also sees the impact of Elephant residing in the dialectic the film establishes between 'documentary-style immediacy and formalist distance'. See Taubin, 'Blurred Exit', 18.
36 De Luca, 'Gus Van Sant and Visionary Realism', 208.
37 As Colin Davis observes, for Derrida melancholia 'is an attempt to preserve the lost other, to keep tangible the sense that the other cannot be assimilated but that proximity to its unspeakable strangeness can nevertheless be maintained. This is, Derrida insists, an *ethical* position; it does not diminish the gap between self and other, and it does not consign the other to oblivion: 'So melancholia *is necessary*.' See Davis, *Critical Excess*, 55.
38 Little, 'Plotting Dead Time in Gus Van Sant's *Elephant*', 126.

7

The Withdrawal of the Body

Ethical experience, if it is an experience, is from the outset an excessive obsession with the other since, in Emmanuel Levinas's thought, 'the subject is affected without the source of the affection becoming a theme of representation'.[1] Of course, a meaning-making process, one that demands and thus calls for a proper context, might be carried out later; but only later and only through a negation that aims at obscuring the meaning of 'affectivity qua affectivity'. This already belated obscuration, already caught up in an economy of retroactivity that corrupts the pre-reflective affect, cannot deny the fundamental fact that the other imposes itself on the self immediately.

For Levinas, proximity to the other arrives 'first' as it takes place before the subject having the privilege to reflect and thematise. The self, in a certain sense, offers itself to the other whereas this offering is not the outcome of a subjective act. The exposure to the other reveals that the subject's existence is first and foremost a passivity before the body of the other.[2] This radical notion of proximity conceives of the subject as that which is always already responding to a welcoming that has happened before the self has a chance to choose. It is an originary welcome – the other is already affecting the self. Hospitality is thus based on an originary sociality that is implicated in the structure not of enclosure but of exposure: not a relation between already formed subjects but the condition for the possibility of being a subject. Hospitality is being exposed to affects that cannot be and should not be considered as cognitive: affects as those experiences that make the subject be, not experiences that the subject simply has. The subject does not have sovereignty over its home and self, for hospitality, in its originary sense, frustrates all sovereignty.

Indeed, the self as the host/hostage can react to the arrival of the other, to its visitation, either by welcoming or rejecting. Yet both Levinas and Jacques Derrida maintain that there nevertheless exists the necessity of responding to 'an incalculable alterity of the other' as the basis of the ethical condition. There must be a response even if there exists no guarantee of the positive fulfilment of the obligation. Hospitality is a welcome before the subject gets the chance to say 'no!' as it is offered prior to consent and the subject is originarily displaced: its welcoming rises not from ability, attitude or will, but from a fundamental structure of exposure. It rises from originary homelessness and vulnerability, from an inability to be self-sufficient or self-determined in the face of the other. As Joanna Zylinska observes, hospitality does not mean that 'the other cannot be ignored, scorned or even annihilated', but rather that the other must be responded to and addressed.[3] The self might have the freedom to react to the arrival of the other by a rejection. However, this freedom (to say 'no!') implies a more originary lack of freedom. The extremity of the ethical commandment – that is, the necessity to respond – has always already positioned the self as 'the accusative' rather than 'the normative', implying an unbearable and excessive responsiveness that displaces the self from its home, divorcing it from the position of the normative while banishing it to a state of being accused.[4]

How does this ethical exposure resonate with the appearance and persistence of the body of the other within the cinematic image? What the cinematic image does is a rewatching of being, as opposed to a representation of it. The presence brought forth within the image and enveloped in fixed durations is irreducible to intentional meaning and resonates with the self-presentingness of the image: the cinematic image brings into being not an object within the frontal visual field but a call to attend oneself to an address that harbours a promise. The filmed body of the other is not real. Having turned into an image within the constraints of the frame, however, the filmed body imposes itself as a powerful impression of presence, thus issuing a call to look. Bearing a certain analogy with Hagi Kennan's notion of the face of the image previously discussed in the book, Karl Schoonover argues:

> Cinema makes possible the rewatching of being. The image invites us to watch while telling us that we are just watching. In other words, the image is a visual field that is becoming, something that just is, but it also asks to be witnessed ... this cinepresence confronts the viewer with the profound ambiguity of the real. This ambiguity is not that of a blank face on which we can project just anything. Fully realized, this realist cinematic body ... makes visible an image that is as open as it is certain, an image degraded when encoded, made discursive, or appended with any semantic stability.[5]

Open yet certain, the filmed body is not sustained by its meaningfulness. A body is rewatched not because it makes sense but precisely because it has been captured by the camera and is preserved within the image. The filmed body is a return to the existential bond between the image and the body-thing. What is pivotal in this reconceptualisation is the prioritising of a rewatching over a representation of the other that domesticates the latter by positing it as a given. The cinematic image, conceived in this manner, is what brings forth a viewing position that attests to its foreignness to the other and thus to the latter's inaccessibility and elsewhereness. For André Bazin, the realist film is not only identified by its ability to capture the contingent, the particular and the local, but is also elevated when it 'privileges the foreignness of the gaze that cinema's image engenders'. The ideal film is one that orients the viewer to 'the contingencies of a foreign moment', while the ideal viewer is 'an outsider, a foreigner'. Cinema, in a certain sense, 'makes us all outsiders'.[6]

Moreover, if we accept that an integral part of the self-presentingness of the cinematic image is its promise of a story on the way to being told, then it is equally important to elaborate the implications of this promise with regard to the subaltern other who falls from the domain of representability. As Schoonover rightly points out in his study on Italian Neorealism and the thought of Bazin, the contention that filmmakers shared in the post-war era could be formulated as a belief that 'a society is dehumanised when a body suffers without eyewitnesses'.[7] And cinema has an important status due to the ways in which it provides the conditions for a certain mode of bearing witness to the world, specifically to the 'imperiled body' of the other. Bazin's defence of the achievements of films like Roberto Rossellini's *Germany Year Zero* (*Germania anno zero*, 1948) resides, on the one hand, in the film's refusal 'to fix the meaning of the events it represents', and on the other, in its deployment of the filmed body 'to accentuate a virtual but nevertheless powerful impression of presence'.[8] This presence, which Schoonover dubs 'cinepresence', not limited to specific filmic styles or movements but resides in film's rendition of bodies, is not to be confused with 'the conventional experience of presence as direct and absolute thereness', despite the often uncanny proximity of the two. Schoonover seems to suggest that what distinguishes cinepresence from the actual thereness of things stems not merely from the virtuality of the filmed body within the cinematic image but more precisely from the fact that the image 'invites us to watch while telling us that we are just watching'.[9] Schoonover goes further – and it is exactly here that his argument becomes pertinent to this book – by conceiving the image as 'a visual field' that 'asks to be witnessed'.[10] Even though Schoonover does not speak of the claim or address of the image and the response it evokes, his conception of the image confronting the viewer structurally resembles the facing of the image as the condition for the possibility of whatever the image conveys while remaining irreducible to what it contains.

The onlooker and the local body

Cinema makes possible the rewatching of being as the cinematic image asks to be witnessed, making possible the response to the precarious body within the image. In Schoonover's formulation, however, this asking to be witnessed appears less as an actuality. It is a potentiality precisely because not only the image but also the body within the image is always in danger of getting digested and therefore 'degraded' through a filling of bodies, faces, looks and gestures with meaning. The body-too-much that film affirms technologically is inevitably compromised and caught up in abstracting forces that work to mediate its literalness, therefore making the address something to be achieved rather than given. This potentiality, of course, bears strong resonances with the facing image, which, as I have shown, must re-earn its facingness through aesthetic negotiations.

In addition, what gives cinema its specificity is the way in which it can evoke the viewer as the one who bears witness to the local body from the position of a foreigner. Cinema can call forth a certain impression of presence, an impression that does something to its viewer. Schoonover's reading of Bazin spotlights the promise that he sees in narrating the local body. At the same time, Schoonover speaks of the foreignness of the gaze, of the viewer as 'the outsider', thus evoking a certain distance between the viewer and what is viewed: a foreigner, who by virtue of the cinematic technology gains the privilege of witnessing what is distant. Yet witnessing is in itself an obliteration of a distance intrinsic to objectifying practices. The promise of the image, an integral part of its self-presentingness, detaches it from mere objecthood.

The image has a certain proximity within its structure that problematises an equation of image with voyeurism. The promise of the image circumvents the assurance that voyeurism offers. Something-to-be-looked-at is not necessarily a spectacle, and the call to look is not necessarily a call to render an object visible. Schoonover seems to imply, and I say rightly so, that quite the contrary is the case – the address of the image is what troubles voyeurism from the outset. This is why voyeuristic impulses tend to conceal the address as their condition of emergence. The viewer of a truly realist film witnesses by looking; a looking, however, that does not desire visibility but is transformed through witnessing. Here, the viewer is thought less as a viewing subject than an 'onlooker' who is first and foremost implicated within the host/hostage aporia. Characterised by their ability to bear witness, the onlooker attends oneself to a rewatching of being while refusing to exercise subjective powers in a digestion of the presences onscreen. And this ability is a gift – there are certain cinematic practices that call into being a viewer as an onlooker; but they do so through a return to, a reaffirmation of, what is there within the structure of the image but is always exposed to the risks posed by the dominant desire for visibility.

With respect to the dynamics of the local and the foreigner, it is crucial to note the conditions under which the latter becomes a voyeur.[11] The film viewer is always already implicated within the structure of being a foreign observer of the body of a distant other – sitting in the dark theatre, watching something that has opened onto them from elsewhere. More significantly, the foreignness of the gaze of the viewer resides in the facing of the image – something is coming from elsewhere, already presenting itself as that which unfolds within the frame to be rewatched. As Schoonover asserts, the onlooker, as an ideal spectator in Bazin's thought, is a viewer who is 'at the crux of a spatial tension between a place of remove and a place of exigent obligation'. The onlooker 'observes without taking part', for they are implicated within 'expanded observation and commitment'.[12] While in voyeurism pleasure is premised upon 'the voyeur's continued remove from the scene', the onlooker is not 'beyond effecting change', because viewing is 'neither purely part of the diegesis nor fully exempt from responsibility for the world viewed'.[13] Following Kenaan's reading of the Levinasian face and its relation to the visual, a voyeur's relation to the viewed can be said to be frontal – it is a viewing position according to which what the image gives is exhausted by what is contained within the visual field. By contrast, the facing image of realism evokes the viewer as an onlooker who is unable to move beyond the giving that is taking place within the image. The onlooker is implicated within the condition that the image is presenting itself to the eye prior to communicating or conveying anything – that there is a call and address that cannot be located within the frontal. The facing image is an affirmative violence against vision and is a staging of the tension between the ethical and the visual precisely because its giving of the filmed body holds the viewer response-able while the viewer is unable to contain the body as given and to respond adequately. There is a presence onscreen that presses itself upon the viewer owing to its persistence within duration. It makes a claim upon the viewer so far as the viewer is unable to respond exhaustively to this uncertain but stubborn presence.

There is a certain literalness in the way the cinematic image evokes its referent – it carries the body of the local other without forcing it to signify localness. It attests to a past presence, therefore pronouncing an other whose actual lived duration is recorded and preserved. Before being projected, and prior to an identification of the body by a conscious subject, the cinematic image, to borrow again from Judith Butler's reading of the Levinasian ethics of the image, in the second chapter, has already assumed the future anterior: 'a life has been lived'. By sustaining the body and imposing duration, the cinematic image humbly assumes an other whose life is precarious and would be grieved if lost. Exoticism, by contrast, is the collapse of cinematic witnessing. It is enacted when the local appears as local, concealing the physical transfer that determines the cinematic rendition of the profilmic. To avoid the voyeuristic impulses of exoticism, it is therefore essential to retain a notion of indexicality with respect to the local body of the other. The existential bond between the filmed body and the profilmic ensures that the body that the image carries within itself is tied to the singularity of a duration that has been automatically captured.

It can be argued, as Schoonover does, that indexicality forms an image that maintains and preserves 'a residue of [man's] historical experience'.[14] The local body stages the historical experience and grants it evidence. It is the vehicle for the gestures and postures, and is the site in which the documentation of the latter is made possible. The bodily documentation within the cinematic image can thus be said to evoke the historical. But it also bears the seeds of the subversion of a proper historicity. Its historicity is bound with the pastness of the profilmic and is thus too particular and therefore exposed to a certain unreadability from the outset. The cinematic image documents a historical duration, yet is unable to move beyond the actuality of its own literalness to signify the absence of a historical time in order to represent it. Speaking of the desire of the modern man to 'observe history-in-the-making'[15] to conceptualise the relevance of an indexicality that transfers the body to film is therefore insufficient in accounting for the peculiar historicity of the formation of the image. History-in-the-making implies a significance that already assumes socially constructed frameworks, which excludes the margins of history. The reality of the body of an outcast, for instance, often falls outside the normative boundaries of history. It is simply too insignificant to be accounted for. Yet many if not most films that fall under aesthetic realism often identify themselves by recourse to ethico-political obligations to narrate the bodies that are deemed unrepresentable. These bodies are rendered unrepresentable precisely because the frameworks that govern the visibility of history are effects of cutting these bodies out as what threaten to disturb the intelligibility of the (historical) narrative. The bodies on the margins are not only non-visible but are invisible as they have no address – they are simply incapable of making a claim as there is no recognition of the grievability of their lives. The inhuman eye of the machine, by contrast, documents the body prior to its identification. The ethical exposure it sets up resides in the fact that it does not interrogate the body as a prerequisite to having it recognised as belonging to the visual field.

Similarly, as Schoonover points out, the filmed body has the potential 'to lead viewers to a dynamically experiential means of thinking about worlds and times beyond their normal purview'.[16] It must also be noted that understanding the other worlds and times in a normative sense (the historically delineated and socially situated other) is equally blind to the radicality of what the camera does. The non-selectivity of the camera first and foremost brings into being the world and the time of the profilmic regardless of the historical significance or situatedness of the latter. The local is brought to life precisely prior to its appearing as local. The voyeur craves the local to look as local, to subsume it under a grand narrative that delineates sameness and difference. The camera at its degree zero, however, brings the local to life and undermines its appearing as local from the outset because it is a machine, the non-selectivity of which is utterly indifferent to the familiar image of the local no matter how socially or historically singular the latter looks. For the ethics of the image, therefore, otherness is not merely a historical or social construct but is an effect of the production of the image that provides the grounds of an encounter prior to the emergence of an active subject that discriminates bodies so as to deliver meaning. The cinematic image opens up to the viewer, giving the foreigner the local body that is already withdrawing from being local. Implicated within the face of the image, the local body is neither a universal body nor a particular body precisely because the singularity of the event of exposure cannot be contained by the givenness of a local image.

Performance and bodily surplus

The cinematic image involves responsibility, for the filmed body is always the body of an other. There is a fundamental ethicity in the manner the body of the other is framed, but also in the way it is given a renewed life. The body being offered to the gaze of the camera while it is watched by the machine does not necessarily assume subsequent rewatching by a viewing subject, and does not readily assume a giving *for* (the viewing eye of the foreigner).

However, its being within the image has this viewing condition as a possibility. The body of the other can remain unprojected. If projected, it happens to and visits the viewer. More significantly, the local body does not readily appear as local. Affirmed by the machine prior to signifying processes and without the condition of being viewed as a necessity, the local body is watched without the necessity of looking local for an eye that recognises and identifies the sameness/difference of localness.

I turn here to a few examples to show how certain intersections of performance and the local body can equip the cinematic image with an enhanced indexicality and a peculiar literalism that defy the frontality of vision. I give an ethical account of the materiality of performance in Carlos Reygadas's *Battle in Heaven* (*Batalla en el Cielo*, 2005), Bruno Dumont's *L'humanité* (1999), Jafar Panahi's *Crimson Gold* (*Talaye sorkh*, 2003) and Amir Naderi's *The Runner* (*Davandeh*, 1984). I particularly look at exemplary scenes illustrating the realisms of the body that these films set forth through a resonance between performance and the automatism of the camera. The scenes demonstrate practices where the filmed body is not tied to intentional meaning while performance brings forth the contingent body and opens the non-frontal aspect of the image. Through a certain dialectic between control and contingency and an admission of indebtedness to the profilmic event, the local body is brought onscreen to be witnessed while its recognition is not reduced to an identification of otherness but is carried out through an exposure to bodily surplus within the image.

Employing mostly non-actors and recounting the stories of outcasts and the marginalised, these films testify to otherness through a disruption of what is typically deemed to be acceptable performance in dominant forms of narrative cinema where 'imitation' and 'emotional verisimilitude' are the criteria for performers' success.[17] Discussing Bazin's argument regarding performance, George Kouvaros reminds us that classic acting is based upon a certain mode of continuity between 'internal psychological causes' and 'external gesture' that is pivotal to performance's 'readability' and 'coherence'. In this formulation, what is perceived as 'the inner world of the character determines the nature of the external gesture; but each determines and legitimates the other'.[18] As Michel Rubin reminds us, performance is assumed to consist of modes of expressions of inner existence and is carried out through external actions that correspond to the interiorities of bodies to create characters. What is assumed here is 'an organic composition between circuits of interiority and action that evolve along linear lines of perception.'[19] These approaches to acting are, in a certain sense, teleological – they rely on an ontology of the body according to which every physiological movement is implicated within an economy that sees the success of acting in mimesis. This functional conception of gestures and movements turns corporeality into the means to create identifiable characters.[20]

While dominant conceptions of performance are invested in recognisable subjective states to render bodies meaningful and readable, Reygadas, Dumont, Panahi and Naderi disrupt the 'mimetic inscription of character' by establishing the performances of their non-actors as an integral part of the formation of their images. What is at stake in these films, as Rubin argues particularly with regards to *L'humanité* and *Battle in Heaven*, is 'a precarious balance between control and contingency in the profilmic world', where the non-actor is physically involved in filming processes. Rather than produce performances that are defined by the 'portrayal of a coherent fictional character' and actions that are consistent with narrative objectives, filmmaking becomes a process where 'the new and unexpected can continually erupt and manifest'.[21]

This is not to suggest that these films are constructed around mere exposure of the artifice of filmmaking – rather, as we shall see, they turn the profilmic bodies into productive elements. Furthermore, in most cases, their aesthetic effects are not necessarily achieved through improvisational methods that would give actors the freedom to compose and create characters. Compositions and *mise en scéne* are controlled to the extent that the peculiar qualities of images are indebted to turning the bodies into automatons within the constraints placed on the actors. Stressing the freedom to improvise would still assume that the materiality of the body is regained, but through a certain skilfulness on the part of the actors. Even though not acting out intentional meanings, the actor is still assumed to possess a certain body-consciousness and an understanding of the potentialities of their bodies to be able to bring forth alternative bodily affects. Here, on the contrary, the non-actors do not manifest this level of awareness. Despite the filmic control over the bodies, contingency is partly produced through a predominant use of long takes and physically demanding performances where a high level of unpredictability is introduced into the images.

Battle in Heaven follows the working class, indigenous Marcos (played by non-actor Marcos Hernández) in Mexico City who struggles with his conscience while deciding whether to turn himself in to the police following the death of a child whom he had kidnapped with his wife's assistance. In recounting Marcos's story, as Rubin observes, Reygadas manifests a concern with the 'possibility of documenting the material deformations, discontinuities and gaps that emerge in the process of filming', where 'unexpected moments' are brought forth to disrupt the articulation of characters, emphasising instead the 'phenomenological weight and surface textures of the performance'.[22] These gaps are not merely narrative; nor are they simply present in the profilmic. They reside in the way the images are set up to perform a certain indebtedness to the profilmic. Through an aesthetic of the long take, Reygadas creates an alternative space for an exposure to bodily surplus via a filming of the body before the action occurs and after it concludes. Emblematic of this approach is the scene in which Marcos visits his employer's daughter Ana, a young woman with whom Marcos has occasional sexual encounters, in her apartment to inform her about his plan to go to the police before murdering her with a knife without known motives in a gruesome display. As Rubin notes in the composition of the scene,

> after Marcos has told Ana he will turn himself in to the police, the camera does not cut immediately, but instead remains filming. Noticeably uncomfortable, the actor stands awkwardly in front of the camera and there is a moment, fleeting yet significant, when he does not know what to do with his body: what he does do is indecisively move his hands towards his pockets. However, he keeps them suspended at his sides, his fingers merely fidgeting nervously. In this disruptive moment, the unpredictable real indeed trumps the staged, as we witness physiological actions that disturb the coherent organisation of a fully realised character existing in a fictional world.[23]

There is a recording of bodies, durations and fragments in *Battle in Heaven* that refers to their literal actuality before the camera rather than being a mere element within a larger articulation. From a Bazinian view, the production of gaps before and after filmic actions can be seen as the foregrounding of '[u]nconcious gestures and movements' that work to 'counter the intended meanings of a rigid script', resulting in an aesthetic structure that 'allows fugitive elements to come through in all their variance, ambiguity, and luminosity'.[24] Contingency in the above shot, however, is not only present within the image (the unintended gesture) but becomes the image itself. Through Reygadas's refusal to cut immediately once an act is concluded, the image is returned to a certain indebtedness to the profilmic – it works as the force of contingency, and its claim on the viewer resides in the unmotivated persistence of the body in a suspended state. This presentational approach releases the physicality of the body from the telos of meaning and visibility – the discontinuities and persistence of the body's movements and gestures within the image are released from the urge to either express the inner life of the character or locate it within an identifiable image of the local.[25]

What Reygadas does in this scene is to highlight the fact that film is a dual operation and the filmed body's opening up within the image is always already in a state of withdrawal. The parallelism that he creates exercises pressure over film's constitutive duality to stage the uncompromising persistence of the filmed body beyond its embodiment of the character. This persistence reintroduces ontological instabilities into the image and amounts to a surplus of irreducible materiality that interrupts readability. By establishing parallelism through its gaps, the image aesthetically enacts a failure in exhausting the filmed body to accentuate the space that is already opened up by the automatic recording. This alternative image bears witness to its own giving of a body that is irreducible to what is posited as a given within the image, for the viewer who hosts the body is unable to properly make sense of the eruption of the impulsive real within the image and adequately respond.

What is pivotal for Reygadas is neither naturalistic performance nor faithful representation; rather, it is 'the actual human presence' as a state of being in the world that, as Troy Bordun observes, revisits the real and the fictional binarism in favour of actual persons performing a scene onscreen 'in the flesh – in their vulnerability, anxiety, and bursts of courage'.[26] This actuality of human presence is particularly evident in the non-actors' engagement in performing real, unsimulated sex. From the opening fellatio scene to the graphic depiction of Marcos having sex with his wife and with Ana, there is a certain materialisation of carnality that is indebted to the profilmic. Similar to Dumont's *La vie de Jésus* (1997) and *L'humanité*, Reygadas employs extreme close-ups of body parts in order, as Tiago de Luca asserts, to 'scrutinize and magnify their fleshy excess'.[27] While fragmentation of the body in, for example, Robert Bresson's films still contributes to the narrative,[28] there is a certain literalism in Reygadas's approach exemplified in unflattering camera angles and close-ups of hands, feet, buttocks and genitalia that exceed beyond narrative function. In the scene following the sexual act between Ana and Marcos, there are several extreme close-up shots 'whose geometric fragmentation of . . . bodies, framed in idiosyncratic positions, discloses a malleable geography of fleshly forms'.[29] What is alternatively achieved through 'an excessive proximity to the human body' is a transformation of 'flesh into unexpected shapes and unusual forms', one that 'threatens to disfigure the legibility of the image'.[30] Drawing on Laura U. Marks's notion of 'haptic visuality', de Luca argues that this proximity diminishes the distance that is required for objects and bodies to appear as recognisable, resulting in an enhanced materiality.[31] What Martine Beugnet argues with regard to 'cinema of sensation'

Figure 7.1 Marcos and Anna, the unlikely couple in *Battle in Heaven* (Carlos Reygadas, 2005).

is equally relevant here: 'In contrast with the body caught in action in medium or long shot, filming in close-up makes it possible to evoke a body that is temporarily freed from its function as social, cultural and even gender signifier.'[32] Owing to its simultaneous closeness to and fragmentation of the body, the camera turns into a device that explores textures and surfaces without contextualising them within a body as a unified whole, thus further problematising the relevance of characters' interiorities to render bodies significant and meaningful or locate them within a broader social context.

A demonstration of evident physical and socio-ethnic disparities, Ana's unlikely infatuation with her chauffeur Marcos in the film is perplexing, particularly because Reygadas, owing to his anti-psychological methods, denies the viewer enough access to characters' interiorities to make sense of this coupling. Here, as de Luca observes, full-frontal nudity and penetrative sex are

> shocking not only because [the couple] are unsupported by a plausible dramatic structure that would explain their incoherence. There is the greater shock of seeing these non-professionals in explicit sexual intimacy. Which is to say that these are impossible fictions authenticated and indeed made possible in reality. More than 'representing' the unlikely encounter of different ethnicities, classes and ages, the sexual intercourse between Ana and Marcos *is* this encounter, registered by the camera lens.[33]

Moving beyond the representation of pre-existing reality or making sense of bodily surfaces, performance becomes ontogenetic[34] – a moment of production of bodily surplus that is indebted to non-actor's real lives overlapping with the lives of the characters they play. This bodily surplus transforms the visual into what asks to be witnessed, yet leaving the viewer unguided in how to respond adequately. The image of performance becomes autonomous, but paradoxically, because of its indebtedness to the profilmic. The cinematic presence, as Schoonover notes, resides in 'the transfer of contingency associated with physical transcription of the discrete moment and specific space of the profilmic to the time and space of exhibition'.[35] The particularity of the image's giving is particular, even if the exact historical moment of giving (of performance presented to the camera) is no longer relevant. The image does not need to refer to the profilmic to claim its force of particularity. In a certain sense, the time of giving is no longer a historical time. The image carries the thrust of profilmic performance within itself and relives the particularity of the profilmic event while giving the latter a new life. The image carries within itself the automatically recorded fragments of performance. This carrying is in itself a displacing – an altering. In the face of the ontogenetic performance, the image gains a peculiar literalness as it testifies to the irreplaceability of bodily performance even if the moment of capturing the performative body is historically insignificant.

These scenes are emblematic of an image whose constitutive factor is the productivity of a maladjustment in relation to the automatism of the camera. Consider Dumont's *L'humanité* – a police procedural fiction on the surface, yet with a detective who, as Douglas Morrey observes, is 'inarticulate to the point of autism',[36] to the point of draining 'all urgency' that is generically expected from a detective drama.[37] Discussing Emmanuel Schotté's performance as Pharaon, Rubin argues:

> Challenging the hard and impenetrable physiognomies frequently seen in conventional representations of detectives, Schotté's body is ungainly and awkward, the buckled shoulders, collapsed chest and protruding stomach antithetical to stereotypical action heroes. Indeed, his drooping flesh and lugubrious movements reveal the remarkable force of gravity and expose a certain passivity in the flux of matter. This incongruity or disjunction between the actor's corporeality and the role he portrays means we cannot see the character as completed and subsequently suspend our disbelief.[38]

Neither a documentary nor a fiction, what the viewer witnesses is a deliberately failed and incomplete participation of the contingencies of the

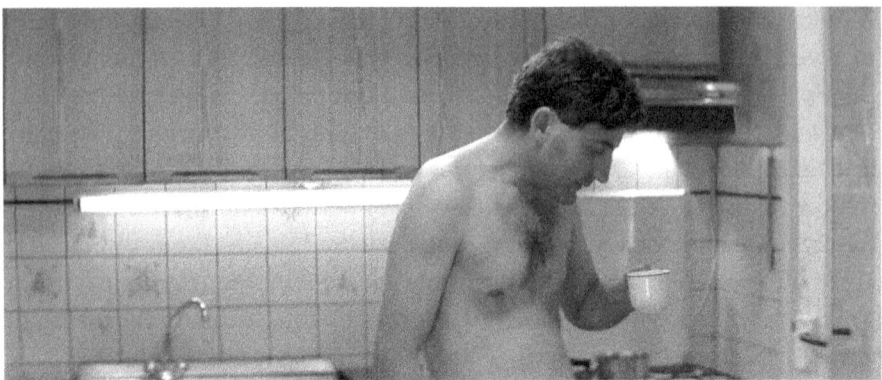

Figure 7.2 The distinctive bodily presence of Pharaon that defies the conventional figure of detectives in *L'humanité* (Bruno Dumont, 1999).

profilmic. Bad casting and spatio-temporal integrity allow the particularity of the reel-time (in which bodies are made available to the camera in their sheer physical presence) to interrupt a reduction of the filmed body to a given. The image becomes indebted, but not reducible. It carries the particularities of the profilmic as a force. In the awkwardness and clumsiness of Pharaon's body, the implausible body of the detective impacts no less as a powerful impression of a literal bodily presence, for physiological gestures carry their own claim as the image stands out and exposes its position as a bearer of particularity. This approach also finds an interesting example in the way Dumont exploits Schotté's inability to drive. As Nikolaj Lübecker observes:

> Emmanuel Schotté, the nonprofessional actor who plays Pharaon, did not know how to drive at the time of filming. However, Dumont decided to take advantage of this, and he put Schotté behind the wheel despite the fact that he was terrified of driving. Schotté's fear is palpable in several sequences, so when Pharaon drives it is slowly, hesitantly, bizarrely.[39]

In *L'humanité*, as well as in *Battle in Heaven*, at the core of the cinematic performance is a certain impotency whereby, as Rubin notes, 'the untrained actor cannot fully imitate or master the gestures expected of him'. What is disclosed instead is the non-actor's vulnerable physicality as the materiality of performance is brought to the fore. This maladjustment generates a certain 'unfinished quality' and grants the character a documentary aspect, while calling the viewer to attend themselves to 'the actor attempting to perform', as opposed to desiring a performance that brings forth 'a stable and completed character in the fictional world'.[40] This surplus of bodily presence creates a hyperbolic parallelism: it is impossible to distinguish between the body of the actor and that of the character, as they both occupy the same space and commit the same gestures. The boundary between the actor and the filmed body giving itself to the gaze of the camera to be automatically recorded is troubled.

The fiction is then indebted to alterity precisely because framing presence to be witnessed constitutes an other time. It is the time of the other – not simply the time of the other's story, which essentially assumes a progression that tells the story of the other in a proper fashion. Otherness is produced by an image that performs its debt to the time of the other giving itself to the gaze of the camera in its literal thereness, inertia and fatigue, to be watched by the camera so that its being might be rewatched and borne witness to. This approach is taken to its extreme particularly in the scenes where the image is turned into a staging of physical feats of endurance:

> Think of the gruelling trudge Marcos endures on his knees through the sweltering streets of Mexico City or the uphill bike ride undertaken by Pharaon where we listen to his heavy breath and see his undulating chest. In these instances, the filmmaking process is less about following a pre-established narrative trajectory and more about provoking corporeal affects through extreme physical situations.[41]

Also consider the lethargic rhythms of the body in Panahi's *Crimson Gold*, which generates similar effects. Based on a screenplay by Abbas Kiarostami, the film recounts the story of a war veteran who now works as a pizza deliveryman. Still suffering from the injuries of war, Hossein rebels against injustice in the city of Tehran by holding up a jewellery store before shooting himself. Countering prevailing modalities of temporal experience, *Crimson Gold* is partly structured around several pauses that put narrative progression on hold and instead provides cues for the non-actor, Hossein Emadeddin portraying the protagonist Hossein, to move (in the profilmic). There is an extended scene in the middle of the film when Hossein is prevented by the police from delivering pizza as they are waiting to arrest the people at a party. Instead of completing the action, Hossein is kept in a confined space, moving around and offering the pizzas to the cops and soldiers. Or think of the shot of Hossein having to walk up numerous stairs while delivering pizza, and what we hear is the sound of his heavy breathing – a scene that is set up to depict the body in feats of physical exertion in an extended, unbroken crane shot. Or consider the scene where, under almost absurd yet

Figure 7.3 Capturing the lethargic rhythms of the non-actor's body in *Crimson Gold* (Jafar Panahi, 2003).

still plausible circumstances, Hossein ends up in a penthouse and is left to himself to walk around for an extended period of time.

The long takes and tracking shots of *Crimson Gold* that record blocs of time and space, and the image that carries these blocs within itself, are not mere inclusions of the everyday of the subaltern other to suggest and produce lifelikeness, the latter strongly tied to the logic of representation. Rather, despite the commitment to portray the injustice in contemporary Tehran, Panahi's shots stage a different sort of engagement with the mundane. Redefining the role of the camera, *Crimson Gold* challenges what it means to cinematically observe. The film's observation is not made possible by a camera that is characterised by the 'happened to be there' or fly-on-the-wall impressions it creates – there is an evident intent in the way scenes are set up so that the body moves for the camera to automatically record it. In these scenes, Panahi's camera is turned into a device that is preoccupied with capturing the movements of Hossein's body. It mobilises corporeal materiality by documenting predominantly the singularity of the manner in which Hossein moves, the latter partly residing in the medication he takes to cope with the side effects of wartime injuries (a condition that the character and the non-actor share).

Using a non-actor to give flesh to a character he resembles is not to grant the images a certain level of authenticity at meaning-making level. Exemplary of the neorealist thread in Iranian cinema, Panahi's methodology clearly demonstrates a debt to Vittorio De Sica's, Cesare Zavattini's and Bazin's shared belief in the potency of using non-professionals, in an approach whose merit is particularly noticeable 'in those amateurs whose life experience weighs heavily on their bodies'.[42] Take Schoonover's observations in relation to De Sica's *Bicycle Thieves* (*Ladri di biciclette*, 1948):

> For Bazin, the purest moments of this film occur when its narration seems to free itself from the dictates of a script and the limits of artificial *mise-en-scene*. Those pure moments appear most readily in the 'natural' action of bodies, which in turn lend the screen image its unique presence, its immediacy, and allow it to emanate a palpable sense of duration. The tics and other specificities of bodies in *Bicycle Thieves* appear to determine the shape of the narrative for Bazin.[43]

What is pivotal for De Sica is not to cast a non-actor to give the images an authenticity that can be validated through a historical knowledge of actual lived experiences but a mere physical existence within the actuality of profilmic duration. According to Bazin,

> [b]efore choosing this particular child, De Sica did not ask him to perform, just to walk. He wanted to play off the striding gait of the man against the short trotting steps of the child, the harmony of this discord being for him of capital importance for the understanding of the film as a whole.[44]

Indeed, Bazin's preference for non-actors does not involve 'an abstract faith in re-enacting recent history with the real agents of history'.[45] In *Crimson Gold*, as in the neorealist films that Bazin tirelessly champions, the non-actors embody a peculiar naturalism – they are chosen precisely because of 'their suitability for the part, either because they fit it physically or because there is some parallel between the role and their lives'.[46] However, the non-actor does not necessarily bring something to the role that can be regarded as reliable in terms of making the body readable and situating it within a given image of the local. Rather, the image of Hossein's body corresponds to that Bazinian view that the value of non-actors 'comes not from any conscious knowledge they might impart to a film'. What instead fascinates Bazin as well as Panahi are their physiognomic peculiarities, 'as if the lives of these amateurs can be read on their bodies and in their movements'.[47]

The thrust of performance fleshes out the transmission that resides in the indexicality of the cinematic image. According to Bazin, photography 'actually contributes something to the order of natural creation instead of providing a substitute for it'.[48] An index is not simply a substitute that is presumed to sit in the place of the absent referent and to fill its absence while associating it with meaning against the backdrop of other objects. While this conception regards the index as what is based on a lack, index-as-testimony implies a fullness. Referring to the world does not contradict the image's being in the world. Being a bundle of traces that attest to a past presence before the camera is not equal to being a secondary copy. The cinematic image carries the traces within itself precisely because it is an image that has the potential of bearing inscriptions. Accordingly, the index does not signify or render its referent meaningful. It is primarily a humble testimony, a minimal assertion that 'something exists' – a presence that is too contingent to be reduced to signifying processes and is therefore always already implicated within a withdrawal from the frontal.

Irreducible to a mere reproduction of scripted dramaturgy, performance becomes a transmission (inscription of traces) that is indebted to the singularity of the event of the profilmic body giving itself to be recorded. Yet speaking of the index, as Schoonover does, is not so much about a unique capacity 'to transmit meaning across a great expanse of time and space'.[49] What the cinematic index does is less a transmission of meaning than an exposure of meaning to uncertainty. The physical continuum that the cinematic index offers transmits 'something', but that very transmission immerses the transmitted thing in a radical degree of particularity that renders impossible an exhaustible ascription of meaning. Even though the scripted meaning motivates the breakthrough of the body within the image, the performative body is always already on the verge of withdrawing from the meaning it is expected to convey, precisely because the automatism of the camera carries a past presence that is already contextualised within the 'elsewhereness' of the profilmic performance. Indeed, the image 'carries the trace of a physical contact with a body'.[50] It is a 'cinematographic report' (of the performative event) insofar as it 'carries a legacy of physical intimacy with the event it represents'.[51] The withdrawal of the performative body from within the frontal visual field resides in this physical, existential bond that transfers the body from the singularity of the moment of its actualisation through performance.

The weightiness of the performative body stubbornly resists being abstracted from the actuality of its initial profilmic context. What Rubin argues with respect to Marcos's body in *Battle in Heaven* applies to Hossein's performance with equal measures. Marcos's as well as Hossein's movements are to a certain extent automated. Throughout the films, they embody 'an uncomfortable awkwardness and uncertainty, the burden of a specific corporeal density that betrays an incapacity to reproduce what is ostensibly expected from [them] by the director'. Instead of emphasising control over the body to achieve 'natural' performance, these bodies manifest a certain literalism of the body, an 'untrained inelegance', the latter as what 'announces itself through an explicit resistance to corporeal movement: the kinesis of the body paradoxically measured and excessive'. While in the extreme scenes both bodies appear restrained – robotic in the case of Marcos and medicated in the case of Hossein – 'a sense of surplus movement' continues to surface.[52]

Naderi's *The Runner* offers an interesting example of literalism by engaging the local body in feats of physical exertion. The film recounts the story of Amiru, an illiterate orphan boy who has lost his home during Iran–Iraq war, and follows him as he engages with several jobs (shining shoes, collecting empty bottles or selling water) on the margins of an industrial region in Iran's southwest. Amiru decides to learn and write, enrols at a school and begins to memorise the alphabets. Intriguingly, Naderi turns this memorisation into a performance that requires bodily engagement on the part of his non-actor, Majid Niroumand. As Hamid Dabashi notes:

> Gradually his memorization of the letters of the alphabet begins to assume rhythmic and melodic tonalities, ebbs and flows, sounds and effects entirely independent of what these letters are supposed to mean and do. A visual and verbal stylization gradually emerges that is in pure and undiluted forms. Amiru memorizes them walking, he memorizes them sitting, he memorizes them at the schoolyard, through the crevices of rocks at the coast of a stormy sea.[53]

This engagement of the profilmic body is further enhanced when Amiru competes with his schoolmates in anguishing practices to see who manages say all the thirty-two Persian alphabets in a single breath, an impossible attempt that Naderi's camera captures in several extended shots. Here, alphabets are dissociated from their ordinary function. They do not give voice to the character to reveal his interiority but rather turns his body into an expression in often choreographed interactions with the camera.

The final scene intensifies the physicality of performance when Amiru, who finds immense joy in running as the viewer has witnessed throughout the film, enters a physical challenge with his classmates. A block of ice is placed near a fire, and the objective is to see who gets there first and gets there before the ice has completely melted:

196 The Eye of the Cinematograph

Amiru and his friends start sabotaging each other's progress, getting in each other's way and knocking each other down as they race toward their goal . . . The kids run, roll, bump, bounce, throw, hit, strike, jolt, jerk, jump, punt, push, pull, drag, and yank – anything and everything to be the first to get to the melting ice by the subterranean fire . . ., or at the very least to prevent anyone else from getting there.[54]

Amiru is eventually the winner as he gets to the ice by the fire first. In slow-motion shots that further emphasise the flames of fire and splashes of water and the actor's bodily engagement in the scene, Amiru begins beating on the barrel triumphantly and holds the piece of ice over his head and joyously dances. Even though the camera 'captures' the event, the performative body exposes the viewer's subjective authority to failure through its bodily expressions, and instead evokes what Maurice Blanchot would call 'visual fascination'. Resonating with Levinasian iconoclasm, Blanchot associates seeing with the subject's power, since 'seeing implies distance, the decision that causes separation, the power not to be in contact and to avoid the confusion of contact'.[55] A proper distance is required for the viewing subject to constitute as object what appears within the frontal visual field and have it

Figure 7.4 Ecstatic bodily expressions of Amiru that defy the activity of the viewing subject in *The Runner* (Amir Naderi, 1984).

always at their disposal – a distance that, at the same time, is the condition for the constitution of the viewer as an active subject.[56] However, Blanchot suggests that the visual also harbours an alternative potentiality that defies the violence of visibility. The power of the 'ego', according to him, is 'ruptured' at the point of visual fascination – a point at which seeing seems to transform into an absolutely altered experience:

> [W]hat happens when what you see, even though from a distance, seems to touch you with a grasping contact, when the matter of seeing is a sort of touch, when seeing is a contact at a distance? What happens when what is seen imposes itself on your gaze, as though the gaze had been seized, touched, put in contact with appearance?[57]

This proximity is simultaneously a demonstration of passivity, and a call to host the body of the other that breaks through the visual in the absence of an exhaustive grasp of what the other is presumed to signify. As Jeffrey Dudiak in his reading of Levinas's ethics reminds us,

> proximity describes a relation with the other that is the erasing of, and that which precedes, the 'safe' distanciation that consciousness establishes with its object in order to 'fix' it as 'there,' at arm's length, the distance necessary for perception, for conceptualization, for the appropriating grasp. Proximity describes the too far to be grasped of transcendence as a too near to be grasped.[58]

Amiru's ecstatic bodily expressions of distress and joy turn the filmed body itself into a filmic drive that disrupts the rule of mediation, instead transforming the image into what asks to be witnessed. Returning to Bazin's humanist trust in the inhuman camera, the filmed body is no longer a vehicle for the filmic event in this alternative emergence of performance. The body itself becomes the event and the thrust of the singularity of ethical exposure that takes place within the visual field without becoming visual content.

The Runner accentuates and foregrounds the anteriority of the profilmic, for the physicality of what the actors engage in in the profilmic takes the upper hand over the actors' function to represent articulated characters. With what Alla Gadassik sees as the film's 'meditative pacing, interest in multi-sensory experience, and blurring of reality with fiction',[59] *The Runner* summons a physicality that owes its existence and motivation to its own literal happening in the profilmic rather than to any narrative or dramatic horizon. This takes the form of a certain literalness, making the filmed bodies and the camera enter into a degree zero interaction – what is suggested is happening in the diegesis is literally taking place in the profilmic. Despite *The Runner*'s relatively shorter takes, there is still a strong literal flow of time that blurs the boundaries between the filmic and the profilmic. The viewer may abstract from the filmic action a sign of destitution, but this abstraction is built upon and thus remaining secondary and heterogeneous to the profilmic act, failing to exhaust the intensities of the profilmic event that have been affirmed by the camera's automatic recording. There is a uniquely cinematic immediacy that is rendered through performance and is imposed on the viewing subject through the image. Ivone Margulies suggests this possibility by asserting that 'literal art', as she calls it, tends to amplify 'what is implicit in any indexical language: its rendering of a first, "immediate" meaning – its referent'.[60] The performative body of the other becomes the origin of the immediate meaning as it no longer owes its actualisation to anything other than its engagement in the profilmic event.

This particular method of involving local child non-actors in the production of films is evident in a considerable number of widely acclaimed Iranian films, including Kiarostami's *Traveler* (*Mossafer*, 1974) and *Where is the Friend's Home?* (*Khaneye doust kodjast?*, 1987), and Mohammad-Ali Talebi's *Willow and Wind* (*Beed-o baad*, 1999), to mention a few examples. Shot on location and largely dependent on what happens on the spot in the profilmic, these films are characterised by a certain reduction in narrative composition, the latter reduced to a local and often ordinary goal defined for the protagonist to follow throughout the course of the film. The filmic structure is turned into providing cues for the child non-actors to move in the diegetic space, attending to everyday yet equally urgent matters and often having to meet a deadline, while engaging in demanding physical tasks. *Traveler* tells the story of ten-year-old Qassem for whom football is not only a passion but also a way to escape the boredom of his hometown, dominated by authoritarian adults. He starts the quest to scrape enough money for him to travel to Azadi Stadium in Tehran to watch his favourite team play. Having found a broken camera, he comes up with the idea of staging a photoshoot, pretending to be taking pictures outside the school, promising to have the photos available and ready the next day. Qassem eventually manages to travel to the stadium, only to realise the match has been sold out. Ahmad, the child protagonist at the centre of *Where is the Friend's Home?*, is a schoolboy searching to find the house of a classmate in a nearby village where he is told he lives, in a journey that involves constant, often perplexing walks and runs up and down the hill. Ahmad's self-imposed mission is to return the notebook he has accidentally brought home, for he is anxious that his classmate might be expelled from school if he is unable to hand in his homework the next morning. Co-written by Kiarostami, Talebi's *Willow and Wind* involves a similarly simple premise that follows the journey of a schoolboy who tries to replace the window in his village school fearing that his classmate, who broke the glass but whose family cannot afford to replace it, will be expelled the next morning. The film follows him as he struggles alone to carry the glass to school in stormy weather.

Bringing about new modes of realism of the body, these films rely on certain literal, unsimulated qualities that result particularly from positioning child non-actors in carefully composed narrative spaces. Countering a working method that would require a certain processing of the script so as to act out intentional meanings, these films present characters who are not articulated through meaning-making frameworks but are an effect of physical engagement in the profilmic tasks. With a focus on the materiality of the environments where the filmic actions take place, the filmmaker prioritises the filming process over the enactment of scripted characters. The non-actors enact their own exertions in response to the surroundings as the shape of the filmic event is indebted to the contingencies that arise during the filming process. Due to its indexical connection to the profilmic, the production of an image of the local is derailed through a spatial expansion in which the body of the other withdraws from representation and form. Lúcia Nagib's notion of 'physical realism' would be revealing here in demonstrating how in these examples a certain 'bodily commitment' is endowed with the 'belief in the reality of the material world', as well as a 'belief in cinema's unlimited power to convey this reality'. In this mode of realist practice,

> [r]ather than symbiosis with fictional characters, the actors' physical engagement with performance is thus as much an engagement with a real context as it is with a film about it. As a film event, physical acting relates to contingency, rather than narrative mimesis, with presentation of reality as it happens, rather than representation, and this is where commitment translates into an ethics.[61]

Representation of characters' psychology is replaced by an intensification of physical engagement, for plots are centred on the precariousness of the lives of characters who are essentially unable to be merely recognised through an identification of their 'voice'. What is pivotal in these films is that there is a coming into being of bodies: a claim to their existence, but an existence that is not to be digested by either the socio-political context or by a supposedly generous act of an individual (the filmmaker) who poses as the one who is giving voice to their precarity. This coming into being is inseparable from the body committed to perform in the profilmic space, creating a surplus that exposes to failure any subsequent attempt to exhaustively recontextualise the body and its precarity through unified characterisation. It is as though the character's history is produced through an exploration of bodily movements and gestures, owing to a camera that sustains the performative body as its visual interest. In these examples, there is not much to distinguish between the body of the non-actors walking and running, uncomfortably carrying objects or being positioned in demanding situations, and a character that is supposed to commit the same acts within the same space. Details and nuances of characters are produced through the profilmic event and cannot be adequately attributed to a scripted production of intelligibility. This cinematic parallelism between the filmic and profilmic bodies does not simply interrupt the integrity of the diegetic space. It exposes the originary tenuousness of a diegesis, which is indebted to the profilmic that the image carries within itself. Most of the time, the non-actors even cease to be themselves: they are effectively reduced to bodies that are compelled to move in space, the duration of which is recorded. The local is therefore not produced through an identification of localness – it is an effect of the body of the other committing to submit itself to the camera and physically engage in the profilmic space. The body enacted in response to surroundings becomes the filmic event to present the character through profilmic happenings, as opposed to a mere creation of a seamless character whose recognition is delayed until after scripted attributes are realised.

Literalism of the body

For Levinas, the other gifts the originary meaning and establishes proximity. The self is therefore responsible for the other, while this responsibility has been brought upon it before it was able to decide.[62] It is a difficult responsibility simply because it obliges the self even before the self is conscious and able to assume responsibility. As Ewa Ziarek observes, granting privilege to reflection and consciousness signifies 'freedom and the coincidence of the self with itself', a coincidence that is possible only at the price of 'the negation of both alterity and the body'. Levinas, of course, locates the foundations of ethical subjectivity not in free will or consciousness, but in the 'extreme way of being exposed'.[63] His ethics is located at the intersection of alterity and the body, positing obligation as 'a displacement of the I from the position of enunciation to the position of the addressee'.[64]

The literal body, actualised in the surplus of performance, brings forth the passivity of the addressee – the viewing act no longer requires the activity of recognising the local body.⁶⁵ In the literalness of the performative body, gaze loses the power that has often been attributed to it as active, revealing a passivity at its very core. What emerges is a seeing that is already charged with the call to bear witness to transient bodily presences – a seeing that, as Blanchot would suggest, is a blindness: 'the gaze of what is incessant and interminable, in which blindness is still vision, vision that is no longer the possibility of seeing, but the impossibility of not seeing, impossibility that turns into seeing.'⁶⁶ Cinematic seeing ceases to be merely a matter of visibility; seeing does not result in absorption or unity. Visual fascination turns seeing into a radical passivity: I, as the viewer, am not able to exercise power over what I see; rather, it is more that, Steven Shaviro notes, 'I am powerless *not* to see'.⁶⁷ In the face of performance, the viewer as the subject becomes accusative rather than normative. I am no longer an active agent inviting the bodies, merely rendering them meaningful by locating them in the world; but rather someone who has been visited, who is being a host, or who, like a hostage, has been forced to be a host before they had had any will or power, consciousness or sovereignty to issue an invitation. Performance transforms film viewing into ethical exposure – not deciding to see or hear the body through the cinematic image but being visited by a body that imposes itself.

As Jacques Rancière reminds us: 'At the origin of the cinema, there is a "scrupulously honest" artist that does not cheat, that cannot cheat, because all it does is record'⁶⁸ – remarks reminiscent of Bresson's famous note: 'What no human eye is capable of catching, no pencil, brush, pen of pinning down, your camera catches without knowing what it is, and pins it down with a machine's scrupulous indifference.'⁶⁹ This honest artist, of course, is not the filmmaker. The latter, as I have tried to demonstrate in several examples in this chapter, stages an unthematisable encounter between the camera and the actualisation of the body in performance. In a certain sense, the human body is no longer recognised through mimesis as performance enacts a return to a bypassing of imitation at work in the photographic base of the film medium. Owing to the existential density and thickness of performance, there is a double subversion of subjective authority: not only is the spectatorial search for recognisability onscreen disrupted, but the body onscreen is giving itself in its inertia, fatigue, exertions and exasperations without rendering its flesh intelligible in the absence of subjective expressiveness.

As performance disrupts the rule of the third and literalises bodily presence, the bodies of Pharaon, Marcos, Hossein, Amiru and others might be said to proceed towards the ideal neorealist body that, according to Schoonover, 'performs without performing'. Regardless of the intensity of the scenes the non-actors are involved in, there is always a certain 'unbelabored labor' as far as performing in a classical sense is concerned, for 'comportment and physicality', in their literal thereness, 'bespeak a character's history and his or her present actuality more than any acting technique'. Indeed, the amateurs are 'chosen for a defining physical characteristic – an automatic quirk or ingrained bearing that was taken to index their personal histories'.[70] Literalism therefore brings about an unfinished quality that makes the bodily surplus explicit. It demonstrates a debt to the profilmic body of the other and exhibits a maladjustment: the properly local body (the body that owes its embeddedness within a matrix of bodies to an identification of its localness) cannot exhaust the bodily presence that is brought to life by the machine to be borne witness to.

Notes

1 Levinas, *Otherwise Than Being*, 101.
2 See Levinas, *Otherwise Than Being*, 111. Also, see Wyschogrod, 'Language and Alterity in the Thought of Levinas', 200–1.
3 Zylinska, 'The Future . . . Is Monstrous', 218–19.
4 Levinas, *Otherwise Than Being*, 123. 'Here I am' as a primordial from of 'response of responsibility'. See Levinas, *Otherwise Than Being*, 142. Also, see Barnett, 'Ways of Relating', 5–21 and Miller, 'Reply to Bernhard Waldenfels', 55.
5 Schoonover, *Brutal Vision*, 27.
6 Ibid., 5.
7 Ibid., xxxi.
8 Ibid., 27.
9 Ibid.
10 Ibid.
11 For discussions of the ethical implications of viewing the distant other particularly with regards to suffering, see Chouliaraki, *The Spectatorship of Suffering*, Sontag, *Regarding the Pain of Others*, and Saxton 'Ethics, Spectatorship and the Spectacle of Suffering'.
12 Schoonover, *Brutal Vision*, 7.
13 Ibid.
14 Ibid., 18.
15 Ibid., 8.
16 Ibid., 4–5.
17 Rubin, 'Corporeal Affects and Fleshy Vulnerability'.
18 Kouvaros, '"We Do Not Die Twice"', 385.
19 Rubin, 'Corporeal Affects and Fleshy Vulnerability'.
20 Ibid.
21 Ibid.
22 Ibid.
23 Ibid.
24 Schoonover, *Brutal Vision*, 46.

25 The hyperbolic application of the long take, as Tiago de Luca would suggest, promotes 'a sensuous viewing experience anchored in materiality and duration', making possible 'a protracted inspection of physical reality'. See De Luca, *Realism of the Senses*, 183. For an audience-orientated approach to studying slow cinema, see Boer, 'As Slow as Possible'.
26 Bordun, *Genre Trouble and Extreme Cinema*, 69.
27 De Luca, *Realism of the Senses in World Cinema*, 49.
28 See Rancière, *Film Fables*, 122.
29 De Luca, *Realism of the Senses*, 62.
30 Ibid., 61.
31 Ibid., 62.
32 Beugnet, *Cinema and Sensation*, 96.
33 De Luca, *Realism of the Senses*, 88.
34 I take this notion here to emphasise a becoming through the profilmic act that defies the fixity of a pre-existing being. According to Elena del Río, 'While representation is mimetic, performance is creative and ontogenetic'. See del Río, *Deleuze and the Cinemas of Performance*, 4 and 9.
35 Schoonover, *Brutal Vision*, 33.
36 Morrey, *The Legacy of the New Wave in French Cinema*, 111.
37 Ibid., 116.
38 Rubin, 'Corporeal Affects and Fleshy Vulnerability'.
39 Lübecker, 'The Poetry of Idiots', 448.
40 Rubin, 'Corporeal Affects and Fleshy Vulnerability.
41 Ibid.
42 Schoonover, 'Wastrels of Time', 69.
43 Ibid., 69–70.
44 Cited in ibid., 69.
45 Schoonover, *Brutal Vision*, 44.
46 Cited in ibid., 45
47 Ibid., 44.
48 Cited in Morgan, 'Rethinking Bazin', 445
49 Schoonover, *Brutal Vision*, 18.
50 Ibid., 49.
51 Ibid., 51.
52 Rubin, 'Corporeal Affects and Fleshy Vulnerability'.
53 Dabashi, *Masters & Masterpieces of Iranian Cinema*, 241.
54 Ibid., 246.
55 Blanchot, *The Gaze of Orpheus*, 75. Cited in Shaviro, *The Cinematic Body*, 45.
56 Shaviro, *The Cinematic Body*, 45–6.
57 Cited in ibid., 46.
58 Dudiak, *The Intrigue of Ethics*, 198.
59 Gadassik, 'Davandeh (The Runner)', 358.
60 Accordingly, 'referentiality is the "natural" given of indexical representation'. See Margulies, *Nothing Happens*, 72.
61 Nagib, *World Cinema and the Ethics of Realism*, 32. It must be noted here that Nagib's notion of ethics diverges from the Levinasian ethical. Nagib particularly refers to Alain

Badiou's critique of the idea of absolute alterity, and defines her ethics as a film's 'commitment to the truth of the unpredictable event'. See ibid., 11.
62 See Levinas, *Otherwise Than Being*, 12, 85. Also, Dudiak, *The Intrigue of Ethics*, 197.
63 Ziarek, 'The Ethical Passions', 78–9.
64 Ibid., 79–80.
65 Performance can be said to stand out as an intensification of the literalism of the 'indexical image' – the latter, Alain Robbe-Grillet suggests, as what blocks interpretation via a direct presentation of the referent as a presence that escapes meaning. See Robbe-Grillet, *For a New Novel*, 72. Cited in Margulies, *Nothing Happens*, 70–1.
66 Cited in Shaviro, *The Cinematic Body*, 47.
67 Ibid. Also, see Benjamin, *Illuminations*, 238.
68 Rancière, *Film Fables*, 2.
69 Bresson, *Notes on Cinematography*, 14.
70 Or in the case of Italian Neorealism in particular, 'national pain, and the aftereffects of a global war on the human community'. See Schoonover, 'Wastrels of Time', 69.

8

The Offscreen and the Promise of the Image

Ossos (1997) is the first part in a trilogy of films directed by the Portuguese filmmaker Pedro Costa that focuses on life in Fontainhas – a poor, ghetto-like suburb of Lisbon that no longer exists today and whose residents were mostly immigrants. With a minimal plot that is constituted of rarefied dramatic elements, *Ossos* is a fiction film based on an including the real residents of the slum as non-actors, and on their hard living conditions and everyday life. The depressed, suicidal Tina has just had a baby with her boyish-looking partner. He takes the baby away to attract pity while panhandling on the streets of Lisbon city. Meanwhile, the father also tries to get rid of the baby by attempting to convince a nurse and then a prostitute to take care of it as Tina's gloom worsens. While one might say that the plot certainly gestures towards a melodrama, *Ossos* embeds the presumably melodramatic elements within a filmic body that de-dramatises what it contains. The film's richness, by contrast, is indebted to how the image is set up – an often rigid, monotone staging of bodies in static shots in which, as we shall see, onscreen presences are entwined with the thrust of the emptiness of the offscreen.

Reading Jean-Luc Godard's famous quote that 'every film is a documentary of its actors', Gilberto Perez argues that a 'fiction movie constructs the fiction of characters from the documentary of actors. It is the documentary of a fiction enacted before the camera.'[1] Costa, in a certain sense, literalises Perez's statement as he casts the real residents of the neighbourhood to play their own selves. Found by Costa's camera, the bodies within the image do not stand in the place of something that is absent – they are, rather, as they appear within the image. More interestingly, Costa constructs his fiction through a documentation of bodies through not only his aesthetics but also his filmmaking methods. As Nuno Barradas Jorge points out,

> Discussions of slowness in contemporary art cinema have been mostly centred on textual properties and aspects of visual and narrative

style ... While aesthetic deceleration is the most predominant criterion in grouping many film-makers commonly subsumed under the term slow cinema, other aspects, related to technology and cinematic modes of production, can also be productively examined through the prism of slowness ... in the case of the Portuguese film-maker Pedro Costa, slowness should be understood as both an aesthetic proposition and as a particular mode of film-making resulting from a specific and patient work method.[2]

It is not that Costa's film is unscripted. Despite relying on 'the social conditions offered by the location' as well as 'the collaborative practices between Costa and its inhabitants',[3] *Ossos* is recounting a fiction but one in which the characters are inseparable from the real bodies involved in it and the real hardship they undergo daily. The script is, in a certain way, what charges Costa's camera with an aesthetic intent and therefore a promise. More importantly, *Ossos*'s bodies do not merely reflect a subjectivity that has been denied due to oppression and marginalisation. The frames of *Ossos* bring the bodies into the visual field. However, bodies are not rendered visible within the frame as they are rewatched in an indifference to making sense of the history of their marginalisation. Significantly, they are rewatched with their history imprinted on their surfaces and empty stares.

The affirmative violence of the frame in *Ossos*

Ossos's shots might appear as portraits of the residents of the neighbourhood. Yet their appearance as 'painterly portraits' does not amount to a mere aestheticism that concerns itself with good framings.[4] As the first shot of *Ossos* discussed previously in this book demonstrates, an investigation of the way the image works in *Ossos* and what it does is inseparable from a discussion of the offscreen, particularly as the film is carefully structured around a refusal to re-establish seer–seen structure. Jean-Louis Comolli's reading of Costa's trilogy is helpful in highlighting the role that the offscreen plays in the film – according to him, '*Ossos* is a film made off-screen'.[5] His understanding of the frame and its relation to the question of visibility provide the premise for a discussion of how the offscreen is an integral part of the viewer's experience of Costa's films.

Framing, according to Comolli, is a cutting. To frame means to cut '[w]hat we see from what we don't'.[6] In addition, framing is not simply defined in terms of what is included by the act of cutting. Comolli evokes André Bazin's metaphor of the mask to stress the significance of what is excluded and left out. Given that 'the proportion of the visible obscured by the framing . . . is quantitatively greater than the framed proportion of the visible',[7] the frame works more as a mask than, one might say, a window onto the world. Comolli's remarks are revealing as they bring to attention an understanding of the frame that does not stop at a mere emphasis on what is framed and brought onscreen. It is precisely in the light of this interconnectedness of the on and offscreen that framing as cutting is regarded as a form of violence: 'To frame is to inflict violence.' It is a violence 'against the field of vision itself'.[8] Framing does something to the world viewed as well as to the viewer. It violates the world by including only a portion of it while cutting the rest out.

Comolli's argument is further promising when he regards framing not simply as what leaves out the unframed but as a kind of opening onto it: 'yet this restriction of the visible brought about by framing is an opening, a call to the non-visible.'[9] This leads Comolli to a critique of images that conceal the violence inherent in framing, of what he dubs as 'the general alienation that merges and confuses the world with its spectacle'.[10] Comolli defends the aesthetic achievements of Costa's cinematic manoeuvre to problematise a naturalism stemming from a will to deny the art-nature distinction. Costa's tireless problematisation of an aesthetics that denies the frame is political precisely because, according to Comolli, the creative deployment of the offscreen challenges the ideology of transparency. What

Figure 8.1 Frame-within-a-frame compositions in *Ossos* (Pedro Costa, 1997).

is needed is a 'critical viewer' who will not fall prey to the illusion that the screen is 'transparent'.[11] Costa's *Ossos* is thus considered by Comolli to be subversive insofar as it brings to the foreground the constitutive role of the offscreen. It does so not only through a framing that constantly truncates bodies and thus exposes the cutting function of the frame but also through a frame-within-a-frame structure that further delimits solitary characters and emphasises the constitutive role that framing plays in providing the viewer's access to a world framed. The framing in *Ossos* can be said to be critical of the act of framing itself, obviously not through a forgoing of framing, but by a certain deployment of the frame that exposes its own artifice to make possible a critical viewing practice that refuses to confuse the world with its spectacle.

Despite its valuable insights into how significant the offscreen is and how it is possible to encourage a new mode of looking through a manipulation of the interrelation between the on and offscreen, Comolli's critique is problematic on several counts. The way he establishes a binary distinction between nature and art is inadequate in accounting for the ways the image is capable of doing a certain affirmative violence to the visual field. There is a violence inflicted upon the viewer that can be accounted for through an exploration of the self-presentingness of the image and its address – of how the image's irreducibility to an object within the frontal visual field acts as a threat to the viewer's habituated perception. Comolli's approach fails to do justice to what *Ossos* has achieved through its radical evocation of the offscreen. What the act of framing potentially does, its violence against the world as well as the viewer's visual field, has little to do with the nature–art binarism. The everyday perception is itself not natural but regulated by certain habits of looking that shape and regulate our way of perceiving the world and rendering it visible. The violence of framing provides the grounds for a disturbance of these habits and not of nature as such, and this is a potential explored by Costa's *Ossos*. While the aesthetic can be said to be ideological insofar as it naturalises the framing of the world, a critique of naturalism should not fall prey to another ideological trap – a belief that the unframed world is natural, that framing is responsible for the artifice of our perception. Critical art does not merely expose the artifice of its own framing. More importantly, it disrupts the naturalism of what is considered to exist prior to form – what is historically contingent but appears in the disguise of nature.

Comolli's approach underplays the richness of the concept of the invisible by reducing it to what is merely not visible. Masking is not simply a violence that cuts the world out of the frame, rendering it non-visible.

Similarly, the world presented through the frame is not constituted merely by what is outside it, by a negative relation to what is left out unframed. The frame itself produces an image of the world. The event of the formation of the image transcends both what the image contains and what it leaves out. It has a promise in its very structure. It opens a certain portion of the world, making a claim and doing something to the visual field. The violence of the frame thus embodies a certain constructive thrust that reaffirms something beyond what is posited as content. It is through the image that the world presses itself upon the viewer. The image is the site in which the world *faces*.

The problem is not only that the world is confused with its spectacle, as Comolli suggests, but that the world turned into spectacle forecloses the possibility of a giving of the world, not to entertain or be digested but to be witnessed. The frame is not simply forgotten by an uncritical viewer – what is most crucial is a trivialisation of the frame that buries the address of the image. Even when Comolli is to acknowledge the affirmative side of framing, his concern is largely limited to the production of the non-visible, regarding the invisible as a derivative, as a secondary term – the invisible is merely something that is not visible. Such a conception fails to account not only for the invisibility of the ethical address, but for the resistance of something that is within the image, and is thus thought to have been already rendered visible, to becoming visible. In *Ossos*, the offscreen is not only not visible, but is what problematises the visibility of what is onscreen. A critique of the ideology of transparency fails to explain the status of the image in general, and the critical way the image is set up in *Ossos*. What is overlooked in the ideology of transparency is less the fact that something has been framed – what Comolli determinedly returns to – than that framing has a promise in itself that is often denied. The fact that Comolli recognises the violence of framing but is less interested in exploring what could be affirmed by this violence demonstrates that his discussion remains tied to the 1970s politics of reflexivity. These discussions were based on questionable binary distinctions, not least the binary opposition between realism and modernism, which the recent scholarly revival of realist theories has problematised. Comolli's discussion comes short of investigating how the modernist thrust of realist filmic practices can enter fruitful negotiations with the ethico-political possibilities of framing the world through the cinematic image. It similarly comes short of demonstrating how an aesthetic reworking of realism can stage reality so as to call forth the claim of the latter upon a viewing subject who has long lost their capacity to be affected by the promise that resides in the structure of the framing. What is achieved in *Ossos* is not what is beyond the frame but the frame itself – the frame not simply as what separates the on from the off, but as what is self-presenting, what refers to itself as a promise. The presence to be witnessed, the being to be rewatched, is witnessed insofar as the event of the image – the event of its facing the viewer, its bringing into being a viewer through the facing – is reaffirmed.

It is important that Comolli evokes a notion of otherness to refer to what is missed in a world saturated with images, in a world where images often fail to address the viewers beyond the content that is given, posited and digested. According to him, the triumph of the ideology of transparency is not only what provides the conditions for a confusion of the world with its spectacle, but is also what forecloses the possibility of a genuine encounter with the otherness of the world: 'What is always framed . . . produces images which appear to resemble . . . what in the world is not framed . . . Goodbye to troubling strangeness, goodbye to irrecoverable otherness, goodbye to a reality that cannot yet be framed!'[12] Indeed, it is equally important to ask: what is 'a reality that cannot be framed', and is it merely the world that has been masked by the frame? A genuinely rewarding critique of the status of the image should also account for another sense of the disappearance of the frame. The viewing that forgets the frame is not a viewing that simply mistakes the world for its spectacle. It is one that conceals the promise residing in the event of framing, denying the peculiar visual being of the image as the site in which the world faces the viewer.

Comolli's argument is revealing again when he remarks that: '[t]he offscreen is the site of what remains: what remains to be shown, to be acted out, to be experienced. A reserve, a surplus, a beyond.'[13] In *Ossos*, what remains to be shown is less a property of the act of framing in the film (its essential consequence) than an effect of a certain mode of viewing the image that expects a reciprocation between the seer onscreen and what is presumed to be seen off it. Speaking of what remains to be seen rightly acknowledges that which habitually evokes the desire to see. But it should not be forgotten that it is just a starting point – *Ossos* evokes the desire just to frustrate it. The 'nothingness' of the offscreen is an effect of the expectation to see what remains to be seen. *Ossos* is structured around a production of an offscreen that is not a full space with determinate content. It is a non-space whose being an extension of the onscreen is problematised by a constant refusal of the film to couple the seer onscreen with a potential seen off it. The offscreen is neither diegetic nor non-diegetic. It is precisely by the film's emphatic evocation of the offscreen that, in a certain sense, there is no offscreen in the film. The offscreen is neither a world overflowing the frame nor what plants the filmed bodies into a specific, determinate socio-political context. It is an elsewhere – the invisible force that evokes the non-frontality of vision by problematising the onscreen space, constantly subtracting something from it.

In *Ossos*, the onscreen space is no longer self-contained or self-evident, not simply because there is an offscreen space beyond it, but because what is inside the image (what the image contains) resists resonance with what is outside of it, thus unsettling the image itself. There is a failure of the image in exhausting whatever is within it – not through a fullness that is offscreen, but through an onscreen body that, by its empty look, creates and enacts a non-space offscreen – an uninhabited, indeterminate space. The body that results from framing – the filmed body – is less a body that is truncated by the frame than a bodily presence presented to be witnessed. The violence of framing in *Ossos* is the violence of producing bodies whose being within the image, whose projection and presence onscreen, carries a claim. Moreover, *Ossos*'s hyperbolic deployment of frame-within-a-frame is not simply exposing the artifice of framing. The inexhaustible persistence of bodies onscreen has already short-circuited the illusion of transparency, since the viewer is forced to revisit, investigate and eventually redefine their relation to the image. What the persistence of bodies onscreen attests to is a staging of a giving: a giving of presences to be witnessed.

Weightiness as subversion of visibility

Assuming a fullness for the offscreen implies that there is a reality that overflows, and that the frame is what stages this overflowing by exposing the mask (a frame that calls forth a critical viewer). It is as if framing necessarily leads to reification and what is most crucial is to acknowledge the overflowing of reality from any framing.[14] Yet an alternative understanding of the too-muchness of reality will prove genuinely fruitful here. The too-much is not simply reality in its irreducible richness and density; rather, it is the opening of the image towards the viewer – its facing. In the absence of the address, the uninvolvedness of the viewing subject persists and is deepened. A critical viewer is not one who is baffled or bewildered in the face of the chaos of the real. Otherness does not simply pre-exist the event of exposure – it is, rather, an effect of the framing, as it is through the image that reality faces the viewer.

There is a certain weightiness to *Ossos*'s bodies onscreen – a weightiness that provides the premise for a reaffirmation of the self-presentingness of the image, for the existential densities of the bodies onscreen help them withdraw from being contained as visual content. Weightiness is indebted to the way the filmed bodies are rendered unsustained mainly through the offscreen thrust of emptiness. According to Comolli,

> This *possible* of the off-screen functions, of course, as a narrative and/or dramatic reserve. But when this reserve is shown to be empty, as it is in *Ossos*, and not just once but every time, the off-screen acts as a threat to the film itself, to the very figuration of the filmed bodies. What is present in the frame is threatened at every moment with being thrust into this essential off-screen space of emptiness or nothingness.[15]

The inexhaustibility of the bodies, as well as the resonance between a look offscreen that disturbs the onscreen space with the self-presentingness of the image, forecloses the reduction of presences to visual content. This weightiness is further emphasised through the pauses where the radical reduction of mobility anchors the filmed bodies in their profilmic material presence, whereas the pause returns the duration of the image to a nonnarrative sustaining of the weightiness.

The narrative contingencies of *Ossos*'s bodies is irreducible to Bazin's discussion of the after-the-fact details of bodily gestures, which, owing to their condition of emergence, cannot be accounted for in advance.[16] In contrast to what I have discussed previously in this book about the affirmative contingencies of bad acting, acting in *Ossos* is evidently underplayed and the

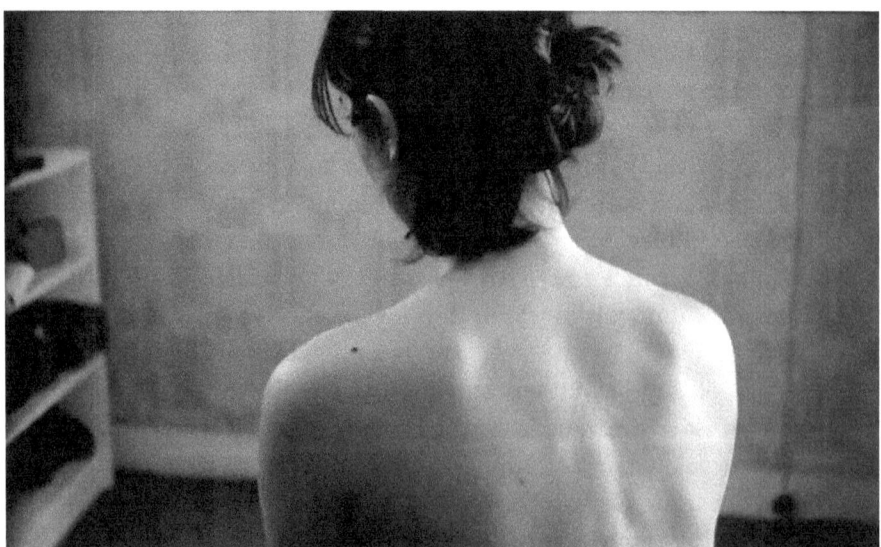

Figure 8.2 Pauses that emphasise the weightiness of onscreen bodies in *Ossos* (Pedro Costa, 1997).

movements are rarefied and reduced to the extent that gestures are minimised and not much room is left for the accidental to take place. Yet the filmed bodies still stand out as the force of contingency – as its facilitator. It is not that the details of gestures are unplanned and thus overflow scripted schemata, but precisely because a radical reduction and sometimes even an absence of mobility, along with the empty time, extended duration and the looking offscreen into nothingness, lead to a certain unreadability of the body's presence onscreen. According to Ira Jaffe, *Ossos* is constituted by images that resist or impede the 'onward movement' of the narrative: 'the individual image or moment acquires independent standing or distinction, apart from its narrative function.'[17] In *Ossos*, the present moment 'is made visually absolute' rather than being subordinated to either 'narrative flow' or 'human psychology'.[18] Contingency in *Ossos*'s realism of the body therefore involves shots that make bodies available, while the 'for' of 'making available for' is incapable of exhaustively justifying the body's emergence and persistence onscreen.

The exposure of the limits of seeing within the frames of *Ossos* also finds revealing examples in the rare instances of two-shots in the film. There is a radical reduction of interaction between the filmed bodies within the two-shots, an evident lack of proximity. What the viewer sees is often nothing but merely a spatial closeness between two bodies within the frame. There is not much dialogue, and there is no reciprocation of gazes. More importantly, both characters are often looking offscreen, just as they do in the single shots, evoking the thrust of emptiness that troubles the onscreen space and its meaningfulness. Proximity is due to the two bodies being present within the same diegetic space. More crucially, their presence within the same frame is justified not by the meaningfulness of their being close to one another but by the mere fact of their being staged for the camera within a shot. Their proximity is forced by the filmic practice of juxtaposing them within the *mise en scène*, as if the bodies onscreen are less actors embodying characters than filmed bodies blocked and staged within the visual field of the lens.

What also needs to be accounted for is the extent to which the conversion of the filmed body in *Ossos* is facilitated or disrupted by the interaction between the shots. The editing that allows for no reciprocation between the seer and what is being seen constantly denies the viewer the solace of motivating the bodies onscreen, of filling them with signification and justifying them. Moreover, deploying ellipsis as a main narrative device (leaving out events that could be dramatically important and instead devoting extended time to non-dramatic durations) further helps the individual shots stand on their own terms in their odd density. This gives the whole film a structure that highlights the contingency – as opposed to the necessity – of the connection of shots and their spatio-temporal threads. The juxtaposition of shots often disorients the viewer as opposed to facilitating the formation of connections between singular shots. This is not only because the link often seems loosely unjustified but also because the shots are often sustained by their own immanent function. A certain reduction of mobility and rationalisation within each shot removes it from merely being a fragment that bears the traces of the editing from the outset – in their spatial density, the shots are too much to be exhausted by their connection. Furthermore, the totality that is expected to result from editing is already a tenuous one due to the reduction of resonance between the shots. As Jaffe observes, the images of *Ossos* are mainly characterised by an extended use of close-ups and medium shots while these shots 'stand by themselves as separate scenes', appearing as 'privileged moments, outside any chain of action'.[19] Editing in *Ossos* becomes an exposure of the failure of what editing is conventionally associated with because the scattering force of individual shots is established within the shots themselves from the outset even before they are juxtaposed to form the film in its entirety. Each shot is disrupted by the thrust of the offscreen but remains self-evident and irreducible.[20]

The local body

The weightiness of bodies and their resistance to a reduction in visual content is peculiarly evident in the ways *Ossos* evokes the local for a foreign onlooker (a cinematic potential discussed in the previous chapter). If we are to speak of a certain 'overflowing', it is the local body that overflows the everydayness of the local world. The failure of the local in locating the body finds its most evident actualisation in the offscreen sound. As Costa himself has remarked, *Ossos* is a 'noisy' film.[21] Almost all scenes, especially those set in the neighbourhood, are saturated with everyday sounds of people chatting, babies crying and televisions and radios being left on. One might consider the omnipresence of everyday sound in *Ossos* as the film's tendency to create the impression that the bodies of the actors/characters are contained by what is going on offscreen in the bigger realm of the neighbourhood life. Such a reading would regard the offscreen sound as simply diegetic, overlooking the ways in which *Ossos* disrupts the simple fitting and synchronisation that diegetic sounds, by definition, assume. The repetitiveness of the offscreen sound, its being an almost unidentifiable mass of noise, and most importantly the absence of meaningful reciprocation between the filmed bodies onscreen and the constant flow of the everyday sound off it, demonstrate that the use of sound is in the service of an abstraction of the filmed bodies rather than embedded within the local community. The sound works as a container (of bodies, of faces), but it is a failure of containment. Sound presents itself as a found thing – as opposed to a sound that is scripted and produced based on a selection, amplification and reduction of sound effects. The detachment of offscreen sound from the filmed body implies a recording of sound that could take place independently, thus staging a return to the automatic recording, to its fundamental contingency, indifference and elsewhereness. Due to a lack of resonance between the offscreen sound and onscreen bodily presences, it is as if the bodies' image is merely put together with the found offscreen sound, thus exposing the artifice of the film's attempt at capturing the local body. The constant, overwhelming presence of sound is less in the service of embedding the bodies within the social milieu than in exposing the failure of the surroundings in exhausting the bodies being filmed.

The contingency of the offscreen sound along with the extended use of close-ups and alienated stares helps to detach the bodies onscreen from their surroundings.[22] Bodies on display are showcasing the failure of the context, which essentially is the failure of representation. The latter is dependent upon a readability of the bodies – here, a readability that sees embeddedness within a wider social realm as its condition for possibility. *Ossos*'s bodies are embedded, but at the same time withdrawn. They reaffirm the fundamental actorlessness of the film medium, for they emerge as the site in which the failure of the local in exhausting the filmed bodies is theatricalised. In a certain sense, *Ossos* flips the hierarchy: the local body, by being presented to the camera in its indeterminacy and in its non-relation to what is not within the visual field of the camera, is less a derivative of the local than a facilitator of it. If any sense of localness is affirmed in the film, it is mediated through the close-ups and medium shots of bodies – shots that withdraw the latter from the broader community, giving them a certain weight in their persistence onscreen. The filmed bodies constantly reflect but also displace the local.

Even in rare cases where the (offscreen) everyday life is shown in its non-dramatic, mundane flow, it is through the frame-within-a-frame structure and the often troubling interaction between the foreground and the background. In a scene in Lisbon city where the father is asking people for money to feed his infant child, there is an odd staging of the foreground in relation to the background in a static, extended shot. With a low-angle shot

Figure 8.3 The prevalence of stares into the offscreen space in *Ossos* (Pedro Costa, 1997).

through a long focal-length lens that compresses the perspective, the foreground paradoxically appears detached from the background as the father's movements seem to be the primary visual interest in the shot while other people move around the market in a manner that is utterly indifferent to the stationary camera. This simultaneous compression and separation of space yields an uncanny feeling, as if there were a screen within a screen, or a rear projection, a re-screening of the everyday. The way the image is set up accentuates its self-presentingness – the everyday is staged to be rewatched. The use of sound in the scene is also troubling as the amplified murmurs of the father asking for money distorts the perspective of sound that we might associate with a believable, realist presentation. At a representational level, it could be said that this peculiar *mise en scène* tends to represent the character as being rejected by the rest of the community. Yet what the scene is most concerned with is a negotiation with the camera's ability to automatically record the real. The everydayness of what is recorded is distorted but is not turned into an unreality; it is more a spatio-temporal block of reality preserved and displaced within the image. The father is not merely an actor enacting intentional meanings. He is also the human subject of a documentary, located on a busy street to be rewatched while the representational thrust of the dramatic action is deprioritised.

Ossos's responsible approach to the hardship of life in the ghetto-like neighbourhood embodies a certain informativeness about a specific social world.[23] Yet the image returns the film to a certain degree zero of recording, to an assertion of the recording abilities of the camera that subverts any presumed representation of subaltern life. Representation assumes and calls forth a viewing subject who comprehends what is onscreen by recourse to what is already familiar, rendering visible what they view through the mediation of the third. In *Ossos*, by contrast, the local is captured by the camera in a way that opens up space for the possibility of a witnessing that challenges the objectification of what is captured. *Ossos* foregrounds the role of the machine in such a capturing precisely to stage the failure of the subsequent capture by the human agent – a failure that is already registered in the originary making available of bodies. As Vered Maimon argues, Costa's films, particularly his Fontainhas trilogy, are 'not "about" the poor, nor do they "represent" the poor' – they rather 'insist on shared common capacities to tell stories that are as rich as countless life experiences'. What is striking is Costa's attempt to locate the ethical in a certain non-frontal aspect of the image: 'in Costa's films characters become storytellers who tell their own stories not as confessions but as reports.'[24] The characters' reports demonstrate an alternative engagement with their bodies where the pre-reflective exposure to the other is cinematically restaged and prioritised over a recognition of otherness.

It is with regard to both the automatism of the film medium and the originary foreignness of the cinematic viewer that Costa's tendency to deploy non-actors and location shooting cannot be simply reduced to a gesture of authenticity.[25] What these aesthetic decisions bring into play is an enhanced indexicality that disrupts attempts to posit the given image of the local. The latter is, in a certain sense, recorded regardless of whether or not it appears as local. As Mary Ann Doane observes, indexicality must be dissociated from intrinsic connections to uncritical notions of realism as 'the reflection of a coherent, familiar, and recognizable world'. Index is a humble denotation of 'this' or 'here it is'; it is a testimony that is 'essentially without content'.[26] Similarly, for Costa, the local imprinting itself on the celluloid is far more crucial than an effort to create the impression of localness. This emphatic exploitation of the non-human relation between the machine and the local troubles any recourse to the logic of impressions – the local that is captured cannot be digested either by a return to the familiar or by an exoticism that itself reaffirms and demarcates familiarity in the disguise of difference. The power of Costa's images resides in their theatricalisation of what Karl Schoonover calls 'the forceful impact of immediate history on the image',[27] but also in a displacement of the local that this impact creates. *Ossos*'s images are less a transference of reality from the world to the image than a displacement of the world that turns the latter into what is coming from elsewhere, and thus is irreducible to what can be located within the frontal visual field.

The lived duration of the suffering body

The demise of the promise of the image is not only contingent upon how an image is set up. In effect, certain viewing practices as well as film criticisms contribute to a concealment of the ethical address of images. In particular, there are critical approaches that tend to explain away the specific viewing position that *Ossos* promotes by a reduction of its experiments to the question of mysteriousness. Speaking of 'mysterious density', reducing the film to an attempt to make things difficult to know,[28] or to 'Costa's disposition . . . to hide or elide information that could illuminate the film's plot and spatio-temporal context as well as its characters,'[29] scholars assume that the power of the image in *Ossos* stems from a regime of revealing and withholding information. The uncritical assumption is that what the viewer goes through in part consists of a game of guessing, inferring, filling the blanks and in fact constant frustration. Even acknowledging otherness by asserting that in *Ossos* 'the characters' mysteriousness indicates that life is too vast and complex to be encompassed and explained in this or any other film'[30] is symptomatic of the problems I discussed earlier with regard to Comolli's reading of Costa's trilogy – a conception of otherness that merely preoccupies itself with an other who overflows the frame. Conflating otherness with mysteriousness, this approach assumes that *Ossos* is based upon a certain denial of information to create a sense of mystery that in its own right testifies to the overflowing of the reality of the other. It is as though otherness is produced by withholding information, which essentially means that otherness is effectively resolved by uncovering it.

Mysteriousness is the term a viewer/critic may hide behind to rationalise the frustrations of the image. Such an approach, despite its apparent attention to the activity of the viewer, to their cognitive endeavour to solve the mystery or appreciate the artifice of creating mystery by manipulating filmic conventions, effectively denies the capacities of a viewer who can revisit their relation to images that unfold in the face of dissatisfactions. The viewer is conceived as an agent who is detached from the temporality of film and is thus incapable of appreciating something alternative beyond the activity of narrative comprehension after early frustrations. Contending, as Jaffe does, that 'events as well as characters in *Ossos* exist in an indeterminate realm or context'[31] does little justice to the film. The only confusing thing about *Ossos*, if any, is the time it takes for the viewer to get a grasp of the film's temporal composition and distinguish between characters – which is more a matter of identifying their physical attributes and distinctions than bestowing interiority on them to render them readable. Such a theoretical craving for interiority fails to reflect on its own assumptions: what is a context? Is the story's context not already there? Is the profilmic not appearing as an adequate context that envelopes the bodies in the flow of duration? Is context necessarily what comprehends and pins down in a cognitive way anything that is found in the frame? Or is context not that which is created by the bodies, by their weightiness within the images and their carrying their histories imprinted on them? A persistent search for interiority neglects the fact that *Ossos* is based on a systematic reduction of interiorities. The hardship of life is simply there onscreen, defining what a body goes through daily, needless of any elaboration.

It is the same desire for visibility that reads *Ossos*'s refusal of verbalisation and expression of suffering as a sort of concealment as if what the film is structured around is a will to hide something that can otherwise be rendered visible. This approach is unable to account for the fact that the reduction of expression in *Ossos* is less a reduction of reality – something real that is left out and thus rendered non-visible – than a reduction that challenges viewing habits of associating the suffering of the other with determinate content. Suffering is not a pre-existing content that *Ossos* simply hides. If this was the case, a conventionally narrative rendition of the other's suffering would be truer and more adequate to reality (and hence, one might convincingly say, 'more ethical'). This approach overlooks the fact that once the other's suffering is objectified – once it is turned into a something that can be easily located within the visual field and filled with determinate content – the claim of the image is lost. *Ossos* does not hide content through its reductions and refusals but disturbs the habit of considering suffering as something that can be rendered visible and thus intelligible.

There is a certain de-hierarchisation in *Ossos* that refuses to highlight the suffering at the expense of the lived duration. At a melodramatic level, it is Tina as the mother who is most evidently suffering, compared with what the other characters undergo. Yet there is not only no expression or verbalisation of her torment but also the film's de-hierarchising structure denies her any special treatment at a formal level. The times Tina appears and persists onscreen are by no means in the service of singling her out, and the way she is framed is not in any form different from the way, for instance, Clotilde (Tina's neighbour) as the seemingly stronger, less fragile female character is framed. Tina is most of the time trapped within the same framing within a frame, but just as much as any other character in the film is.

Reducing the other and its suffering to visual content jeopardises the address and claim of the image, turning it into a (successful) work of mourning that evokes the other to leave its precarious body behind. Through such a reduction, the image can no longer work as an opening onto the other. It initiates a movement towards the other that constantly returns to the same. By contrast, Costa's images can be said to be melancholic precisely because they foreclose any subsumption of the other, refusing the objectification of its agonised body. The viewer-as-onlooker is affected by the imperilled body onscreen, by the suffering inscribed on its body and face and its empty look, but is denied any verbalisation or expression of what turns the suffering into a spectacle to be looked at. Returning Judith Butler's reformulation of the Levinasian face, *Ossos*'s images can be said to evoke the face, insofar as what the images communicate is wordless but can still be traced on the agonised body of the other. Suffering in *Ossos* is invisible precisely because it is within the image, facing the viewer without the need to be verbalised or signify anything. It does not need to stand for anything, to evoke the third or represent something else. The filmed body is dense precisely because it does not present itself as a derivative. It is as it appears, a body enveloped in literal durations, unfolding in an already present but equally distant pro-filmic time.

An apparently benevolent portrayal of the suffering of the other can never convey the senselessness of suffering simply because its will to narrativise always bears the seeds of a rationalisation of suffering within the constraints of a story proper to conjure it away.[32] Nor is it willing to admit, or capable of admitting, that the gap inherent in otherness is falsely bridged in such an apparently benevolent viewing practice, in what can be called a mystified 'tele-intimacy'.[33] Compassion in its true sense must be distinguished from a voyeuristic consumption of the agonised body. What *Ossos* does is eliminate suffering, not from the reality of the body, but from the ideological, naturalised unreality of historically dominant modes of storytelling, according to which the other must be told regardless of the fact that what gives the suffering its weight is its being alien to the realm of representation. Jaffe refers to this 'untoldness' when he remarks that '[t]he faces especially of Tina and the baby's father suggest untold need and suffering'.[34] To follow the implications of this untoldness, I would ask: What is it that is kept untold? Is it a pre-existing content that is left unrevealed? Or is it what is produced or is expected to be produced by the act of telling? Who is the agent of the untelling? And who is the one who desires the telling, longing for a rendition of the visibility of the bodies?

Suffering, in its either physical or psychological essence, is invisible. It resists reduction to visual content. And its power to address resides in its irreducibility – in, one might say, its withdrawal from the domain of visibility. There is a certain materiality to the suffering of the subaltern other that *Ossos* respects in a profound way. Materiality becomes a mode of being. It is an effect of being a non-member of a community; of being a body living in proximity to other bodies but precisely by having a material body and not by belonging to and participating in the discursive formation of a culture.[35] The otherness of the human other in *Ossos* is therefore not the predefined otherness of a socio-cultural situatedness, despite the fact that the marginalisation of the residents of the ghetto effects as a hard, concrete fact. The precarious body of the other is a marked one – marked not least by its suffering. Precisely due to its being marked, however, the body is unidentifiable. It cannot be simply located within a history. Its being marked does not lead to its signifyingness within meaningful relations to other bodies.

Costa's preoccupation with filming bodies within controlled and static shots undermines the assumption that an enacted story precedes the event of the image opening up within the visual field. While a story proper desires a body born out of the script, a body that fits a pre-existing scheme, *Ossos*'s bodies are a theatricalisation of a bodily surplus that dictates its being within the image as the source of the story. Bearing witness to the hardship of life in the Fontainhas neighbourhood is therefore inseparable from the present tense of a filming that is only virtually present. The ghostly weightiness of the filmed body onscreen disrupts the inviting powers of the viewing subject. Rewatching an other onscreen who owes their cinematic presence to a machine that watches the bodies and *not* the characters, the viewer's grip over the other is tenuous.

Ossos reaffirms the facing of the image through its ethico-aesthetic of incompleteness – one that does not anticipate a future or possible completion; not a failure that sets up the success to come. What is not-yet is a promise that cannot be fulfilled. It is that which cannot be grasped by a better framing, a better production of the visible. The images in *Ossos* stage the tension between the ethical and the visual to perform their anxiety in the face of the senselessness of the suffering of the other – one that, ethically speaking, addresses insofar as it resists translation into any figuration.

Notes

1. See Leigh, 'Ontology, Film and the Case of Eric Rohmer', 165.
2. Jorge, 'Living Daily, Working Slowly', 169.
3. Jorge, *The Films of Pedro Costa*, 34.
4. As an example, *The Criterion Collection* release of the trilogy that describes the films as 'spare, painterly portraits of battered, largely immigrant lives in the slums of Fontainhas'.
5. Comolli, 'Frames and Bodies', 65. Also, see Heath, 'On Screen, In Frame', 251–65. For a discussion of different offscreen zones, see Burch, *Theory of Film Practice*, 17–32.
6. Comolli, 'Frames and Bodies', 64.
7. Ibid.
8. Ibid.
9. See ibid.
10. Ibid., 67.
11. Ibid.
12. Ibid.
13. Ibid., 65.
14. Comolli evokes the offscreen as a sort of threat, possibility and promise. See ibid.
15. Ibid.
16. For Bazin, according to Schoonover, the filmed body is the site in which 'the radical potentialities of contingency' are manifested. See Schoonover, *Brutal Vision*, 3–4.
17. Jaffe, *Slow Movies*, 124–5.
18. Cited in ibid., 125.
19. Ibid.
20. *Ossos* is less emphatic in terms of its deployment of extended duration compared to most of the films discussed in this book. But the shots of the film certainly make their passing felt. See Jaffe, *Slow Movies*, 4–5.
21. Visit 'Pedro Costa and Jean-Pierre Gorin on Ossos', uploaded to YouTube on 4 May 2013, <youtu.be/nDvPO9tqKSk> (last accessed 25 April 2022). The conversation was recorded for Criterion Channel in August 2009 in New York.
22. For an in-depth discussion of sound, body and presence, see Doane, 'The Voice in the Cinema'.
23. As Flanagan argues, 'the distinctive aesthetics of slow films tend to emerge from spaces that have been indirectly affected or left behind by globalisation, most notably in the films of Alonso, Bartas, Jia, Costa and Diaz'. See Flanagan, '"Slow Cinema"', 111. What Dominique Nasta argues about New Romanian Cinema (poverty being a central theme) to a certain extent applies to the stylistic patterning of *Ossos*. See Nasta, *Contemporary Romanian Cinema*, 157.
24. Vered Maimon, 'Beyond Representation', 339–41.
25. As Bárbara Barroso observes, *Ossos* is not 'aiming for a kind of documentary "look" as an immediate tip to the "authenticity" of its setting'. See Barroso, 'Ossos/Bones'.
26. Doane, *The Emergence of Cinematic Time*, 25.
27. See Schoonover, *Brutal Vision*, xvi.
28. Tag Gallagher, Cyril Neyrat and Shigehiko Hasumi are among several critics who agree with Wall. Gallagher writes that 'Costa denies us entry to his characters', Neyrat remarks that the characters 'preserve their mysterious density until the end', and Hasumi notes

that their 'identity' and 'interrelations' are 'difficult to know'. Cited in Jaffe, *Slow Movies*, 120. See Hasumi, 'Adventure', Gallagher, 'Straub Anti-Straub' and Neyrat, 'Rooms for the Living and the Dead'.
29 Jaffe, *Slow Movies*, 124.
30 Ibid., 120.
31 See ibid., 124.
32 In his discussion of J. M. Coetzee, Sam Durrant speaks of 'a base level of suffering that resists narrativization'. See Durant, *Postcolonial Narrative and the Work of Mourning*, 18. James Phillips, in his analysis of Kenji Mizoguchi's realism, opposes the latter to a 'pornography of human misfortune' where the 'creation and consumption of suffering as an object' works to 'avoid having to confront the actual unobjectifiability of suffering'. See Phillips, 'The Fates of Flesh', 20.
33 According to Susan Sontag, the 'imaginary proximity to the suffering inflicted on others that is granted by images suggests a link between the faraway sufferers – seen close-up on the television screen – and the privileged viewer that is simply untrue, that is yet one more mystification of our real relations to power'. See Sontag, *Regarding the Pain of Others*, 104. Cited in Saxton, 'Ethics, Spectatorship and the Spectacle of Suffering', 66.
34 Jaffe, *Slow Movies*, 125.
35 For Durant's discussion of the extra-discursive materiality of the bodies who have acquired a certain materiality 'precisely because they have been denied access to the discursive realm of culture', and of a 'material level of suffering' that refuses to be translatable, see Durant, *Postcolonial Narrative and the Work of Mourning*, 112–14.

Coda

How is it possible to admit that an image of the body of the other assumes that 'a life has been lived', and that in the absence of the image, the other is 'sustained by no regard or testimony, and ungrieved when lost', and still engage with Emmanuel Levinas's antipathy for the image and art in general? It has been my objective in this book to demonstrate that what Levinas's thought offers to film studies is more than a critique of the altericidal violence of the image or an acknowledgement of images that are critical of their own visual being. Levinas's conception of the face and his understanding of the tensions between the ethical and the visual are nuanced such that there can emerge alternative possibilities from within his iconoclasm to think and appreciate the image in affirmative ways. Levinas assists us to see the tensions that are constitutive of vision while the thrust of a Levinasian approach can reveal what the image does to vision in order to restage these tensions. The image can even be taken to show attributes analogous to the ethical epiphany of the face, as an originary meaningfulness, rather than the meaningfulness of intentionality. The image is where the breakthrough of the other, but also its withdrawal, takes place.

Whereas Levinas founds his ethics on a condemnation of ontological regimes that dominate vision, I have attempted in this book to demonstrate how his ethics can be hospitable to notions of cinematic realism that resonate with the originary structure of exposure. At the same time, I have tried to show how the thought of André Bazin, revered as one of the prominent ontologists of cinema, and several other film theorists can assist us to locate the ethical in the body–camera encounter where 'otherwise than being' can be borne witness to. While Levinasian ethics can be read to appreciate the visuality of the cinematic image, Bazinian realism can similarly be reworked to map out the ontological instabilities of the filmic rendition of the body which alter a gaze that would otherwise grasp the other to return to the familiar.

Through discussions of several films I have tried to demonstrate that, while the camera automatically records the world and makes it available to a conscious subject, there is already something in this automatic formation that bears the seeds of a certain withdrawal of what is offered by the camera from being neatly recognisable by the viewing subject. The cinematic image can stage proximity to the automatically captured body, enabling us to bear witness to our hospitality to the other as that which has taken place prior to our leisure, privilege or power to identify the other. The cinematic image can be set up in creative ways to assist us to dissociate otherness from a recognition of sameness and difference, and relocate it in the structure of exposure. To respect the other no longer entails tailoring a subjectivity for the other to fill them with interiority. To respect is to rewatch the body of the human other that was first watched by the inhuman eye of the machine. Not exhaustively making sense, the other addresses the viewer – owing to the way the cinematic image sustains what resists appropriation.

As the existing literature on Levinasian film scholarship testifies, my emphasis in this book on aesthetic realisms of the body is by no means the only approach to demonstrate the revelation of the Levinasian ethical in cinema. Nor can these realist practices, of course, be limited to the cases studied in the scope of this project. In my arguments and film analyses, I have been inspired by the possible partnerships between Levinas's ethical thought and film theory to articulate what fascinates me about cinema – its capacity to tell stories, while the real, existing bodies that host these stories can impact as powerful impressions of human presence onscreen without having to be remarkable or even knowable in order to belong to the screen. This capacity has always been for me a sort of incompleteness where I as the viewer have been moved, not by a desire to ask for more meaning and visibility to reach completion, but by a peculiar, perhaps inexplicable but no less powerful appreciation of human presence in its precarity and vulnerability.

Even though there are newly emerging forms of film viewing practices and spectatorial modes particularly due to new technologies, my assumption has been that films are viewed under the specific conditions intended by their filmmakers that involve fixed-time circumstances where a film dictates its own temporality. Indeed, I even go further to argue that the ethical relevance of experiencing the films studied here to a certain extent resides in their resistance to assimilation into our current image-saturated cultures and mediatised environments. This resistance is beyond the mere application of certain filmic techniques or aesthetic decisions that can often be reappropriated by dominant regimes of image formation, but involves the experience that a film provides in its entirety.

Whereas throughout the book I have defended the images that resist meaning, I have also been conscious to diverge my interest from part of the dominant contemporary forms of making and circulating images whose success in commodification is often carried out through a reduction of meaning to facilitate the production and consumption of visual and aural excesses. I have preferred to speak not so much of excess but of surplus as a demonstration of the originary refusal of the other to merely grant a given image, and of the body–camera interaction as what brings into being a life that defies the necessities of intelligibility. Furthermore, to establish a different significance that is meaningful, I have tried to locate meaningfulness not in active contemplation but in a commitment that watching certain films demands.

I have hoped to demonstrate throughout this project how certain aesthetic experiments with the eye of the cinematograph can help us resist and counter the hegemony of the eye and engage with alternative ways of encountering the other through the cinematic image. This encounter can turn the image into a gift, into an openness towards the other in our shared vulnerability. This hospitality of the image, perhaps, may come close to what Jacques Derrida would call a being 'unprepared, or prepared to be unprepared, for the unexpected arrival of *any* other'.[1]

Note

1 Derrida, 'Hospitality, Justice and Responsibility', 70.

Bibliography

Agacinski, Sylvaine. 2003. *Time Passing: Modernity and Nostalgia*. New York: Columbia University Press.
Ahern, Mal. 2018. 'Cinema's Automatisms and Industrial Automation.' *Diacritics* (Cornell University) 46 (4): 6–33.
Alligier, Martline. 2012. *Bruno Dumont: l'animalité et la grâce*. Aix-en-Provence: Rouge Profond.
Andrew, Dudley. 1976. *The Major Film Theories: An Introduction*. New York: Oxford University Press.
Andrew, Dudley. 1978. *André Bazin*. New York: Oxford University Press.
Andrew, Dudley. 2004. 'Foreword to 2004 Edition.' In *What is Cinema?*, vol. 2, by André Bazin, xi–xxvi. Berkeley, Los Angeles and London: University of California Press.
Backman Rogers, Anna. 2009. 'Realism and Gus Van Sant's Elephant.' In *Realism and the Audiovisual Media*. Edited by Lúcia Nagib and Cecília Mello, 85–95. London: Palgrave Macmillan.
Balaisis, Nicholas. 2007. 'The Risk of Ambiguity: Reconsidering Zavattini's Film Ethics.' *CineAction* 72: 42–5.
Barnett, Clive. 2005. 'Ways of Relating: Hospitality and the Acknowledgement of Otherness.' *Progress in Human Geography* 29 (1): 5–21.
Barroso, Bárbara. 2009. 'Ossos/Bones.' *Senses of Cinema*. <https://www.sensesofcinema.com/2009/cteq/ossos/> (last accessed 28 June 2022).
Barthes, Roland. 1993. *Camera Lucida: Reflections on Photography*. London: Vintage.
Barzanji, Arta. 2020. 'A Still Cinema.' *Film Matters* 11 (2): 7–17.
Bataille, Georges. 1985. 'Base Materialism and Gnosticism.' In *Visions of Excess: Selected Writings, 1927–1939*. Translated by Allan Stoekl, 45–52. Minneapolis, MN: University of Minnesota Press.
Bazin, André. 1949/1971. 'Bicycle Thief.' In *What is Cinema?*, vol. 2. Translated by Hugh Gray, 47–60. Berkeley, Los Angeles and London: University of California Press.
Bazin, André. 1949/1971. 'In Defense of Rossellini.' In *What is Cinema?*, vol. 2. Translated by Hugh Gray, 93–101. Berkeley, Los Angeles and London: University of California Press.
Bazin, André. 1949/1971. 'The Evolution of the Language of Cinema.' In *What is Cinema?*, vol 1. Translated by Hugh Gray. Berkeley, Los Angeles and London: University of California Press.

Bazin, André. 1949/1971. 'The Ontology of the Photographic Image.' In *What is Cinema?*, vol. 1. Translated by Hugh Gray. Berkeley, Los Angeles and London: University of California Press.

Bazin, André. 1949/1971. 'The Virtues and Limitations of Montage.' In *What is Cinema?*, vol. 1. Translated by Hugh Gray. Berkeley, Los Angeles and London: University of California Press.

Bazin, André. 1949/1971. *What Is Cinema?, vol. 1*. Translated by Hugh Gray. Berkeley, Los Angeles and London: University of California Press.

Bazin, André. 1949/1971. *What is Cinema?, vol. 2*. Translated by Hugh Gray. Berkeley, Los Angeles and London: University of California Press.

Bazin, André. 1973. *Jean Renoir*. Edited by Francois Truffaut. Translated by W. W. Halsey II and William H. Simon. New York: Simon & Schuster.

Bazin, André. 1973. 'The French Renoir.' In *Jean Renoir*, 74–91. New York: Simon & Schuster.

Bazin, André. 2002. 'Will CinemaScope Save the Film Industry?' *Film-Philosophy* 6 (1). <https://www.euppublishing.com/doi/10.3366/film.2002.0002> (last accessed 28 June 2022).

Beardsworth, Richard. 1996. *Derrida and the Political*. London: Routledge.

Benjamin, Walter. 1969. *Illuminations: Essays and Reflections*. Edited by Hannah Arendt. Translated by Harry Zohn. New York: Schocken Books.

Bennington, Geoffrey. 2000. 'Deconstruction and Ethics.' In *Deconstructions: A User's Guide*. Edited by Nicholas Royle, 64–82. Basingstoke: Palgrave Macmillan.

Bergren-Aurand, Brian. 2009. 'Film/ethics.' *New Review of Film and Television Studies* (Taylor & Francis) 7 (4): 459–74.

Bergstrom, Janet. 1977. 'Jeanne Dielman, 23 quai du Commerce, 1080 Bruxelles, by Chantal Akerman.' *Camera Obscura: A Journal of Feminism and Film Theory* 2: 115–21.

Beugnet, Martine. 2007. *Cinema and Sensation: French Film and the Art of Transgression*. Edinburgh, UK: Edinburgh University Press.

Birks, Chelsea and Coulthard, Lisa. 2019. 'Divine Comedies: Post-Theology and Laughter in the Films of Bruno Dumont.' *Film-Philosophy* 23 (3): 247–63.

Blanchot, Maurice. 1981. *The Gaze of Orpheus*. Translated by Geoffrey H. Hartman. New York: Station Hill Press.

Blanchot, Maurice. 1987. *Everyday Speech*. Translated by Susan Hanson. New Haven, CT: Yale University Press.

Blanchot, Maurice. 1992. *The Infinite Conversation*. Translated by Susan Hanson. Minneapolis, MN: University of Minnesota Press.

Boer, Jakob. 2015. 'As Slow as Possible: An Enquiry Into the Redeeming Power of Boredom for Slow Film Viewers.' *Arts, Culture and Media* (University of Groningen).

Bond, Lewis Michael and Luiza Liz Bond. 2021. 'The Tragic Side of Cinema | Video Essay.' The Cinema Cartography YouTube channel, 22 January. <youtu.be/toQ1W_ILpBU> (last accessed 25 April 2022).

Bordun, Troy. 2017. *Genre Trouble and Extreme Cinema: Film Theory at the Fringes of Contemporary Art Cinema*. Cham: Palgrave Macmillan.

Bowles, Brett. 2004. 'The Life of Jesus (La Vie de Jésus).' *Film Quarterly* (University of California Press) 57 (3): 47–55.

Bresson, Robert. 1977. *Notes on Cinematography*. Translated by Jonathan Griffin. New York: Urizen Books.

Burch, Noel. 1981. *Theory of Film Practice*. Translated by Helen R. Lane. Princeton, NJ: Princeton University Press.

Burns, Gerald L. 2004. 'The Concepts of Art and Poetry in Emmanuel Levinas's Writings.' In *The Cambridge Companion to Levinas*. Edited by Simon Critchley and Robert Bernasconi. Cambridge: Cambridge University Press.

Butler, Judith. 2006. *Precarious Life: The Powers of Violence and Mourning*. London and New York: Verso.

Butler, Judith. 2009. *Frames of War: When is Life Grievable?* London and New York: Verso.

Çağlayan, Emre. 2018. *Poetics of Slow Cinema: Nostalgia, Absurdism, Boredom*. Cham: Springer International Publishing.

Cardullo, Bert. 2011. 'Defining the Real: The Film Theory and Criticism of André Bazin.' In *André Bazin and Italian Neorealism*. Edited by Bert Cardullo. New York: Continuum.

Cardullo, Bert. 2011. 'Cinematic Realism and the Italian School of the Liberation.' In *André Bazin and Italian Neo-realism*. Edited by Bert Cardullo. New York: Continuum.

Carroll, Noël. 1988. *Philosophical Problems of Classical Film Theory*. Princeton, NJ: Princeton University Press.

Chouliaraki, Lilie. 2006. *The Spectatorship of Suffering*. London: Sage.

Comolli, Jean-Louis. 1978. 'Historical Fiction: A Body Too Much.' *Screen* 19 (2): 41–54.

Comolli, John-Louis. 2010. 'Frames and Bodies – Notes on Three Films by Pedro Costa: Ossos, No Quarto da Vanda, Juventude em Marcha.' *Afterall: A Journal of Art, Context and Enquiry* (24): 62–70.

Conley, Tom. 2005. 'Cinema and Its Discontents: Jacques Rancière and Film Theory.' *SubStance* 34 (3): 96–106.

Cooper, Sarah. 2007. 'Mortal Ethics: Reading Levinas with the Dardenne Brothers.' *Film-Philosophy* (Edinburgh University Press) 11 (2): 66–87.

Cooper, Sarah. 2007. 'The Occluded Relation: Levinas and Cinema.' *Film-Philosophy* (Edinburgh University Press) 11 (2): i–vii.

Cooper, Sarah. 2008. *Selfless Cinema? Ethics and French Documentary*. UK: Modern Humanities Research Association and Maney Publishing.

Costello, Diarmuid and Dawn M. Phillips. 2009. 'Automatism, Causality and Realism: Foundational Problems in the Philosophy of Photography.' *Philosophy Compass* (Blackwell Publishing) 4 (1): 1–21.

Crignon, Philippe. 2004. 'Figuration: Emmanuel Levinas and the Image.' *Yale French Studies* 104: 100–23.

Critchley, Simon. 2004. 'Introduction.' In *The Cambridge Companion to Levinas*. Edited by Simon Critchley and Robert Bernasconi, 1–32. Cambridge: Cambridge University Press.

Criterion Channel, August 2009. 'Pedro Costa and Jean-Pierre Gorin on Ossos.' Available at <citerionchannel.com/ossos/videos/pedro-costa-and-jean-pierre-gorin-on-ossos> (uploaded to YouTube 4 May 2013; last accessed 20 June 2022).

Crowley, Patrick and Paul Hegarty. 2005. 'The Interminable Detour of Form: Art and Formless.' In *Formless: Ways In and Out of Form*. Edited by Patrick Hegarty and Paul Crowley, 185–92. Bern: Peter Lang.

Dabashi, Hamid. 2001. *Close Up: Iranian Cinema, Past, Present and Future*. London and New York: Verso.
Dabashi, Hamid. 2007. *Masters & Masterpieces of Iranian Cinema*. Washington, DC: Mage Publishers.
Daney, Serge. 1983. *La rampe: Cahier critique, 1970–1982*. Cahiers du cinéma Paris: Gallimard.
Daney, Serge. 2003. 'The Screen of Fantasy (Bazin and Animals).' In *Rites of Realism: Essays on Corporeal Cinema*. Edited by Ivone Margulies and translated by Mark A. Cohen, 32–41. Durham, NC: Duke University Press.
Davis, Colin. 2000. *Ethical Issues in Twentieth-Century French Fiction: Killing the Other*. London: Palgrave Macmillan.
Davis, Colin. 2010. *Critical Excess: Overreading in Derrida, Deleuze, Levinas, Zizek and Cavell*. Stanford, CA: Stanford University Press.
De Luca, Tiago. 2011. 'Sensory Everyday: Space, materiality and the body in the films of Tsai Ming-liang.' *Journal of Chinese Cinemas* 5 (2): 157–78.
De Luca, Tiago. 2013. *Realism of the Senses in World Cinema: The Experience of Physical Reality*. London and New York: I. B. Tauris.
De Luca, Tiago. 2013. 'Gus Van Sant and Visionary Realism.' In *Realism of the Senses in World Cinema: The Experience of Physical Reality*. London and New York: I. B. Tauris.
De Luca, Tiago. 2016. 'Slow Time, Visible Cinema: Duration, Experience, and Spectatorship.' *Journal of Cinema and Media Studies* (University of Texas Press) 23–42.
De Luca, Tiago and Nuno Barradas Jorge. 2016. 'Introduction: From Slow Cinema to Slow Cinemas.' In *Slow Cinema*, 1–21. Edinburgh, UK: Edinburgh University Press.
Del Río, Elena. 2008. *Deleuze and the Cinemas of Performance: Powers of Affection*. Edinburgh: Edinburgh University Press.
Derrida, Jacques. 1984. *Signéponge/Signsponge*. Translated by Richard Rand. New York: Columbia University Press.
Derrida, Jacques. 1992. *Acts of Literature*. Edited by Derek Attridge. London and New York: Routledge.
Derrida, Jacques. 1997. *Adieu to Emmanuel Levinas*. Translated by Pascale-Anne Brault and Michael Naas. Stanford, CA: Stanford University Press.
Derrida, Jacques. 1999. 'Hospitality, Justice and Responsibility: A Dialogue with Jacques Derrida.' In *Questioning Ethics: Contemporary Debates in Philosophy*. Edited by Mark Dooley Richard Kearney, 65–83. Psychology Press.
Derrida, Jacques. 2007. 'A Certain Impossible Possibility of Saying the Event.' *Critical Inquiry* 33 (2): 441–61.
Derrida, Jacques, and Anne Dufourmantelle. 2000. *Of Hospitality*. Stanford, CA: Stanford University Press.
Devismes, Brigitte. 2020. 'On Theory: An Interview.' In *Jean-Francois Lyotard: Interviews and Debates*, by Kiff Bamford, 17–28. London and New York: Bloomsbury.
Doane, Mary Ann. 1980. 'The Voice in the Cinema: The Articulation of Body and Space.' *Yale French Studies* (Yale University Press) 60: 33–50.
Doane, Mary Ann. 2002. *The Emergence of Cinematic Time: Modernity, Contingency, the Archive*. Cambridge, MA and London: Harvard University Press.
Downing, Lisa. 2007. 'Re-viewing the Sexual Relation: Levinas and Film.' *Film-Philosophy* (Edinburgh University Press) 11 (2): 49–65.

Dudiak, Jeffrey. 2001. *The Intrigue of Ethics: A Reading of the Idea of Discourse in the Thought of Emmanuel Levinas*. New York: Fordham University Press.
Durrant, Sam. 2004. *Postcolonial Narrative and the Work of Mourning: J. M. Coetzee, Wilson Harris, and Toni Morrison*. Albany, NY: SUNY Press.
Eisaesser, Thomas, and Malte Hagener. 2009. *Film Theory: An Introduction Through the Senses*. New York: Routledge.
Eisaesser, Thomas, and Malte Hagener. 2009. 'Cinema as Window and Frame.' In *Film Theory: An Introduction Through the Senses*, 13–34. New York: Routledge.
Eliaz, Ofer. 2014. 'Acts of Erasure.' *Discourse* 36 (2): 207–31.
Finnegan, Elizabeth Hope. 2018. 'To See or Not to See: A Wittgensteinian Look at Abbas Kiarostami's Close-up.' *Film-Philosophy* (Edinburgh University Press) 22 (1): 21–38.
Flanagan, Matthew. 2012. '"Slow Cinema": Temporality and Style in Contemporary Art and Experimental Film.' *Dissertation*. University of Exeter.
Flitterman-Lewis, Sandy. 2003. 'What's Beneath Her Smile? Subjectivity and Desire in Germaine Dulac's *The Smiling Madame Beudet* and Chantal Akerman's *Jeanne Dielman, 23 Quai du Commerce, 1080 Bruxelles*.' In *Identity and Memory: The Films of Chantal Akerman*. Edited by Gwendolyn Audrey Foster, 27–40. Carbondale, IL: Southern Illinois University Press.
Fried, Michael. 1996. *Manet's Modernism: or, The Face of Painting in the 1860s*. Chicago and London: University of Chicago Press.
Fried, Michael. 2008. *Why Photography Matters as Art as Never Before*. Yale University Press.
Frodon, Jean-Michel. 1997. 'À bras le corps dans l'enfer du Nord.' *Le Monde* 5 (June).
Gadassik, Alla. 2010. 'Davandeh (The Runner).' *Quarterly Review of Film and Video* (Taylor & Francis) 27 (5): 358–60.
Gallafent, Ed. 2005. 'The Dandy and the Magdalen: Interpreting the Long Take in Hitchcock's Under Capricorn (1949).' In *Style and Meaning: Studies in the Detailed Analysis of Film*. Edited by John Gibbs and Douglas Pye, 68–84. Manchester: Manchester University Press.
Gallagher, Tag. 2007. 'Straub Anti-Straub.' *Senses of Cinema* (43).
Garber, Marjorie B., Beatrice Hanssen and Rebecca L. Walkowitz. 2000. *The Turn to Ethics*. London and New York: Routledge.
Gies, Nathan. 2015. 'Signifying Otherwise: Liveability and Language.' In *Butler and Ethics*. Edited by Moya Lloyd, 15–40. Edinburgh: Edinburgh University Press.
Girgus, Sam B. 2007. 'Beyond Ontology: Levinas and the Ethical Frame in Film.' *Film-Philosophy* (Edinburgh University Press) 11 (2): 88–107.
Girgus, Sam B. 2010. *Levinas and the Cinema of Redemption: Time, Ethics, and the Feminine*. New York: Columbia University Press.
Girgus, Sam B. 2017. 'Existential Presence and the Cinematic Image: Ethics and Emergence to Being in Film.' *New Review of Film and Television Studies* 15 (4): 481–95.
Girgus, Sam B. 2018. *Time, Existential Presence and the Cinematic Image: Ethics and Emergence to Being in Film*. Edinburgh: Edinburgh University Press.
González, David. 2017. 'Interview (with Bruno Dumont).' cineuropa, 24 May. <cineuropa.org/en/interview/324938/> (last accessed 20 June 2022).
Greenberg, Clement. 1961. 'Modernist Painting.' *Arts Yearbook* 4: 5–10.
Grist, Leighton. 2009. 'Whither Realism? Bazin Reconsidered.' In *Realism and the Audiovisual Media*. Edited by Lúcia Nagib and Cecília Mello. London: Palgrave.

Grønstad, Asbjørn. 2016. 'Slow Cinema and the Ethics of Duration.' In *Slow Cinema*. Edited by Tiago de Luca and Nuno Barradas Jorge, 273–84. Edinburgh: Edinburgh University Press.

Gunning, Tom. 2004. 'What's the Point of an Index? or, Faking Photographs.' *Nordicom Review* 25 (1–2): 39–49.

Gunning, Tom. 2007. 'Moving Away from the Index: Cinema and the Impression of Reality.' *Differences* 18 (1): 29–52.

Haase, Ullrich, and William Largte. 2001. *Maurice Blanchot*. New York: Routledge.

Hand, Seán. 1996. 'Shadowing Ethics: Levinas's View of Art and Aesthetics.' In *Facing the Other: The Ethics of Emmanuel Levinas*, 63–91. Richmond: Routledge.

Hand, Seán. 2009. *Emmanuel Levinas*. London and New York: Routledge.

Hansen, Miriam Bratu. 1997. 'Introduction.' In *Theory of Film: The Redemption of Physical Reality*, by Siegfried Kracauer, vii–xlv. Princeton, NJ: Princeton University Press.

Hasumi, Shigehiko. 2005. 'Adventure: An Essay on Pedro Costa.' Rouge. <http://rouge.com.au/10/costa_hasumi.html> (last accessed 8 July 2022).

Heath, Stephen. 1975. 'Film and System: Terms of Analysis.' *Screen* 16 (1): 91–113.

Heath, Stephen. 1976. 'On Screen, In Frame: Film and Ideology.' *Quarterly Review of Film Studies* 1 (3): 251–65.

Heath, Stephen. 1981. 'Body, Voice.' In *Questions of Cinema*, 176–93. Bloomington, IN: Indiana University Press.

Henderson, Brian. 1976. 'The Long Take.' In *Movies and Methods: An Anthology*. Edited by Bill Nichols, 314–24. Berkeley, CA: University of California Press.

Henderson, Brian. 1980. *A Critique of Film Theory*. New York: Plume.

Hole, Kristin Lené. 2016. *Towards a Feminist Cinematic Ethics: Claire Denis, Emmanuel Levinas and Jean-Luc Nancy*. Edinburgh: Edinburgh University Press.

Horowitz, Gad. 2004. 'Bringing Bataille to Justice.' *Religiologiques* 30: 127–40.

Hughes, Darren. 2002. 'Bruno Dumont's Bodies.' *Senses of Cinema* (19).

Ingawanij, May Adadol. 2021. 'Philippine Noir: The Cinema of Lav Diaz.' *New Left Review* 130: 53–71.

Jaffe, Ira. 2014. *Slow Movies: Countering the Cinema of Action*. New York: Columbia University Press.

Jay, Martin. 1993. *Downcast Eyes: The Denigration of Vision in Twentieth-Century Thought*. Berkeley, CA and London: University of California Press.

Jayamanne, Laleen. 2001. 'Modes of Performance in Chantal Akerman's Jeanne Dielman, 23 Quai du Commerce, 1080 Bruxelles.' In *Toward Cinema and Its Double: Cross-Cultural Mimesis*. Edited by Laleen Jayamanne, 149–60. Bloomington, IN: Indiana University Press.

Jones, Kent. 2000. 'L'Humanité.' *Film Comment* 33 (6): 73.

Jordan, Randolph. 2012. 'The Ecology of Listening while Looking in the Cinema: Reflective audioviewing in Gus Van Sant's Elephant.' *Organised Sound: An International Journal of Music Technology*, 248–56 (Cambridge University Press).

Joret, Blandine. 2019. *Studying Film with André Bazin*. Amsterdam: Amsterdam University Press.

Jorge, Nuno Barradas. 2016. 'Living Daily, Working Slowly: Pedro Costa's In Vanda's Room.' In *Slow Cinema*. Edited by Tiago de Luca and Nuno Barradas Jorge, 169–79. Edinburgh: Edinburgh University Press.

Jorge, Nuno Barradas. 2020. *ReFocus: The Films of Pedro Costa*. Edinburgh: Edinburgh University Press.

Kael, Pauline. 1987. 'At Fifteen.' *The Current Cinema*: 74.

Kasman, Daniel, and Kurt Walker. 2017. 'On the Verge of Heaven: An Interview with Bruno Dumont.' mubi, 26 May. <youtu.be/PBYlxdIomPc> (last accessed 20 June 2022).

Keathley, Christian. 2005. *Cinephilia and History, or The Wind in the Trees*. Bloomington, IN: Indiana University Press.

Kelley, Kathleen. 2012. 'Faithful Mechanisms: Bazin's Modernism.' *Angelaki, Journal of the Theoretical Humanities* 17 (4): 23–37.

Kenaan, Hagi. 2011. 'Facing Images: After Levinas.' *Angelaki, Journal of the Theoretical Humanities* 16 (1): 143–59.

Kenaan, Hagi. 2013. *The Ethics of Visuality: Levinas and the Contemporary Gaze*. London and New York: I. B. Tauris.

Kendall, Tina. 2013. '"No God But Cinema": Bruno Dumont's.' *Contemporary French and Francophone Studies* (Taylor & Francis) 17 (4): 405–513.

Keohane, Elizabeth Geary. 2019. 'Dismembering and Remembering Childhood in Bruno Dumont's *P'tit Quinquin*.' In *Screening Youth: Contemporary French and Francophone Cinema*, 234–5. Edinburgh: Edinburgh University Press.

Kinsman, Patrick. 2007. 'She's Come Undone: Chantal Akerman's Jeanne Dielman, 23 Quai du Commerce, 1080 Bruxelles (1975) and Countercinema.' *Quarterly Review of Film & Video* 24 (3): 217–24.

Koutsourakis, Angelos. 2012. 'Cinema of the Body: The Politics of Performativity in Lars Von Trier's Dogville and Yorgos Lanthimo's Dogtooth.' *Cinema: Journal of Philosophy and the Moving Image* 3: 84–108.

Koutsourakis, Angelos. 2019. 'Modernist Belatedness in Contemporary Slow Cinema.' *Screen* 60 (3): 388–409.

Koutsourakis, Angelos. 2021. 'A Modest Proposal for Rethinking Cinematic Excess.' *Quarterly Review of Film and Video* (Routledge) 38 (8): 700–26.

Kouvaros, George. 2008. '"We Do Not Die Twice": Realism and Cinema.' In *The Sage Handbook of Film Studies*. Edited by James Donald and Michael Renov, 376–90. London: Sage.

Krueger, Joel W. 2008. 'Levinasian Reflections on Somaticity and the Ethical Self.' *Inquiry* 51 (6): 603–26.

Kuhn, Annette. 1982. *Women's Pictures: Feminism and Cinema*. London: Routledge.

Law, Jonathan. 2011. 'Stasis and Statuary in Bazinian Cinema.' *Critical Quarterly* (Blackwell Publishing) 53 (1): 107–22.

Leigh, Jacob. 2009. 'Ontology, Film and the Case of Eric Rohmer.' In *Realism and the Audiovisual Media*. Edited by Lúcia Nagib and Cecília Mello. London: Palgrave.

Levinas, Emmanuel. 1969. *Totality and Infinity: An Essay on Exteriority*. Translated by Alphonso Lingis. Pittsburgh, PA: Duquesne University Press.

Levinas, Emmanuel. 1981. *Otherwise Than Being or Beyond Essence*. Springer Science & Business Media.

Levinas, Emmanuel. 1985. *Ethics and Infinity*. Translated by Richard A. Cohen. Pittsburgh, PA: Duquesne University Press.

Levinas, Emmanuel. 1986. 'The Trace of the Other.' In *Deconstruction in Context*. Edited by Mark C. Taylor and translated by Alphonso Lingis, 345–59. Chicago: University of Chicago Press.
Levinas, Emmanuel. 1987. 'Reality and Its Shadow.' In *Collected Philosophical Papers*. Translated by Alphonso Lingis, 1–14. Springer Netherlands: Martinus Nijhoff Publishers.
Levinas, Emmanuel. 1987. *Time and the Other*. Translated by Richard A. Cohen. Pittsburgh, PA: Duquesne University Press.
Levinas, Emmanuel. 1996. 'Enigma and Phenomenon.' In *Emmanuel Levinas: Basic Philosophical Writings*. Edited by Adriaan T. Peperzak, Simon Critchley and Robert Bernasconi, 65–77. Bloomington, IN: Indiana University Press.
Levinas, Emmanuel. 1996. *Emmanuel Levinas: Basic Philosophical Writings*. Edited by Adriaan T. Peperzak, Simon Critchley and Robert Bernasconi. Bloomington, IN: Indiana University Press.
Levinas, Emmanuel. 1996. 'Transcendence and Height.' In *Emmanuel Levinas: Basic Philosophical Writings*. Edited by Adriaan T. Peperzak, Simon Critchley and Robert Bernasconi, 11–31. Bloomington, IN: Indiana University Press.
Levinas, Emmanuel. 1998. *Discovering Existence with Husserl*. Translated by R. Cohen and M. Smith. Evanston, IL: Northwestern University Press.
Levinas, Emmanuel. 1998. 'Meaning and Sense.' In *Collected Philosophical Papers*. Translated by A. Lingis. Pittsburgh, PA: Duquesne University Press.
Levinas, Emmanuel. 1998. 'Philosophy and the Idea of Infinity.' In *Collected Philosophical Papers*. Translated by A. Lingis. Pittsburgh, PA: Duquesne University Press.
Levinas, Emmanuel. 1999. *Alterity and Transcendence*. Translated by Michael B. Smith. London and New York: Columbia University Press.
Lim, Song Hwee. 2016. 'Temporal Aesthetics of Drifting: Tsai Ming-liang and a Cinema of Slowness.' In *Slow Cinema*. Edited by Tiago de Luca and Nuno Barradas Jorge, 87–98. Edinburgh University Press.
Lippit, Akira Mizuta. 2012. *Ex-Cinema: From a Theory of Experimental Film and Video*. Berkeley, CA: University of California Press.
Little, William G. 2013. 'Plotting Dead Time in Gus Van Sant's Elephant.' *Film-Philosophy* (Edinburgh University Press) 17 (1): 115–33.
Loader, Jayne. 1977. 'Jeanne Dielman: Death in Installments.' *Jump Cut: A Review of Contemporary Media* 16: 10–12.
Longfellow, Brenda. 1989. 'Love Letters to the Mother: The Work of Chantal Akerman.' *Canadian Journal of Social and Political Theory* 13 (1–2): 73–90.
Lübecker, Nikolaj. 2013. 'The Poetry of Idiots: Siegrid Alnoy, Lars von Trier.' *New Review of Film and Television Studies* 11 (4): 438–54.
Lyotard, Jean-Francois. 1984. *The Postmodern Condition: A Report on Knowledge*. Translated by Geoff Bennington and Brian Massumi. Minneapolis, MN: University of Minnesota Press.
Lyotard, Jean-Francois. 1992. *The Postmodern Explained: Correspondence 1982–1985*. Translated by Bernadette Maher, Julian Pefanis, Virginia Spate and Morgan Thomas Don Barry. Minneapolis, MN: University of Minnesota Press.
Lyotard, Jean-Francois. 1997. *Postmodern Fables*. Translated by Georges Van Den Abeele. Minneapolis, MN: University of Minnesota Press.

Lyotard, Jean-Francois. 2010. 'The Sublime and the Avant-Garde.' In *The Sublime: Documents in Contemporary Art*. Edited by Simon Morley. London: Whitechapel Gallery; Cambridge, MA: MIT Press.

McCarthy, Todd. 2003. 'Elephant.' *Variety*. 18 May. <variety.com/2003/film/awards/elephant-2-1200541588> (last accessed 25 April 2022).

Mai, Joseph. 2010. *Jean-Pierre and Luc Dardenne*. Urbana, Chicago, Springfield, IL: University of Illinois Press.

Mai, Joseph. 2011. '*Lorna's Silence* and Levinas's Ethical Alternative: Form and Viewer in the Dardenne Brothers.' *New Review of Film and Television Studies* 9 (4): 435–53.

Maimon, Vered. 2012. 'Beyond Representation: Abbas Kiarostami's and Pedro Costa's Minor Cinema.' *Third Text* 26 (3): 331–44.

Malpas, Simon. 2003. *Jean-Francois Lyotard*. London and New York: Routledge.

Manafi, Keyvan. 2013. 'The Ethics of the "Listening Eye": Exploring the Critical Excesses of Iranian "Social Films".' *Senses of Cinema* (68). <https://www.sensesofcinema.com/2013/feature-articles/the-ethics-of-the-listening-eye-exploring-the-critical-excesses-of-iranian-social-films/> (last accessed 28 June 2022).

Margulies, Ivone. 1996. *Nothing Happens: Chantal Akerman's Hyperrealist Everyday*. Durham, NC: Duke University Press.

Margulies, Ivone. 2003. 'Bodies Too Much.' In *Rites of Realism: Essays on Corporeal Cinema*, 1–23. Durham, NC: Duke University Press.

Margulies, Ivone. 2003. 'Exemplary Bodies: Reenactment in Love in the City, Sons, and Close Up.' In *Rites of Realism: Essays on Corporeal Cinema*, 217–44. Durham, NC: Duke University Press.

Miller, Hugh. 2005. 'Reply to Bernhard Waldenfels, "Response and Responsibility in Levinas".' In *Ethics as First Philosophy: The Significance of Levinas for Philosophy, Literature and Religion*. Edited by Adriaan T. Perperzak, 53–8. London and New York: Routledge.

Mills, Catherine. 2015. 'Undoing Ethics: Butler on Precarity, Opacity and Responsibility.' In *Butler and Ethics*. Edited by Moya Lloyd, 41–64. Edinburgh, UK: Edinburgh University Press.

Morgan, Daniel. 2006. 'Rethinking Bazin: Ontology and Realist Aesthetics.' *Critical Inquiry* 32: 443–81.

Morrey, Douglas. 2020. *The Legacy of the New Wave in French Cinema*. London and New York: Bloomsbury Publishing.

Mroz, Matilda. 2012. *Temporality and Film Analysis*. Edinburgh, UK: Edinburgh University Press.

Mulvey, Laura. 2006. *Death 24x a Second: Stillness and the Moving Image*. Chicago, IL: Reaktion Books.

Naficy, Hamid. 2011. *A Social History of Iranian Cinema*. Vol. 2: *The Industrializing Years, 1941–1978*. Durham, NC and London: Duke University Press.

Naficy, Hamid. 2020. 'Slow, Closed, Recessive, Formalist and Dark: The Cinema of Sohrab Shahid Saless.' In *ReFocus: The Films of Sohrab Shahid Saless: Exile, Displacement and the Stateless Moving Image*. Edited by Azadeh Fatehrad, 7–27. Edinburgh University Press.

Nagib, Lúcia. 2011. *World Cinema and the Ethics of Realism*. New York: New York: Continuum.

Nagib, Lúcia, and Cecilia Mello. 2009. *Realism and the Audiovisual Media*. London: Palgrave.

Nasta, Dominique. 2013. *Contemporary Romanian Cinema: The History of an Unexpected Miracle*. London: Wallflower.

Neyrat, Cyril. 2010. 'Rooms for the Living and the Dead (DVD booklet).' Criterion Collection. <criterion.com/current/posts/1425-pedro-costa-s-fontainhas-trilogy-rooms-for-the-living-and-the-dead> (last accessed 20 June 2022).

Nichols, Bill. 2001. *Introduction to Documentary*. Bloomington, IN: Indiana University Press.

Noys, Benjamin. 1998. 'Georges Bataille's Base Materialism.' *Journal for Cultural Research* 2 (4): 499–517.

Oliver, Kelly. 2001. *Witnessing: Beyond Recognition*. Minneapolis, MN and London: University of Minnesota Press.

Overbey, David. 1979. *Springtime in Italy: A Reader on Neo-Realism*. Hamden, CT: Archon Books.

Parna, Karen. 2001. 'Narrative, Time and the Fixed Image.' In *Time, Narrative and the*. Edited by Mireille Ribière and Jan Baetens. Amsterdam: Rodopi.

Pasolini, Pier Paolo. 2005. *Heretical Empiricism*. 2. Translated by Ben Lawton and Louise K. Barnett. Washington, DC: New Academia Publishing.

Perlmutter, Ruth. 1979. 'Feminine Absence: A Political Aesthetic in Chantal Ackerman's Jeanne Dielman, 23 Quoi de commerce, 1080 bruxelles.' *Quarterly Review of Film Studies* 4 (2): 125–33.

Perpich, Diane. 2005. 'Sensible Subjects: Levinas and Irigaray on Incarnation and Ethics.' In *Addressing Levinas*. Edited by Eric Sean Nelson, Antje Kapust and Kent Still, 296–309. Evanston, IL: Northwestern University Press.

Perpich, Diane. 2010. 'Levinas, Feminism, and Identity Politics.' In *Radicalizing Levinas*. Edited by Peter Atterton and Matthew, 21–40. Albany, NY: SUNY Press.

Phillips, James. 2013. 'The Fates of Flesh: Cinematic Realism Following Bazin and Mizoguchi.' *Angelaki, Journal of the Theoretical Humanities* 17: 9–22.

Phillips, James. 2019. *Sternberg and Dietrich: The Phenomenology of Spectacle*. New York: Oxford University Press.

Rancière, Jacques. 2006. *Film Fables (Talking Images)*. Translated by Emiliano Battista. Oxford and New York: Berg.

Raphael, Melissa. 2009. *Judaism and the Visual Image: A Jewish Theology of Art*. London: Continuum.

Raviv, Orna. 2016. 'Andy Warhol's *Screen Tests*.' *Angelaki, Journal of the Theoretical Humanities* 21 (2): 51–63.

Raviv, Orna. 2019. *Ethics of Cinematic Experience: Screens of Alterity*. London and New York: Routledge.

Remes, Justin. 2015. *Motion(less) Pictures: The Cinema of Stasis*. New York: Columbia University Press.

Rennebohm, Kate. 2019. '"A Pedagogy of the Image"': Chantal Akerman's Ethics across Film and Art.' *Moving Image Review & Art Journal* (Intellect) 8 (1–2): 40–53.

Rich, Jennifer A. 2012. 'Shock Corridors: The New Rhetoric of Horror in Gus Van Sant's Elephant.' *Journal of Popular Culture* 45 (6): 1310–29.

Riera, Gabriel. 2004. '"The Possibility of the Poetic Said" in Otherwise than Being (Allusion, or Blanchot in Levinas).' *Diacritics* 34 (2): 13–36.

Robbe-Grillet, Alain. 1965. *For a New Novel: Essays on Fiction*. Translated by Richard Howard. New York: Grove Press.
Robbins, Jill. 2005. 'Aesthetic Totality and Ethical Infinity: Levinas on Art.' In Emmanuel Levinas: Critical Assessments of Leading Philosophers, vol iv. Edited by Claire Katz and Laura Trout, 356–68. Routledge, London and New York.
Rosen, Aaron. 2011. 'Emmanuel Levinas and the Hospitality of Images.' *Literature and Theology* 25 (4): 364–78.
Rosen, Philip. 2001. *Change Mummified: Cinema, Historicity, Theory*. Minneapolis, MN: University of Minnesota Press.
Ross, Alison. 2009. 'The Aesthetic Fable: Cinema in Jacques Rancière's "Aesthetic Politics".' *SubStance* 38.1 (118): 128–50.
Rubin, Michel. 2016. 'Corporeal Affects and Fleshy Vulnerability: Nonprofessional Performance as Process in L'humanité and Battle in Heaven.' *Senses of Cinema* (80). <https://www.sensesofcinema.com/2016/new-directions/nonprofessional-performance-process/> (last accessed 28 June 2022>
Russell, Catherine. 1995. *Narrative Mortality: Death, Closure, and New Wave Cinemas*. Minneapolis, MN: University of Minnesota Press.
Saxton, Libby. 2007. 'Fragile Faces: Levinas and Lanzmann.' *Film-Philosophy* (Edinburgh University Press) 11 (2): 1–14.
Saxton, Libby. 2008. *Haunted Images: Film, Ethics, Testimony and the Holocaust*. London: Wallflower.
Saxton, Libby. 2009. 'Blinding Visions: Levinas, Ethics, Faciality.' In *Film and Ethics: Foreclosed Encounters*. Edited by Libby Saxton and Lisa Downing, 95–106. London and New York: Routledge.
Saxton, Libby. 2009. 'Ethics, Spectatorship and the Spectacle of Suffering.' In *Film and Ethics: Foreclosed Encounters*. Edited by Libby Saxton and Lisa Downing, 62–75. London and New York: Routledge.
Schonig, Jordan. 2018. 'The Chained Camera: On the Ethics and Politics of the Follow-shot Aesthetic.' *New Review of Film and Television Studies* 16 (3): 264–94.
Schonig, Jordan. 2020. 'Italian Neorealism and Gesture: De Sica's Umberto D and Bresson's Mouchette' (video essay). Film & Media Studies with Jordan Schonig YouTube channel, 6 December. <youtu.be/A3tdDdKDCv8> (last accessed 25 April 2022).
Schoonover, Karl. 2012. *Brutal Vision: The Neorealist Body in Postwar Italian Cinema*. Minneapolis, MN: University of Minnesota Press.
Schoonover, Karl. 2012. 'Wastrels of Time: Slow Cinema's Laboring Body, the Political Spectator, and the Queer.' *Framework* 53 (1): 65–78.
Schrader, Paul. 2018. *Transcendental Style in Film: Ozu, Bresson, Dreyer*. Berkeley, Los Angeles and London: University of California Press.
Schroepfer, Helen. 2014. 'Hospitality and Hope: Self and Other in the Work of Jacques Derrida and Jean Piaget.' *Political Theology* 15 (4): 353–69.
Shaviro, Steven. 1993. *The Cinematic Body*. Minneapolis, MN: University of Minnesota Press.
Singer, Ben. 1989–90. 'Jeanne Dielman: Cinematic Interrogation and "Amplification".' *Millenium Film Journal* 22: 56–75.
Sinnerbrink, Robert. 2011. *New Philosophies of Film: Thinking Images*. London: Continuum.

Sinnerbrink, Robert. 2015. *Cinematic Ethics: Exploring Ethical Experience through Film*. London and New York: Routledge.
Sinnerbrink, Robert and Trahair, Lisa. 2016. 'Introduction: Film and/as Ethics.' *SubStance* 45.3 (141): 3–15.
Snyder, Joel and Allen, Neil Walsh. 1975. 'Photography, Vision, and Representation.' *Critical Inquiry* 2: 143–69.
Sontag, Susan. 2004. *Regarding the Pain of Others*. London: Penguin.
Steimatsky, Noa. 2017. *The Face on Film*. Oxford: Oxford University Press.
Tancelin, Philippe, Sébastien Ors and Valérie Jouve. 2001. *Bruno Dumont*. Éditions Dis Voir.
Taubin, Amy. 2005. 'Blurred Exit.' *Sight and Sound* 15 (9): 16–9.
Thompson, Kristin. 1977. 'The Concept of Cinematic Excess.' *CINÉ – TRACTS* 1 (2): 54–64.
Trahair, Lisa. 2012. 'Godard and Rancière: Automatism, Montage, Thinking.' In *Jacques Rancière and the Contemporary Scene: The Philosophy of Radical Equality*. Edited by and Alison Ross Jean-Philippe Deranty, 43–66. London: Bloomsbury Publishing.
Trahair, Lisa. 2014. 'Being on the Outside: Cinematic Automatism in Stanley Cavell's *The World Viewed*.' *Film-Philosophy* 18: 128–46.
Treanor, Brian. 2006. *Aspects of Alterity: Levinas, Marcel, and the Contemporary Debate*. New York: Fordham University Press.
Trifonova, Temenuga. 2011. 'The Twilight of the Index.' *Cinema: Journal of Philosophy and the Moving Image* 2: 61–89.
Tuck, Greg, and Havi Carel. 2011. *New Takes in Film-Philosophy*. London: Palgrave Macmillan.
Tweedie, James. 2004. 'The Afterlife of Art and Objects: Alain Cavalier's "Thérèse".' *SubStance* (University of Wisconsin Press) 33 (3): 52–79.
Vasse, David. 2008. *Le Nouvel Âge du cinéma d'auteur français*. Paris: Klincksieck.
Vertov, Dziga. 1984. *Kino-Eye: The Writings of Dziga Vertov*, edited by Annette Michelson. Berkeley, Los Angeles and London: University of California Press.
Wagner, Jon. 1988. 'Lost Aura: Benjamin, Bazin and the Realist Paradox.' *Spectator* 1: 57–69.
Walton, Saige. 2015. 'Film and/as Devotion: Bruno Dumont's Enworlded Cinema.' *Australian Journal of French Studies* 52 (2).
Watkins, Raymond. 2016. 'Robert Bresson's Heirs: Bruno Dumont, Philippe Grandrieux, and French Cinema of Sensation.' *Quarterly Review of Film and Video* 33 (8): 761–76.
Webber, Insook. 2018. 'Dumont, Bataille, and the Materialist Sacred.' *French Studies* 72 (1): 73–86.
Welten, Ruud. 2005. 'Image and Oblivion: Emmanuel Levinas' Phenomenological Iconoclasm.' *Literature & Theology* 19 (1): 60–73.
Williams, James S. 2013. 'Topographies of Being: Space, Sensation, and Spectatorship in the Cinema of Bruno Dumont.' In *Space and Being in Contemporary French Cinema*, 41–100. Manchester: Manchester University Press.
Wollen, Peter. 1972. *Signs and Meaning in Cinema*. London: Secker & Warburg.
Wollen, Peter. 1976. '"Ontology" and "Materialism" in Film.' *Screen* 7–23.

Wyschogrod, Edith. 2004. 'Language and Alterity in the Thought of Levinas.' In *Cambridge Companion to Levinas*. Edited by Simon Critchley and Robert Bernasconi, 188–205. Cambridge: Cambridge University Press.

Yervasi, Carina. 2000. 'Dislocating the Domestic in Chantal Akerman's *Jeanne Dielman*.' *Journal of the Twentieth-Century/Contemporary French Studies* 4 (2): 385–98.

Zavattini, Cesare. 1953. 'Some Ideas on the Cinema.' *Sight and Sound* 23 (2): 64–9.

Ziarek, Ewa. 2001. 'The Ethical Passions of Emmanuel Levinas.' In *Feminist Interpretations of Emmanuel Levinas*. Edited by Tina Chanter, 78–95. Pennsylvania, PA: Pennsylvania State University Press.

Ziarek, Krzysztof. 1999. 'Semantics of Proximity: Language and the Other in the Philosophy of Emmanuel Levinas.' *Research in Phenomenology* 19: 213–47.

Zylinska, Joanna. 2002. '"The Future . . . Is Monstrous": Prosthetics as Ethics.' In *The Cyborg Experiments: The Extensions of the Body in the Media Age*. Edited by Joanna Zylinska, 214–36. London and New York: Continuum.

Zylinska, Joanna. 2005. *The Ethics of Cultural Studies*. London: Continuum.

Index

abstraction, 26, 28, 71–2, 74, 76, 104, 109, 112, 147, 198, 215
actorlessness, 62, 131–2, 139, 150, 215
adequation, 13–14, 16, 52, 79, 154, 156–7, 161–3
aesthetic realism, 8, 29, 68, 84, 182, 225
affirmative violence, 24, 60, 130–1, 181, 208
Akerman, C., 3, 29, 88, 99–122
allusion, 3, 5, 91, 104, 166
alterity aesthetics, 23
ambiguity, 69, 91, 108, 116, 130, 140, 178, 186
anthropocentrism, 25, 27, 114, 130
anti-humanism *see* humanism
anti-psychologism, 52, 116, 188
anxiety, 54, 61, 99, 119, 156, 187, 221
archetype, 98, 141, 148, 159, 165–7
audio close-up, 134
automatism, 26, 28–9, 67–8, 73–4, 77–8, 81, 84–5, 88, 92, 109–13, 147, 152, 184, 189, 194, 217
autonomy, 22, 43, 105, 164–5, 189

Baláz, B., 78
Barthes, R., 77, 87, 89, 95, 110
Bataille, G., 144, 147, 152
Battle in Heaven, 184–8, 190, 194
Benjamin, W., 89
betrayal, 55, 59, 61–2, 155
Bicycle Thieves, 69, 114, 193
Blanchot, M., 13, 32, 52, 120, 196–7, 201
body-object, 34, 173
body-thing, 27, 34, 53, 72, 128, 135, 173, 179

Breillat, C., 35
Bresson, R., 65, 121, 125, 135, 147, 152, 187, 201
broken shot, 28, 104, 110, 112, 163, 172
Butler, J., 57–9, 182, 220

Camille Claudel 1915, 146
caress, 35, 40, 54, 148, 153
Cavalier, A., 90
CCTV, 156, 167
celluloid, 19, 74, 76, 109, 113, 128, 217
choreography, 145, 165, 170, 195
cinema of sensation, 135, 187
cinepresence, 178–9
Close-Up, 45–62
Comolli, J. L., 26, 70–1, 206–12, 218
compassion, 48, 159, 220
concreteness, 23, 31, 76, 124, 144, 147
constitutive outside, 51, 118
continuity, 26, 93, 103, 117, 145, 168, 184
corporeality, 55, 105, 170, 185, 190–2, 195
Costa, P., 1–2, 29, 91–3, 205–23
countenance, 37, 58
Crimson Gold, 184, 191–3
cut-in, 102, 120

dailiness, 103, 120
Dalí, S., 89
De Sica, V., 50, 69, 125, 193
dead time *see* temps mort
Decouflé, P., 145
deep-focus, 22, 126, 129
de-hierarchised space and time *see* hierarchy

Denis, C., 23, 35
derivative, 1, 40, 43, 50, 75, 138, 161–2, 167, 209, 215, 220
Derrida, J., 34, 39–40, 63, 65, 176–7, 226
diegesis, 22, 25, 121, 124, 127, 134, 139, 148, 159, 181, 198, 200, 210, 213–14
documentary, 27, 46, 67, 70, 74, 95, 124–5, 131, 139, 169–72, 174, 190, 205, 216, 222
domestication, 4, 20, 89, 163, 173, 179
dramatisation, 4, 104, 109, 112, 118, 157–8, 161, 164, 168
dramaturgy, 74, 194
Dreyer, C. T., 147
Dumont, B., 29, 132–50, 184–5, 187–91

egology, 13
Elephant, 154–76
ellipsis, 112, 125, 213
elusiveness, 55, 62, 67, 75, 149
embodiment, 71, 104, 109, 115, 172, 187
enigma, 10, 17
epiphany, 24, 35, 41–2, 56, 79, 224
Epstein, J., 73, 78
equivalence, 93, 102, 104, 118
essentialism, 81–2, 97, 104–5, 112, 120
excess, 15, 87, 99, 106, 114, 119, 124, 145, 187, 226,
existential density, 87, 201, 211
exposition, 3, 652, 108
extended duration, 4, 54, 103–6, 112–19, 164, 166, 167, 213
exteriority, 9, 12–13, 31, 39, 59
eye-line match, 105

faithfulness, 26, 28–9, 69, 76, 81, 86, 97, 108, 113, 141, 144, 147, 149, 155, 161, 169, 173, 187
fatigue, 54, 191, 201
fidelity, 81, 131
figurality, 13
film-philosophy, 6, 21, 31
Flandres, 132, 138
flesh, 7, 134, 148, 150, 187, 190, 201
Fontainhas, 205, 217, 221–2
foreginer, 179–81, 183

formlessness, 66, 81, 123, 125, 135, 138, 141, 143, 145–50, 152
frame-within-a-frame, 207–8, 211, 215
Fried, M., 44
fullness, 49, 75, 108, 125, 147, 194, 211

Germany Year Zero, 179
gift, 25, 30, 39, 45, 59, 181, 200, 226
givenness, 10, 18, 26, 53, 62, 81, 86, 109, 155, 161, 168, 183
Godard, J. L., 121, 205
gravity, 106, 156,162, 190
grievability, 58–9, 182–3, 224

Hadewijch, 132, 142
haptic visuality, 187
Heath, S., 26, 70, 93
hierarchy, 28, 102–3, 126, 162, 165, 167, 215, 219
Holocaust, 20
Hors Satan, 132–3, 138, 141–2, 149
host, 37, 39–40, 63, 177, 181, 201
hostage *see* Host
humanism, 9, 27, 104–5, 124, 131
Husserl, E., 9
hyperrealism, 100, 104–5, 114

iconoclasm, 6, 8, 13, 18–20, 35–6, 41, 45, 48, 67, 196, 224
iconophobia, 13, 19, 29
ideology, 207, 209–10
Igorrr, 145
imposition, 13, 26, 91, 106, 130
indebtedness, 82, 184, 186, 189
indexicality, 26, 68, 74–7, 88, 104, 111–14, 149, 169. 182, 184, 193, 217
indifference, 3–4, 9, 12, 71, 73, 75, 77, 83, 109–10, 126, 131–2, 140, 183, 201, 206, 215–16
inertia, 191, 201
inference, 109
inhuman eye, 26–7, 86, 123, 130, 183, 225
insert shot, 102
intentionality, 10, 13, 24, 35, 127, 148, 224

intertextuality, 115, 147
invitation, 93, 101, 201
irreplaceability, 28, 111, 113, 171, 189
irreversibility, 28, 111–13, 129–30, 171

Jeanne Dielman, 3, 88, 99–122
Jeannette, l'enfance de Jeanne d'Arc, 143–7
Joan of Arc, 143–4, 147, 149
juxtaposition, 92, 166, 214

Kael, P., 90
Kiarostami, A., 29, 45–62
kino-eye, 123
Kracauer, Sigfried, 141

La vie de Jésus, 132, 138, 140, 142, 150
lack, 24, 27, 52–3, 75, 111, 125, 147, 194
Lanzmann, C., 20
L'humanité, 132–3, 138–49
lifelikeness, 51, 110, 192
lip-synching, 145
literal duration, 141, 147, 173, 220
literalness, 73–4, 80, 106, 114, 118, 122, 180, 182, 189, 197, 201
long shot, 51, 133–5, 137, 149, 188
long take, 49, 103–4, 109, 112, 119, 121–2, 126, 128–9, 163, 168, 170, 173, 185–6, 192, 203
Lyotard, J. F., 85, 97–8

Makhmalbaf, M., 46
maladjustment, 26, 70, 72, 125, 145, 189–90, 202
mimesis, 83–4, 96, 108, 185, 199, 201
mise-en-scène, 21, 49, 119, 124, 149–50, 185, 193, 213, 216
Mitry, J., 78
model/copy binaries, 161–2
modernism, 28, 83–4, 88, 96, 121–2, 209
monotony, 49–50, 107
Mouchette, 125
Mulvey, L., 34, 74–6
mutism, 135–6

Naderi, A., 29, 184–5, 195–6
narrative privilege, 56

naturalism, 83, 187, 193, 207–8
neorealism, 27, 68–9, 96, 102, 114, 127, 179, 192–3, 201, 204
noemata, 9
noeses, 9
non-actors, 27, 138–9, 141, 143–5, 149, 155–6, 163, 169–70, 184–5, 187–93, 195, 198–201, 205, 217
non-anthropocentrism *see* anthropocentrism
non-narrative, 110, 212
non-professional actors *see* non-actors
non-relationality, 10–12, 14, 31–2, 38–9, 41, 215
non-selectiveness, 73, 109, 183

obituary, 58–9
objecthood, 26, 29, 41, 43–5, 96, 123, 180
oblivion, 48, 58, 86, 176
one-to-one relation, 109, 115
onlooker, 180–1, 214, 220
ontology, 9–11, 20–2, 26–8, 34, 36, 38–9, 42–3, 53, 55, 65–6, 68, 85, 87–8, 93, 112, 121, 128–9, 147, 184, 187, 224
openness, 29–30, 36, 40, 86–7, 226
oscillation, 26, 104, 171
Ossos, 1–2, 91–2, 205–23

Paisà, 69
Panahi, J., 29, 184–5, 191–3
panim, 42, 64
pan-shot, 138, 149, 167
passivity, 8, 25, 40, 54, 74, 81, 89, 97, 130, 177, 190, 197, 200–1
peniyya, 42–4, 59, 64
phenomenology, 9–10, 102, 141, 186
physical realism, 1999
physiognomy, 27, 133, 135, 147, 190, 193
point-of-view shot, 105
post-action lag, 105
protagonist, 22, 105, 108, 114, 117, 133, 141–2, 191, 198
proximity, 19, 39–42, 56, 110, 137, 148, 177–80, 187, 197, 200, 213, 221, 225

Rancière, J., 73, 95, 201
readability, 26, 28, 48, 71–2, 77, 99, 113, 115, 139, 156, 182, 184, 187, 213, 215
reality effect, 110, 129
real-time, 103, 112–13, 118, 156, 167–8
receptivity, 38–40, 87, 148, 153
reel-time, 171, 173, 190
re-enactment, 46, 57, 91, 155, 158, 162, 167, 169, 173–4, 193
reflexivity, 117, 209
reification, 100, 127, 211
responsibility, 5, 7, 18, 20–1, 39, 49, 56, 63, 157–8, 161, 168, 181, 183, 200, 202
Reygadas, C., 29, 184–8
Rivette, J., 147
Rosselini, R., 69, 179

self-narration, 56
semantics, 27, 74, 77, 82, 124, 127, 178
senselessness, 129, 155–6, 173, 220–1
sensibility, 40, 48, 55, 78, 105, 140, 148
Shahid Saless, S., 29, 45–62
sheer recording, 28, 77–8, 81–2, 104, 112, 119, 145
Shoah, 20
shot/reverse shot, 105, 137
singularity, 16, 23–4, 28, 31, 34, 42, 48, 61, 63, 65, 76, 105, 109, 111–13, 124, 136, 138, 166, 182–3, 192, 194, 197
slow cinema, 49, 88–9, 98, 121, 129, 175, 206
slow-motion, 79, 196
sovereignty, 9, 177, 201
spatialisation, 159–65, 172
stasis, 54, 89, 105–6, 136, 146
Still Life, 45–62
story proper, 53–4, 65, 93, 103, 174, 220–1
surplus, 4, 27, 29, 51, 65, 72, 79, 87, 89, 99–100, 104, 109, 114–15, 132, 136, 141, 147, 184, 186–7, 189, 191, 195, 200, 202, 210–11, 226

Talebi, M. A., 198–9
technological realism, 84, 97, 140, 155
tediousness, 49, 103, 107
teleology, 53, 184

telos, 26, 186
temporal elongation, 106, 151
temporal instability, 68, 128
temps mort, 49, 51, 88, 93, 101
texture, 93, 135, 172, 186, 1888,
the Dardenne Brothers, 21–2
the fourth wall, 144, 170–1
the local, 179–84, 186, 193, 195, 199–201, 214–15, 217
the non-dramatic, 93, 101–4, 118, 164, 213, 215
the offscreen, 1–2, 91–2, 105, 138, 205–16, 222
the outsider, 179–80
the profane, 140–1, 147
the quotidian, 27, 49, 126, 168
The Runner, 184, 195–8
the said, 8, 17, 38–9, 41–2, 55–6, 60–2, 82, 155–6
the saying, 8, 17, 24, 30, 38–42, 55–6, 60–1, 82, 155–6
the third, 13, 52–3, 57, 125, 201, 217, 220
thematisation, 13, 38–9
thereness, 4, 50, 73, 109, 150, 179, 191, 202
Thérèse, 90
Thompson, K., 87, 103
totality, 11, 13, 25, 30, 54, 92, 114, 214
touch, 39–41, 54, 111, 123, 148, 197
trace, 10, 22, 33, 41, 52, 56, 58–62, 74–5, 77, 77–8, 80, 82, 109, 111, 113, 194
transcendence, 10, 12–13, 18, 20–1, 114, 141, 144, 197
Traveler, 198

Umberto D., 50, 114, 125–6
unbroken shot *see* broken shot
unsimulated sex, 187

Van Sant, G., 29, 154–76
vantage point, 121, 163, 174
verisimilitude, 26, 76, 108, 149, 184
Vertov, D., 123
Visconti, L., 124
visitation, 8, 39, 42, 44, 177
visual fascination, 196–7, 201

voyeurism, 180–3, 220
vulnerability, 36, 40, 178, 187, 225

Warhol, A., 78–81, 89, 114
Where is the Friend's Home?, 198

wholeness, 27–8, 108–9, 121
Willow and Wind, 198–9
witnessing, 34, 49, 73, 75, 105, 133, 180–2, 217
work of mourning, 65, 157, 172, 220, 223

EU representative:
Easy Access System Europe
Mustamäe tee 50, 10621 Tallinn, Estonia
Gpsr.requests@easproject.com